THE
COMMODORE

Center Point
Large Print

Also by P. T. Deutermann and available from Center Point Large Print:

Sentinels of Fire
The Last Man

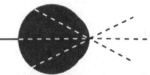

THE COMMODORE

P. T. DEUTERMANN

CENTER POINT LARGE PRINT
THORNDIKE, MAINE

This Center Point Large Print edition
is published in the year 2017 by arrangement with
St. Martin's Press.

The text of this Large Print edition is unabridged.
In other aspects, this book may vary
from the original edition.
Printed in the United States of America
on permanent paper.
Set in 16-point Times New Roman type.

ISBN: 978-1-68324-269-7

Library of Congress Cataloging-in-Publication Data

Names: Deutermann, Peter T., 1941– author.
Title: The commodore / P. T. Deutermann.
Description: Center Point Large Print edition. | Thorndike, Maine :
Center Point Large Print, 2017.
Identifiers: LCCN 2016048890 | ISBN 9781683242697
   (hardcover : alk. paper)
Subjects: LCSH: United States. Navy—Officers—Fiction. | World War,
1939–1945—Naval operations, American—Fiction. | Large type books. |
GSAFD: War stories. | Historical fiction.
Classification: LCC PS3554.E887 C66 2017 | DDC 813/.54—dc23
LC record available at https://lccn.loc.gov/2016048890

This book is dedicated to
the thousands of American sailors still on duty
in the depths of Ironbottom Sound,
off Guadalcanal, in the South Pacific.

ACKNOWLEDGMENTS

I want to acknowledge and highly recommend James D. Hornfischer's book *Neptune's Inferno*, which inspired me to create a novel about a destroyer commander from that period of the Navy's Pacific war.

THE
COMMODORE

PART ONE

THE MAKEE-LEARN

ONE

USS John B. King, *Guadalcanal*

The sound-powered phone mounted above his rack squeaked.

No-o-o, he moaned. Too early. His eyelids felt like they were glued together.

A second squeak, slightly more emphatic. With his eyes still closed, he groped for the handset, pressed the button, and said, "Captain." Croaked was more like it.

"Good morning, Captain, Ensign Belay, junior officer of the deck, here," said an annoyingly bright voice. "The *Frisco*'s coming in."

Frisco, he thought, ordering his right eye to open. It refused. The heavy cruiser *San Francisco*. She'd been the flagship during the big dustup last night. Everyone was wondering how the cruisers had fared this time. Hopefully better than the first time they had gone up against Jap cruisers out in the waters around Savo Island.

"How's she look?"

"Beat up, sir," the JOOD said. "Especially up in the pilothouse, flag bridge area. Somebody worked 'em over pretty good."

"Somebody," he thought, would be the Japanese cruiser formation known as the Tokyo Express.

He sighed. The damned Japs were still the masters of the night fight, them and their horrendous Long Lance torpedoes.

"She under her own power?" he asked.

"Yes, sir, but there's no waterline showing, and her forwardmost turret doesn't look right. Pointed over the side instead of centerlined. It also looks like they're doing a water washdown topside, for some strange reason."

"They're probably washing debris, blood, and human body parts over the side, Mister Belay."

He could actually hear the JOOD gulp at that. Ensign Brian Belay, God love him. The jokes had been endless. He reminded himself once again to stop picking on the ensigns. "I'll be up," he said. "But I need some coffee, please."

"Right away, Cap'n."

He hung up the Bakelite handset and finally convinced his right eye to open. His cabin didn't look any different. Sixteen feet long, seven feet wide, a gray steel bureau with drawers, a tiny closet for hanger gear, and a built-in desk. The bed folded back into the bulkhead and became a couch. One desk chair. One porthole, dogged shut. A tiny head forward with a shower, steel sink, and steel commode. The cabin had been carpeted when the ship was first commissioned, but the carpeting had been ripped out back in Pearl when they took off all the nonessential combustibles.

He'd hit the sack well after midnight still in his uniform, which hadn't done its military bearing any good. He had managed to get his sea boots off. Well, mostly off. They were both still on the end of the bed. With two eyes open now he looked at his watch. Zero five thirty. Reveille in a half hour. He tried to shake the cobwebs out of his brain. He'd once entertained the quaint notion that once he became the captain, he might get to sleep in from time to time. Fat chance, especially these days.

The ship, USS *John B. King*—*his* ship, he reminded himself—was supposed to chop to the Guadalcanal cruiser group at noon today, which meant he'd probably be taking a boat ride once the flagship anchored. If he was going to see the admiral, he needed a shower and a clean, pressed set of khakis. He wondered if there was fresh water available. Even his brand-new destroyer barely distilled enough fresh water for a day's consumption by a crew of 330, and that was only *after* the boiler feed-water tanks had been topped off.

He swung out of the bed, pushed it back up into the bulkhead, and headed for the shower, recalling the sweet-mannered Marine captain back during plebe summer yelling "Aw-*right,* maggots, off your dead asses and on your dying feet!" at every reveille. And then blowing a trumpet over the amplified announcing system. Sixteen years ago.

No—that's when he'd graduated. *Twenty* years ago, when he'd been a brand-new plebe.

Great God, he thought, he was truly getting old. But: in command, and in command of USS *John B. King*, DD-711, a brand-new, 2,100-ton, Fletcher-class destroyer, no less. He was one of only six commanders from his class in command in this year of our Lord 1942. He smiled at the thought of what his superior brethren back at the Boat School would have thought of that. Sluff Wolf? In *command?* No way in hell, that's what they would have thought. Showed them.

His real name was Harmon Wolf. He was a Naval Academy graduate from the class of 1926. His parents were both from the Iron Range territory of Minnesota. His father had been a full-blooded Red Lake Chippewa who drove the giant ore trucks from the taconite open-pit mines to the railhead. His mother was the daughter of an Irish family who'd emigrated to the United States from Canada. Since the little town he'd grown up in was adjacent to the Red Lake reservation, his father had insisted that he spend time on the reservation learning about his Indian heritage. His mother tried equally hard to enmesh young Harmon in the clutches of the Roman Catholic Church. When he'd finally submitted to the coming-of-age ceremony on the reservation, he'd been given the Indian name of Wolf Who Walks in Smoke. Neither of his parents could quite figure that one out, and young Harmon had later come to believe that it had been his paternal uncle's idea of a joke, the smoke an oblique reference to the Catholic High Mass tradition of the priest walking down the main aisle swinging a censer. His uncle was the tribe's Mide, which loosely translated to Medicine Man, although he was also a fourth-degree member of the tribe's Midewiwin and thus one of the most powerful mystical councillors.

The young Wolf did well in school, excelling in mathematics and becoming something of a star on the school's football team as a kicker. His success at school was the result of his mother's Irish heritage and her conviction that education was the best and probably the only way to keep her son out of the taconite pits of the Mesabi Range. That notion was strongly reinforced when Harmon's father overturned an ore truck crossing a river bridge during a rainstorm. They eventually found the truck, but not the driver. Without his father's income, Harmon and his mother moved onto the reservation as wards of the tribe, and in particular his uncle, the Mide. Having been to the white man's school for several years, Harmon was more than a little skeptical of all the mysterious ceremonies and secret signs surrounding his uncle. His mother, ever practical, told him to be politely respectful and to keep his mouth shut.

The contrast between Harmon's academic achievements and those of the rest of the reservation children led to a scholarship to Saint John's University, northwest of the Twin Cities. During his first year there the country went into a sharp depression and he began to wonder what he would do after college. When two military recruiters showed up on campus extolling the good deal offered by the two service academies— four years of college for free—he jumped at it and went after an appointment to both the Naval Academy and West Point. He made the cut for both, but gained only a third alternate appointment. Since all he knew about West Point was that there was a mountain nearby called Storm King, and since he'd had enough of cold dark mountains, he concentrated on the Navy appointment. When the principal appointee and the first two alternates to Annapolis failed their physical exams, Harmon got the nod.

He had no problem passing the physical. He wasn't very tall, only five-eight, but he was built like a steel fire hydrant, all chest and shoulders, and somewhat bandy-legged, like his father. He was undoubtedly the homeliest candidate the entrance examining board had ever seen, with deeply tanned skin, spiky black hair, a huge nose, piercing black eyes, pronounced cheekbones, and a downturned, almost scowling mouth. *He* didn't know he was scowling—that was just his face. He was very strong, having worked as a choker setter for a logging firm in the north woods every summer during high school. Thanks to his mother he'd been an avid reader since childhood and thus had an exceptional vocabulary, but his physical appearance made him stand out from the almost homogeneous stream of young, white, middle-class men flowing through the physical exam center.

His prospective classmates didn't know quite what to make of him, and there were certainly racial underpinnings to how they looked at him. Harmon knew all about that, having taken quite a bit of racial crap from white kids in the town. His uncle had taught him how to fold into himself when the taunts came. He would hunker down, settle his face into a cold mask, condense his body into a posture that hinted at explosive rage, and then lock those obsidian eyes on the biggest and noisiest of his tormentors. Just as his uncle had predicted, that pose made anyone picking on him suddenly uneasy. The admission docs passed him, but without much enthusiasm. The full admissions board noted his math score on the academy entrance exam plus his record of athletic ability, and he was in.

His name at the academy was simply Harmon Wolf, the mystical Indian name having been set aside by the academy's entrance examination board with much rolling of eyes. Some of his classmates joked that Wolf must have been the inspiration for the so-called buffalo nickel, and even he had to admit the resemblance. In those days, as now, it was important that every midshipman eventually acquire his academy nickname. There were, of course, complicated and deeply traditional rules about that. If a midshipman named William dated or eventually became engaged to a woman named Mary, for instance, then her nickname became Billy and *his* nickname became Mary. All Gibsons became Hoot. Anyone with an obviously German name was called Dutch.

Harmon Wolf posed something of a problem in this regard, and he didn't acquire his academy handle until he first went out for varsity football as a walk-on in the beginning of his second year.

Two seniors from the varsity team dressed out in workout gear took one look at the short stack walking into the locker room and burst out laughing. One asked the young Harmon Wolf what his name was.

"Sluff Wolf," he said.

"Sluff?" the biggest guy said. He was probably six-three in height and just as wide. "What kinda name is that?"

"It's easier than saying short little ugly fat fucker," Harmon replied as he began to change out of his class uniform and into sweats.

That produced more laughter, but one of them still wanted to know what a guy his size was doing here trying out for Navy varsity football. "So," he continued, a lineman trying for wit, "Sluff.

20

You here to play football or *be* the football?"

More laughter. Sluff finished changing and went to the footlocker to find some cleats. "I'm here to kick the football," he said. "Don't have to be cow-sized to kick a football."

"Who you calling a cow, there, half-pint," the monster said, getting a little angry now. Sluff turned around.

"Can you catch a football?" he asked quietly.

The lineman said of course he could.

"Okay, then," Sluff said. "See you at the tryout."

"We're already varsity, dumb-ass," another guy said, looking around at his buddies. "We're not here to try out. We're here to show you what the front line looks like when *you* try to get past *us*."

"I'm a kicker," Sluff said. "I don't mess with front lines. Front lines are there to keep *me* safe until I get that kick away. Anyway, how's about I boot one to you and see if you can hold on to it?"

"Is that some kinda challenge, there, shrimp?"

"It's Sluff, not shrimp. But if you're afraid, well . . ."

The big guy hooted and said he'd see him out there. "You kick one to me," he said. "Then I'll throw a tackle to you, how 'bout it?"

Sluff smiled and strolled out to the field. He joined about two dozen other sophomores who were there to try out. An assistant coach put them all into a calisthenics drill, followed by some sideline sprints, which were the quickest way to weed out the absolutely hopeless ones. Then they divided up into their purported specialties. Sluff was the only candidate for kicker. The main reason that he was trying out was that he'd found out the varsity kicker had failed two of his end-of-term exams in May and had been sent home. The Naval Academy took good care of its football team, but every one of them still had to take eighteen credit hours of an engineering curriculum and pass every course, every semester. The vacancy was a matter of some concern to the coaching staff.

Another of the assistant coaches came over, introduced himself, and asked if Sluff had ever played ball before. He said yes, high school, but he hadn't had time during his plebe year for any sports other than the required extracurricular stuff. The coach took him out to the thirty-yard line, handed him a football, and asked him to punt one through the goalposts. Harmon rolled the ball around in his hands for a moment, nodded, and then began to walk away in the opposite direction, toward midfield.

"Hey, sport," the coach called after him. "Where you goin'?"

"Need more room," Harmon said over his shoulder.

He stopped when he got to the fifty-yard line, and then did some stretching exercises for a couple of minutes. The guys who'd been harassing him were over on the sideline now, and his new best friend was making sarcastic comments about ratey youngsters, "youngster" being the academy term for a sophomore. The assistant coach was still down on the thirty, looking pointedly at his watch. Sluff did a couple of jumping jacks; then, cradling the ball between his two hands, he kicked it high over the goalposts and all the way into the end-zone stands, where it bounced back down to the field. He kicked it so hard that the sound caught the attention of the other coaches and most of the varsity team members, all of whom turned to look as that ball sailed over the goalposts. When the ball finally landed, there was a momentary hush on the practice field. The assistant coach looked at the ball and then back up field at Sluff Wolf.

"Can you do that again?" he called.

"All day, coach," Sluff called back. "But I need a football."

To his surprise the big lineman came trotting out onto the field with a couple of footballs. He handed one to Sluff and then said, "Welcome to varsity ball, there, Sluff Wolf." Then he grinned and offered a paw.

Sluff played for three years and made the difference in enough games to become something of a sports celebrity in the Brigade of Midshipmen. When the team was in a tight spot and this short fella with the birth-control face ambled out onto the field, the Brigade would start chanting, "Sluff,

23

Sluff, Sluff," getting a little louder with each chant. The Navy side would go silent when the ball was finally snapped, and then, when it sailed through the goalposts and up into the stands, they'd roar one last *"Sluff!"* In unison. For the rest of his Navy career, Sluff it was.

Sluff Wolf did well academically at the academy, finishing up eleventh in his class of the 424 midshipmen who were actually commissioned. During the winter athletic season he liked to box, and he helped take the Navy intercollegiate boxing team to a divisional championship in his senior year. After graduation he served in the typical career pattern of shipboard assignments in battleships and cruisers. At one point in the early thirties he'd tried out for the nascent naval aviation program, but failed out for what the instructors called "inappropriate temperament." One of his instructors had sneeringly called him a jumped-up woods nigger. Sluff had picked him up and thrown him through a window—from the second story of the hangar building, where the classrooms were. The instructor fell on a biplane wing and thus survived the fall, but Sluff's aviation career was over.

That incident also ended his traditional career path in the spit-and-polish battleship navy. He was subsequently detailed to the wild and woolly destroyer force. There he found his niche. Destroyers were small, fast, heavily armed for their size, and hard-riding fighting ships, manned by men who *liked* to fight. Everyone knew everyone in the destroyer force, and Wolf's personality and even his fierce appearance became a perfect fit. Now, after sixteen years of commissioned service, Sluff Wolf had made it to his own destroyer command. He was not entirely sure how that had happened, because he'd always had the feeling that he'd never quite achieved full acceptance into the all white, all-academy, and still very formal Navy officer corps.

At the beginning of the Pacific war, the Navy could accurately be described as a thoroughly hidebound, white-gloved, tradition-jacketed bureaucratic institution ruled by aging officers who stayed in at their current rank until someone senior to them retired—or died. Then and only then could they move up in the Navy's glacially slow promotion system, especially during the Great Depression. Change, especially any technological advance, was viewed with deep suspicion, sometimes to the point of absurdity: on the Day of Infamy, as Franklin Roosevelt labeled the Pearl Harbor attack, the call to battle stations on every one of the doomed battleships moored at Ford Island had been sounded by a bugler stationed in the "top hampers" of those cage masts. Horatio Lord Nelson would have recognized that bugle call.

And now, Sluff thought, we're finally here, the

ship patrolling two miles off bloody Guadalcanal, where the sounds of desultory artillery fire were audible over the noise of the ship's vent fans. They'd pulled in at 0130, having safely escorted four transports from the port of Nouméa in New Caledonia up to Guadalcanal to bring desperately needed supplies to the Marines, who were apparently clinging to their dusty airfield by their tobacco-stained fingernails. The transports had gone to their anchorages and begun unloading in the dark, trying to get as much stuff as possible off-loaded before Jap torpedo bombers showed up at midmorning. A second tin can prowled the coastline, shooting back at the occasional Jap shore battery trying its luck in the transport anchorage area. *J. B. King* had set up a patrol box to the south of the transports, guarding against Jap subs sneaking in from the Sealark Channel.

During the early hours of the morning he'd received voice radio reports that the American cruiser force was returning to Lunga Point, right off Henderson Field. Between the rainsqualls and the overcast, it had been so dark that none of *King*'s people could make out what kind of shape the cruisers were in, but the radar had shown at least four big ships entering the area. That meant they were still afloat, which was an improvement over the first engagement with the Tokyo Express.

Emerging from the head after his badly needed shower, he found his steward, a gray-headed black man whom the entire crew called Old Mose, laying out a clean uniform. There was a tiny silver tray on his desk with a mug of fresh coffee and a sweet roll nestled in a white linen napkin. Mose knew his captain's fondness for fresh-baked cinnamon rolls.

"Mornin' Cap'n," Mose intoned with a bright smile. Nothing fazed Old Mose. Not yet, anyway. Not for the first time Sluff reflected that the ship and her eager but green crew had not yet "faced the elephant," as they used to say during the Civil War. And neither have I, he had to admit.

"Mose, how are you?" he said, as if nothing was bothering him, either. "What's the weather topside?"

"Hit gonna rain, sure as anythin'," Mose said, nodding wisely. "Already done did. Like a damn cow pissin' on a flat rock, too. Man alive, it was pone down."

Sluff told Mose that he expected to be summoned to the flagship sometime that morning, assuming there was no air raid.

"Lemme give them dress shoes a lick and a polish, then," Mose said, handing over a clean and pressed khaki shirt and trousers, the shirt sporting two bright silver oak leaves on the collars. Still getting used to being a three-striper, Sluff gave them a proud glance. Then the sound-powered phone squeaked again.

"Captain."

"We're getting a flashing light from the *Helena*, Captain," Ensign Belay reported.

"What are they saying, Mister Belay?" Sluff asked. Mose, eavesdropping as always, grinned. Everyone knew that there wasn't an ensign in the entire fleet who could read flashing light.

"I'll find out, sir," Belay answered promptly. "Oh, and we've also IDed *Atlanta* and *Juneau* in the area."

"How do *they* look?"

"*Juneau*, well, XO says she's sagging amidships. He thinks her keel's broken. And *Atlanta* has a big port list on her and she's black from stem to stern. She looks pretty bad, Cap'n. XO thinks he can see Mike boats alongside, like maybe they're taking people off."

Oh, shit, not again, Sluff thought as a chill gripped his bowels. "Very well," he sighed. "What's the air picture look like?"

"Combat reports nothing on our air search, but Cactus says *they'll* be launching strikes at first light. They're going after a Jap convoy northwest of Savo Island. Also, there's radio scuttlebutt that there's a Jap battlewagon still out there, just north of Savo."

Savo Island wasn't that far away, Sluff thought. If there was a wounded Jap battleship out there, nobody here was safe. "Lemme talk to XO," he said.

Lieutenant Commander Bob Frey, his executive officer and second-in-command, picked up. A Steady Eddy if there ever was one, he'd been three years behind Sluff at Annapolis.

"Another bloodletting, XO?"

"Sure looks like it, Cap'n. One of the signalmen's been shooting the breeze with *Frisco*, and they're saying there were two Jap battlewagons out there, and that both of our admirals were killed. Skipper of *Helena* has assumed command."

Sluff felt another cold shock. Admirals didn't get killed. Did they? Please God, not again, he thought. We don't have any more heavy cruisers.

"And what's this about a Jap BB still out there?"

"That's what Combat's hearing over the Cactus control nets. Some of their strikes are going after a troop convoy up the Slot; others are going to finish off a Jap battlewagon who's out there going in circles."

"All right," Sluff said. "I think we better get to GQ, then. All those Japs on Guadalcanal will see and report the cripples, and then Rabaul's gonna send a bunch of Bettys down here to finish it."

"If I may suggest, I recommend sounding reveille first," Frey said. "Then tell everyone what's going on. Give 'em fifteen minutes to hit the head and get some coffee, *then* go to GQ. We should be safe as long as there's no bogeys actually inbound."

"Make it so," Sluff said. "I'll be right up."

He reflected that this was one of his exec's strengths: consideration for the crew. It wasn't as if they weren't trained. Sound GQ, they'd all be on station with the ship buttoned up in under three minutes. If an attack was actually inbound, that's what they'd be doing. But this way the crew would be able to wake up, learn what was going on, have time to do their morning necessaries, and then hustle to their GQ stations.

The radio messenger knocked and came in, bearing a sheaf of naval messages bound onto a steel medical clipboard. Outside, the announcing-system speaker in the wardroom passageway cut loose with the shrill whistle of the bosun's call, sounding reveille. This was followed by the exec, explaining what was going on and urging all hands to be ready to answer the GQ alarm in fifteen minutes.

"Anything hot, Rogers?" Sluff asked, still trying to digest what the exec had told him. It was then that he noticed that Radioman Third Class Rogers looked positively pale as he handed over the clipboard. "The op report from last night, sir," he said, shaking his head. "They got creamed, sir. They ran into fuc—uh, *battle*ships."

Rogers left the cabin without another word. That was unusual. The crew depended on gossip from the radio gang to find out what was going on. The radio messengers would usually linger in the captain's cabin to find out what the ship was going to do next. As if the captain knew, Sluff thought. Destroyers were the workhorses of the fleet, and any given day's plans usually changed hourly as admirals or commodores made snap decisions. A day on a destroyer where everything went by the plan for that day usually meant that the ship had missed a message.

He finished dressing, sat down at his desk, and opened the metal clipboard, while Mose perched on the couch and gave Sluff's uniform shoes a quick polish. His heart sank as he read the short but sad report, sent out by the skipper of the *Helena*. While *John B. King* had been making the milk run from the U.S. base at Nouméa, six hundred miles away, the cruiser force had gone out into the waters north of Guadalcanal looking for trouble. Trouble, in the form of a Jap surface-action task group containing not one but *two* battleships, had more than obliged. For some odd reason there had been two admirals in the task group last night, Rear Admiral Dan Callaghan, embarked in heavy cruiser *San Francisco*, in charge, and Rear Admiral Norman Scott, embarked in light cruiser *Atlanta*, apparently just along for the ride. The report confirmed that both flag officers had been killed in the ensuing gunfight.

That was stark enough news. The senior officer left alive in *San Francisco*, the flagship, was a

31

lieutenant commander. *Four* American destroyers had been sunk outright. The other two, although damaged, were out there now searching for survivors. The antiaircraft light cruiser *Atlanta*, anchored now somewhere nearby and barely afloat, was so badly damaged that the Marines were indeed shuttling landing craft out to her to take her crew to safety ashore. Given the Marines' situation, surrounded by Jap army units, "safety" was a relative term, so *Atlanta* must be in imminent danger of sinking.

The antiaircraft light cruiser *Juneau* had been torpedoed and was also barely afloat, apparently with a broken keel. The heavy cruiser *Portland* was going around in circles out in the sound after being torpedoed in the stern. The skipper of the heavy cruiser *Helena*, which had also been damaged, had assumed command of what was left of the cruiser force. Amazingly, the report was claiming that one of the Japanese battleships had been knocked out of the fight. Who the hell managed that, Sluff wondered.

He downed his coffee and then decided he'd better get topside right now. As dawn broke, there'd almost certainly be Jap air raids from the airfields up in the Shortlands, or even Rabaul itself. As he opened his cabin door he almost collided with the chief signalman, Chief Hawkins, who had a visual signal pad on a clipboard, which he handed to the captain. The chief had that "stand by, everything's changed again" expression on his face.

"What now, Chief?" Sluff asked as he scanned the brief message, knowing that the chief would have read it on his way down from the signal bridge. Like the radio gang, the signalmen were a prime source for the hot scoop.

"Gonna go find the *Washington* and the *South Dakota* and report for duty," Hawkins answered crisply. He was a short but muscular man, mid-thirties, with a permanently sun- and wind-burned face and startling white eyebrows, the product of hours spent topside supervising the guys who worked the signal lights and the flag bags.

"Right," Sluff said, initialing the message form. "Take this to XO on the bridge and tell him I said to get the navi-guesser to lay out a track. Make sure they see this in Combat, too."

"Aye, aye, sir," the chief said, and took the ladder up to the bridge two steps at a time. Sluff followed, trying to ignore the growing pit in his stomach. Last night our cruiser force got mauled by Jap battleships. Apparently Admiral Halsey, in command of everything but back in Nouméa, had decided to up the ante.

You wanted to see some action, he told himself. Here it comes.

TWO

Guadalcanal

A chorus of "Captain's on the bridge" greeted him as he stepped through the pilothouse door. He refilled his coffee mug from the chart-table coffeepot and then went over to his captain's chair on the starboard side of the bridge. Outside, it had begun to rain again, a heavy South Pacific squall that drummed on the overhead and made conversation pointless and visibility impossible. The only benefit was that these heavy showers washed the paint-eating salt and boiler soot off the weather decks. Sunrise was a half hour away, but the tropical dawn made the ship plenty visible should Jap torpedo bombers appear out of the rain clouds.

"Where's XO?" he asked.

"Gone down to Combat," the officer of the deck, Lieutenant Junior Grade Heimbach, replied.

He reread the visual signal: *J. B. King* detached first light. Proceed RDVU with TF 64, est. posit. 80 miles west of Cape Esperance. Report for screening duty NLT 1800K. Maintain strict radio silence. Advise CTF 64 fuel and ammo status en route. Hoover sends. Acknowledge.

Sluff didn't know the complete composition of

Task Force 64, so he called down to Combat on the bitch-box and asked them to look it up. Then he called the chief engineer to get a fuel report. They'd topped off before leaving Nouméa, and the transit to Cactus had been done at a relatively slow twelve knots to accommodate the transports, so they should be at 80-something percent. The engineer, Lieutenant Cliff Harper, called back and reported 80 percent on the nose.

Sluff considered that number. They were ten miles south and east of Cape Esperance, so a ninety-mile transit to the rendezvous, assuming the big guys showed up on time. That meant they would join up at something less than 80 percent. On the other hand, there were fuel barges only about twelve miles away in the harbor of Tulagi. *J. B. King* didn't have to make the rendezvous until 1800, so they basically had all day. He decided to divert into Tulagi, top off the fuel, and then take off for the rendezvous. At twenty knots, it should only take five and a half hours.

The XO called back up to the bridge and reported that Task Force 64 was composed of the fast battleships *Washington* and *South Dakota*, accompanied by just two destroyers, the *Calhoun* and the *Morgan*. Rear Admiral W. A. "Ching" Lee was the task force commander. Sluff told the XO that they would first divert to Tulagi to scrounge more fuel, and then head for the rendezvous. The exec acknowledged and said they'd send up a course recommendation for the drive over to Tulagi, which was an excellent harbor on Florida Island, visible across the sound.

A battleship force, Sluff thought. The situation after last night's engagement was bad enough that Halsey had cut loose two battleships from the *Enterprise* carrier group to come up to Guadalcanal to revisit last night's debacle? It frustrated him that he didn't know what was planned for tonight, but that was life in the fleet. The big bosses often left their destroyers completely in the dark as to what the immediate plan was, relying instead on voice radio orders telling them to go there or to do this as the tactical situation dictated. The destroyers' principal mission was to "screen" the heavies. If they were in transit from point A to B, look and listen for lurking Jap subs. If an air raid developed, close the big guys and shoot down attacking torpedo bombers while trying not to get run over by the capital ships as they twisted and turned to get away from approaching ordnance. The good news was that the bosses rarely told the destroyermen *how* to do their jobs. The bad news was that the tin can sailors never quite knew what the hell was going on until it landed on them.

The rain stopped suddenly, as it usually did. One minute, a deluge. The next, a steam bath as the hot steel decks evaporated all that moisture. Sluff looked out the porthole nearest his chair, which gave him a view of the dirt-strip Marine air base known as Cactus, which was the field's radio call sign. He saw a veritable parade of aircraft taking off, one after another, with their landing lights flickering through the palm trees as the pilots tried to see through the clouds of dust each time one left, their massed engines sounding like a disturbed hornets' nest in the light of dawn.

The bosun's mate of the watch opened the side doors that led out to the bridge wings, so Sluff got out of his chair, grabbed his binocs, and went out to take a look. Behind them was the *San Francisco*, not anchored, but not moving either. *Helena*, who'd sent them the flashing light message earlier, was not in sight. Two miles behind the *Frisco* was what looked like the *Juneau*. She and *Atlanta* were the same class, designated as antiaircraft light cruisers, mounting eight twin-barreled five-inch mounts, six in line, three forward, three aft, and two more on the hip. He was pretty sure he was looking at *Juneau* because he could see the sag the exec had been talking about. There was a hundred-foot-long black smudge along her port side where the torpedo had gone off. He realized that, if he could see that sag in her hull from here, she was not likely to make the trip back to safety at Nouméa, some six hundred sea miles away.

He looked around for the *Atlanta*, but couldn't find her. Then he saw a small swarm of boats congregating in an area closer to shore, where there seemed to be a cloud of steam, light smoke, and disturbed water, about one mile inshore of *Juneau*. Good grief, he thought, has she gone down? He looked hard to see what they were doing over there, but the lenses were so badly fogged he couldn't make out anything. He stepped back in and called the signal bridge on the bitch-box.

"Where's *Atlanta*?" he demanded.

"She went down about five minutes ago, Cap'n," Chief Hawkins replied. "Just before that squall came in on us. Turned turtle, and then disappeared. They'd been taking people off for an hour, so . . ."

"Damn," he said. "Okay, so is *Helena* still within flashing-light range?"

There was a moment's pause, and then the chief said yes, although she was hull-down on the southeastern horizon.

"Wilco his last visual signal to us, if you can raise her."

The chief acknowledged. "Wilco" was short for "I will comply," which was a message that only a ship's captain could send. "Wilco" told the boss that the captain had seen and understood the order, *and* that his ship was able to carry it out.

Combat came up with a course for Tulagi Harbor, and the ship turned northeast to go find some fuel oil. As they came out from under the lee of Lunga Point, they saw the Cactus dive-bombers working over something large just beyond Savo Island. Whatever their target was, she was still capable of shooting back, as the sky filled with black puffs of AA smoke. It was good to know that the Japs had some cripples out there, too.

The exec came up to the bridge from the Combat Information Center, two decks below. The ship was still at general quarters, and Sluff intended to keep the ship at GQ until they made it into Tulagi Harbor. It was only twelve miles from Guadalcanal's Lunga Point to Tulagi, but he felt pretty exposed out there in the sound. The Jap air forces could come in at any time after sunrise, looking for the cripples, and he did not want to get caught napping if they did. General quarters meant the bridge was crowded with extra people: GQ phone-talkers, the officer of the deck and the junior officer of the deck, all the quartermasters, extra lookouts, with everyone dressed out in a steel helmet, a kapok life jacket, and personal battle-dressing medical kits. There wasn't much noise as there wasn't anything happening, yet, and he'd clamped down on unnecessary chitchat on the sound-powered phone circuits that spread throughout the ship like nerve bundles.

"Officer of the deck, increase speed to twenty-seven knots," Sluff ordered. "Broad weave."

"Speed two seven, broad weave aye, sir," the OOD replied, and then gave the orders to the lee helmsman. Sluff could almost feel her jump when the snipes opened the main steam throttles and poured on the oil. Normally he'd make a transit at a more economical speed, but if they were going for fuel, why not get over there in a hurry? Twenty-seven knots and the broad weave also made it harder for any lurking Jap subs to set up a good solution.

"*Atlanta*'s gone," Sluff said to the exec, who was standing next to his captain's chair.

"I heard," Bob said. "Gotta wonder what were they thinking, putting light AA cruisers in the line against Jap battleships."

"Yeah," Sluff said, quietly. "You see the signal from *Helena*?"

"Yes, sir," the exec said. "A battleship formation. That means that what happened last night isn't over."

"Precisely," Sluff said. "The Japs are trying to get a bombardment group down here to smash the Marines' airfield once and for all. As long as the Cactus air force is intact, they can't resupply their army guys on the 'Canal."

At that moment, they both heard the sound of very large shells coming in, making a heavy, sheet-ripping, wa-wa-wa sound as they rotated out of the sky and smashed into the sea around them, raising bright green waterspouts a hundred feet into the air.

"*Right* full rudder," Sluff shouted, jumping out of his chair. "Captain has the conn."

The ship heeled to port as she cut her way around from an east-northeast heading toward Florida Island to due south. "What the hell was that?!" Bob said, hanging on to the bridge counter as the ship's heel increased.

"Steady one eight zero, then broad weave again," Sluff ordered. He turned to the exec. "That's that wounded Jap battlewagon."

"Ain't wounded nowhere enough," the bosun's mate of the watch observed, as another four-gun salvo came howling in from the northwest, raising four thundering waterspouts in their wake.

Amen to that, Sluff thought, as he silently urged his ship to open the range, and now would be nice. Battleships could shoot three-thousand-pound shells from sixteen to twenty miles, and he had no idea how far away that Jap was. He ordered another sharp course change to the east, keyed the bitch-box, and asked Combat for a range to the battleship.

"He's not showing on radar, Cap'n. He's probably up there north of Savo Island, in the island's radar shadow."

"How far is that?" Sluff asked.

"Twenty-eight thousand yards, Cap'n." Fourteen miles, Sluff thought. Still too close.

Then the incoming ceased. The signal bridge gang, using their big-eyes telescopes, had finally spotted the battleship. "There's a crowd of dive-bombers over Savo," the chief reported.

"Looks like they're goin' after that sumbitch."

Sluff felt a wave of relief. None too soon, he thought. One fourteen-inch-shell hit could break *J. B. King* into little-bitty pieces.

He ordered the officer of the deck to take the conn and resume the course for Tulagi. The exec went to the chart table to confirm the proper heading. Sluff sensed the crewmen on the bridge exhaling after seeing those monstrous shell splashes rising up like watery giants all around them. Talons of doom, reaching for them, by name. Some of the younger sailors were joking about getting away from a Jap battleship.

Wait until tonight, Sluff thought. This grudge match isn't over. Somewhere out there was another Jap battleship, with friends.

THREE

Fifty miles southwest of Cape Esperance

The signal bridge called down at 1630 that they had the *Washington*'s director tower in sight on the big-eyes. The rest of her thirty-six thousand tons was still hull-down on the horizon.

"Send CTF Sixty-Four a 'reporting for duty' signal," Sluff ordered. "Once you establish comms, tell him we're at ninety-five percent fuel and ammo."

Combat called up and reported they held the two American battleships on radar twenty-five miles out, headed north at twenty knots. There were three smaller pips out ahead of the big ships. Sluff scanned the horizon for a sight of the big boys, but as yet couldn't see them. Even the horizon itself was hard to distinguish through all the humidity in the air. And that's why we paint our ships haze gray, he thought.

J. B. King was making twenty-seven knots on an intercept course that should put her in front of the battleship column. The seas were smooth, the air was oppressive, and the sun, lower in the west, looked like a menacing bronze disk. Combat had sent the day's recognition codes up to the bridge and signal bridge, just in case the big boys thought they might be a Jap tin can approaching and challenged them via flashing light.

Fueling had been a nonevent until a fleet tug brought the *Portland* into the harbor. The heavy cruiser was down by the stern, where a Long Lance torpedo had smashed her rudder and broken two of her four propeller shafts. Because Florida Island was actually the top of a steep submerged mountain, the water in the harbor dropped off precipitously. That enabled the Seabees to pull the damaged ship right up to the bank and then drape her in camouflage netting from stem to stern to hide her from air attack.

King went alongside a fuel barge and topped off

in thirty minutes. The next problem was to get across the northern coast of Guadalcanal to make the rendezvous without attracting more attention from that Jap battlewagon. They set condition II, which allowed half the crew to get some rest while the other half stayed on watch. In the event, the Cactus air forces, assisted by some Helldivers from the carrier *Enterprise*, had smashed the big ship into a grudging silence. She was still afloat, but wrecked to the point where someone in the Jap high command had to be talking about scuttling her. Even so, *J. B. King* had hugged the coast of Guadalcanal, not wanting to tempt fate. By the time they passed the vicinity of Henderson Field and Lunga Point, the crippled cruisers were no longer in evidence, except for a massive oil slick where the remains of *Atlanta* lay bleeding three hundred feet down off Lunga Point. Once they got around Cape Esperance, they headed south-west to find the approaching battleship group.

"Time to intercept a station four thousand yards ahead of *Washington* is ninety minutes," the OOD reported. "Her three escorts are each stationed at one-thousand-yard intervals ahead of the main body."

"Very well," Sluff said. He leaned forward in his chair and buzzed the wardroom pantry. Mose picked up. Sluff asked for a tray on the bridge whenever Mose could manage it.

When a destroyer approached a formation of

capital ships, her captain did not leave the bridge. He wondered when they'd have to go back to GQ. Probably after dark. He sat back and relaxed, determined to enjoy his new ship's ride as they plowed through calm waters toward the setting sun, as the pestilential, dark green mountains of Guadalcanal receded into the evening mist. There was a swell under that deceptively flat sea, and the ship was gracefully rising and falling in time to huge, deep, and invisible waves that had probably originated on the other side of Borneo.

Twenty-one hundred tons light, twenty-five hundred tons fully loaded, 376 feet long, and capable of thirty-five knots, *J. B. King* sported five single five-inch gun mounts, two torpedo mounts carrying five fish apiece, a bristling nest of smaller AA weapons, depth charges, and, most importantly, a Combat Information Center supported by a full radar suite. There were 329 officers and men assigned to run and fight her, and he was still so proud of her that he smiled every time he even thought about being the skipper.

A sudden breeze washed through the pilothouse, rattling the charts on the chart table and blowing a bluish cloud of cigarette smoke, coffee fumes, and human perspiration out to the leeward bridge wing, to be replaced by the smells of the evening meal coming up from the ship's galley. He became aware of the periodic thrumming vibration as her twin screws lifted and settled back into that deep swell.

"Bridge, Sigs," the bitch-box squawked.

He held down the talk key. "Bridge, aye."

"Captain, message from CTF Sixty-Four in *Washington*: Take station one thousand yards astern *South Dakota*. Night action expected."

He acknowledged the message and pressed the key for the Combat Information Center, two decks below. "Combat, put us on an intercept course at twenty-five knots to take station one thousand yards astern of *South Dakota*, second capital ship in line."

"Course is two three five, Cap'n," Carl Nelson, the navigation officer, replied.

Sluff smiled. Nelson had already gotten the word from the signal bridge and computed the correct intercept course before even being asked. What was that famous saying? The difference between a good officer and an outstanding officer was about three minutes? He told the OOD to change course to 235 and take station as ordered. Mose came out into the pilothouse, bearing a tray covered by a white napkin. The ship heeled to starboard as she came around to the southwest to intercept her station, a point in the water behind *South Dakota*, which was moving north at twenty knots in the wake of the *Washington*.

He lifted the napkin: it looked like meat loaf, mashed potatoes, and green beans. The meat loaf was real; the potatoes had been reconstituted from a white powder, and the beans canned. He picked up a fork and dutifully ate all of it without tasting much of anything. He finished with a fresh cup of coffee from the chart-table pot. The sun was now a reddish disk on the western horizon, and he could just make out the black silhouettes of two battleships rising from a shimmering horizon. The three destroyers ahead of the main body were still not visible. He called the signal bridge and asked who the escorts up front were. The chief told him they were the *Calhoun*, the *Walke*, and the *Morgan*. Sluff asked the chief if there was a division commander embarked. Negative.

A real pickup team, he thought, based probably on which tin cans had the most fuel. If Halsey had sent his only two available battleships to Guadalcanal, things must really be getting desperate. The tattered remains of the cruiser force he'd seen this morning reinforced that notion. Wow.

Mose came back out for the tray and asked if the captain wanted dessert. Sluff shook his head. The more he thought about what might be coming tonight, the less he was interested in food. He would have liked to gather his department heads together in the wardroom and brief them on what to expect later tonight. The problem was that he didn't know. In all probability, the admiral over in the *Washington* probably didn't know either.

Clearly, the two admirals in the cruiser force last night had been in the same predicament, and now they were both dead.

He glanced sideways at the bridge team—the officer of the deck, the junior officer of the deck, the helmsman, the lee helmsman, the bosun, the quartermaster, the messenger of the watch, the lookouts on either bridge wing. He wondered what *they* were thinking now as the ship closed in on that dark line of ships whose silhouettes were becoming more and more distinct as they approached. At some point he was going to have to get on the ship's announcing system, the 1MC, and tell them what was going on.

"Approaching station," the officer of the deck announced. The battleships were clearly visible now in the orange light of sunset, beautiful and deadly, their huge sixteen-inch guns carried low and flat along their seven-hundred-foot length, their towering fire-control structures reaching over 150 feet into the air. He'd had the stations wrong, it turned out. *South Dakota* was in the lead and *Washington* second in the line, and this presented a problem: Their orders had been to take station astern of *South Dakota*, but that would have put them alongside *Washington*. The officer of the deck had just seen the problem and turned to Sluff.

"Take station astern of *Washington*, Mister Heimbach," Sluff said. "Somebody screwed it up. And tell Combat the order is reversed."

"Aye, aye, sir," the OOD replied. He took a bearing on *Washington*'s stern, now only three miles distant, and adjusted *King*'s course to intercept a station one thousand yards astern and right in the battlewagon's boiling white wake.

The exec materialized next to Sluff's chair. "Anything on the Fox sked about tonight's operation?" Sluff asked, as he watched LTJG Heimbach conn *J. B. King* smoothly into *Washington*'s broad wake.

Now there was a whiff of stack gas on the breeze from ahead, courtesy of the battleship's eight boilers directly ahead of them. The bosun closed the pilothouse's windward door.

"Not a word," Bob said. "I keep hoping for a visual signal, but nobody's talking. We got a radio check from CTF Sixty-Four on the TBS, but that's it. They know we're here."

The bitch-box light came on. "Bridge, Sigs, signal in the air: Corpen zero four fie-yiv tack speed two-zero."

The OOD looked over at Sluff, who nodded that he understood the maneuver being ordered. A phone-talker reported that Combat recommended following in *Washington*'s wake and slowing to twenty knots when the signal was executed.

The OOD told the signal bridge "signal understood." Thirty seconds later the signalmen reported that the signal had been executed. Four thousand yards ahead they could see the lead destroyer turning to the new course of 045, or due northeast.

"Heading toward Savo Island," the exec said.

"And over the bones of how many ships?" Sluff muttered. He glanced to his right to look at the looming bulk of Guadalcanal, some thirty miles distant. Like most naval officers, he had never even heard the name Guadalcanal until last August, when news of the invasion had spread through the American fleet. There was an entire Marine division there now, clinging to one Japanese-built dirt airfield while the Japanese Imperial Army fought to take it back.

Fifteen minutes later, after the column was steady on the new course and speed, the red light on the bitch-box lit up.

"Bridge, Sigs, signal in the air from CTF Sixty-Four. Take station in the van."

"That's it?" Sluff asked.

"Yes, sir."

"Okay, Sigs, roger for it. Officer of the deck, haul out to starboard at thirty knots and take station one thousand yards ahead of *Walke*."

The OOD gave the necessary orders and *J. B. King* lunged ahead as she turned out of the *Washington*'s wake and started up the line, passing *Washington*, then *South Dakota*, and then overhauling the three destroyers in the lead of the formation. The Combat Information Center made course and speed recommendations to land the ship three thousand yards ahead of *South Dakota*, taking over the lead position in the formation.

"God, I wish I knew what the hell was going on," Sluff said to the exec, who'd come out to the bridge wing with him. The glistening hulls of the huge battlewagons were barely visible now that the sun had gone down. None of the ships were showing navigation lights, so from here on out Sluff knew it was going to be a radar game. The two battleships looked like castles of steel as they plowed through the darkening waters of Ironbottom Sound.

"You better get below," Sluff said. "Make sure everyone's had chow and then we'll have to set GQ pretty soon. I don't think there *is* a plan, other than going up around the top of Savo Island and seeing who shows up."

"The Japs show up, they're gonna get the surprise of their lives," Bob said.

Sluff looked over at his exec in the gloom. "So far, it's been the Japs who've done all the surprising. They're pretty damned good at this night stuff. Most of the iron on the bottom of Ironbottom Sound is ours."

"It's their torpedoes," Bob said. "We see a Jap destroyer or cruiser, we have to assume their torpedoes are already on their way."

"Damned right, so once we determine that they've seen us, we maneuver. Change course. Change speed. Do something—*anything*—to disrupt their torpedo firing solution."

"But we're in formation," Bob protested. "We can't maneuver out of the line without orders."

Sluff shook his head. "They haven't even had the courtesy to tell us what they *think* is going to happen tonight," he said. "We get into it, XO, I'm going to do what it takes to keep us alive and *then* to go after the bastards. You can bet your ass the battleship guys are not going to be thinking about their destroyers once the shit starts."

"Yes, sir," Bob said, his voice neutral.

"You disagree?"

"No, sir. I like the hell out of that 'keeping us alive' plan."

Sluff laughed as the exec left the bridge and headed for the CIC. The OOD reported that the ship was on station at the head of the line plowing through the black waters of Ironbottom Sound. His exec was absolutely correct, though. A warship in formation was supposed to stay in formation until ordered otherwise. In Sluff's opinion, however, that's why there were so many American ships lying beneath them in Ironbottom Sound. This rigid adherence to formation doctrine gave the enemy an immense advantage: Once they could see an American formation, they knew that their fire-control solution wasn't going to change much, which was perfect for a torpedo attack.

Four destroyers, two battleships, looking for trouble. He stared into the blackness ahead. The night air seemed to be oppressively hot and humid, even with the sun down. The twenty-knot breeze coming over the bow gave scant comfort. He looked at his watch. Twenty thirty. Most of the night actions around Guadalcanal had erupted around midnight. The Japs timed their arrival at their objective area so that they could do what they'd come to do and then be out of range of the Cactus air forces by daylight. But what if they came early? As if to accentuate that question, lightning erupted way over on the northwestern horizon, too far away to be heard but bright enough to paint the huge steel towers of the battleships looming behind them in a brief, yellow glaze. That's what battleship guns probably looked like at night when they started shooting at you from over the horizon.

Change of plan.

"Officer of the deck," Sluff called into the pilothouse. "Pass the word: GQ will go down in five minutes."

He went to his sea cabin as the shrill notes of the bosun's call pierced the 1MC speakers on the weather decks and every space within the ship. He'd told the XO to plan on GQ in twenty minutes or so, but those distant flashes bothered him. The captain's sea cabin was more like a steel box right behind the bridge than a real cabin. It measured six feet by eight and contained a fold-down bunk, a sink, and a steel commode. It was designed so that an exhausted captain could lie down for a few minutes while not being more than three steps away from the bridge. His battle-dress gear hung on a bulkhead.

He used the head, washed his face, then changed into a long-sleeved khaki shirt, buttoned to the throat. Then came his kapok life jacket, which he tied across his chest with three strings before he pulled up the two straps that went between his legs and back up to the waist. There were two tiny flashlights pinned to the bulky jacket, one red-lens, one white. There was also a police whistle on a cord attached to the jacket's lapel.

Already beginning to sweat from all the layers, he strapped on his steel helmet with the letters CO painted front and back. He could hear the tramp of men hurrying to their GQ stations, along with the first sounds of hatches going down. He bent over with difficulty to stuff his khaki trouser hems into his socks. Finally came the utility belt, which contained a packet of morphine syringes, a full-sized red-lensed flashlight, a pouch of battle-dressing bandages, a sheath knife, and a holstered .45 semiautomatic.

He stood up and inhaled, feeling a little like a knight about to climb up on his charger. The gear hanging from his belt and life jacket was mostly for use in the water or in a life raft. He'd often wondered about the utility of the pistol, but the idea was that if all the officers carried a sidearm and the ship went down, there would be some guns aboard the life rafts. That was the published version, anyway. The officers all knew there were other uses for a pistol should battle damage, horrible wounds, or a hysterical crewman require it. Unlike in a land battle, retreat was not an option in a naval gunfight.

The GQ alarm finally sounded, almost as an afterthought, since most of the men were already on station. He could hear the phone-talkers out on the bridge taking manned-and-ready reports from GQ stations throughout the ship. He took a deep breath and went back out onto the bridge. The usual chorus greeted his arrival. The OOD reported that the ship was manned and ready for general quarters. It was fully dark now, with only a faint moon showing through a high overcast. He went out onto the bridge wing, where he could just barely make out the white bow wave of the destroyer next behind the *King*. The battleships, one and a half miles back, were now lost in the gloom.

He went back into the pilothouse area to the chart table, which was illuminated by a dim red light. The navigation plot showed that the formation was north-northwest of Savo Island, about ten miles behind them. He wondered how long they'd head northeast up the channel, called the Slot by the Americans, that ran all the way through the Solomon Islands chain to New Britain and the Japs' big naval base at Rabaul, almost six hundred miles from Guadalcanal. As if in answer to his question, the signal bridge called down with another course change, this time to the southeast. Admiral Lee, embarked in the *Washington*, obviously suspected that the Japs were listening to American tactical radio frequencies, so he was staying off the radio until the action started. Sluff acknowledged the visual signal and then told the OOD to initiate the turn when the signal was executed. A minute later the bitch-box sounded off with a single word: "Execute."

The ship heeled gently as she came right to the newest course. The rest of the formation would do likewise, each ship turning in the same spot where *King* had put the rudder over until the entire column was steadied up on a southeasterly heading. He picked up the sound-powered phone handset next to his chair, dialed CIC, and asked for the exec.

"XO, here," Bob answered a moment later.

"I think I need to tell the crew what's going on," Sluff said.

"Yes, sir?"

"So you're in charge of the Combat *Information* Center. What the hell's going on?"

Bob laughed. "Um, well, we're on course one three five, speed twenty, and it's, uh, dark outside?"

Sluff smiled. "Tell me something I don't know," he said. "Like: Has the boss transmitted a battle plan of any kind?"

"No, sir, not that we've seen. After what happened last night, I'm guessing they have intel that the Japs will be back, and hopefully our battleships'll surprise them. But for right now, we're in the mushroom mode for sure."

The mushroom mode: in the dark and up to their necks in manure. "Okay," Sluff said. "I wish I had that radar display up here, but I don't, so I'm depending on you and your radar guys to keep me informed as to enemy contacts and what the big boys are doing. If nothing else, when the battlewagons start to maneuver, I do *not* want to get in the way of either one of them."

"Got it, Cap'n," Bob said. "Right now all the ships are on station and there are no unknown radar contacts. *Washington*'s radar is mounted about a hundred feet higher than ours, so they should see any Japs first. I assume that's when Admiral Lee will start using the radio instead of flashing light."

"Yeah, I agree," Sluff said. "It's a pity they don't turn the destroyers loose to go up the Slot and see what's what."

"No squad dog or divcom," Bob pointed out. "I think the admiral's pretty much winging it."

"Sounds familiar," Sluff said. "Okay, I'm gonna get on the 1MC and do the same thing."

He hung up the phone and told the bosun to pipe all-hands and then give him the 1MC microphone.

"This is the captain speaking," he began. "As

most of you know we've joined up with a formation of two battleships, the *South Dakota* and the *Washington*. Right now we're steaming in a southeast direction headed down toward the eastern side of Savo Island. The admiral in the *Washington* expects the Japs to come down tonight to finish whatever they came for last night when they ran into our cruisers."

He paused to take a breath. "You saw our cruisers this morning. That fight did not go well for us, except for the fact that the Japs turned back when it was over. But they have to know they kicked ass last night and that our cruisers are not likely to be out here tonight. What they *don't* know is that two battleships have taken their place, so hopefully we're going to surprise them when they come. If they come, they usually show up around midnight, so that's when I would expect action. Until then, stand easy on station while we wait to see what happens. Hopefully I'll have time to give you a heads-up before the shooting starts. I need all hands who are topside to keep a watch out for torpedo wakes—that's how the Japs usually start a night fight. That is all."

He handed the microphone back to the bosun as the echo of his voice died out on the weather decks. He wished he could have told them more, but at least his crew now knew as much as he did, which admittedly wasn't much. He wondered what the admiral back there on the flagship knew.

"Bosun's mate of the watch," he called. "How's the coffee supply?"

"Hot, black, and ready for paving, Cap'n," the bosun responded.

FOUR

The port of Nouméa, New Caledonia

Vice Admiral William F. Halsey looked out at the darkened anchorage and saw not very much. It was nearly midnight. The South Pacific breezes tried their best, but his cabin still reeked of cigarettes and human stress. His flagship, an elderly submarine tender called USS *Argonne*, had no air-conditioning, even in the flag spaces. Have to do something about that, he thought. Maybe run that arrogant Frenchman out of his expansive offices. It wasn't like the French colonial government had anything to do these days but maintain their notorious pride.

He'd sent his remaining operations staff officers to get some sleep. One of them had asked him, pointedly, if perhaps disrespectfully, if *he* was going to get some sleep. Halsey had banished him from his office with a growl and a beetling of his bushy eyebrows, followed by a small smile. His chief of staff, Captain Miles Browning, had stayed behind. He was in the outer office, reading the message traffic and nursing his many ulcers.

It was up to Ching Lee now, Halsey thought, especially after the mauling his cruisers had taken last night. *San Francisco*, *Portland*, and *Helena* were still limping their way back. As the remnants of the cruiser force had started back to Nouméa, *Juneau* had been torpedoed with the apparent loss of all hands just below Florida Island. *Atlanta* had succumbed even before the retreat began. Two flag officers lost: Dan Callaghan had been Ghormley's chief of staff right here in Nouméa, and Norm Scott—another big loss. Should've kept Scott back here at headquarters. In retrospect, Scott had simply been a supernumerary last night.

He fired up the umpteenth cigarette of the evening. Sending his only two battleships up to Ironbottom Sound was most certainly a calculated risk. Chester Nimitz might not agree, but Chester was back in Pearl, while he, Halsey, was right here with a real crisis in his lap. Battleships were designed for Jutland, with great formations of huge ships blasting away at each other at eighteen miles. That's how battleships fought. Sending *Washington* and *South Dakota* into the narrow confines of the waters around Guadalcanal defied every tenet of naval tactics. Battleships with sixteen-inch guns were practically invincible against other battleships mounting fourteen-inch guns, as long as they tried conclusions at battleship ranges. But last night, Dan Callaghan had taken a cruiser and destroyer formation into something resembling one of Nelson's close-in melees, where destroyers set the top hampers of battleships afire from ranges of less than a quarter of a mile, and the Japs' Long Lance torpedoes had harvested almost his entire cruiser force.

He mentally recited the butcher's bill again. *Atlanta*, gone. *Juneau*, her back broken by a Long Lance, vaporized by a Jap sub on the way back to Noumea. *San Francisco* shredded. *Portland* with her propellers blown off by another Long Lance. Not to mention all the destroyers lost. The only bright spot: The Jap battleship *Hiei*, admittedly something of an antique herself, had been rendered helpless by gunfire from a dozen American ships and then wrecked the next day by vengeful aviators launching from the dirt field at Guadalcanal. The Japs had brought two of their battleships, *Hiei* and *Kirishima*, to bombard Henderson Field and then cover the landing of a fresh infantry division on the island. Dan Callaghan had stopped that effort, at the cost of his life, but tonight Pearl was warning him that the Nips were coming back to finish the job. Pulverize the airfield, then land an entire convoy's worth of replacements. *Then* crush the Marines.

They couldn't know that they'd face two American battleships tonight. They'd never expect Halsey to leave his carrier force, or what was left of it, unescorted like that.

No one else would expect that, either, especially his distant masters back at Pearl and Washington, DC. Ernie Jesus King would be suitably aghast—unless, of course, it worked. It had better work.

"Miles, I need a drink," he announced to his empty cabin.

FIVE

Ironbottom Sound, Guadalcanal

"Bridge, Combat."

"What've we got?"

"They're here. Multiple radar contacts, northeast of Savo, coming south. One big, four smaller. Maybe more. Twenty-four thousand yards, closing at twenty-seven knots."

"Okay," Sluff said. "Send a flashing-light report to the boss."

"On the way," Bob said.

"Officer of the deck," Sluff called. "Pass the word throughout the ship: Enemy ships approaching. All stations: Button up tight and stand by."

Sluff checked the gyrocompass. They had just turned west, having circled Savo Island. The formation hadn't changed: destroyers *J. B. King*, *Walke*, *Calhoun*, *Morgan*, followed by battleships *South Dakota* and *Washington*. They were passing through the waters between Guadalcanal and Savo Island, the site of too many defeats for the American forces. They were running downwind now, so there was no longer any cooling relief from the relative wind. The tropical night was so hot and humid that the sea haze was almost a fog. After Sluff's announcement, the men on the bridge stood a little straighter, and the idle chitchat of a moment ago subsided into frightened silence.

"Bridge, Sigs. From the boss: We see them. Open fire when we do."

"Bridge, aye," Sluff said. He relayed the message to the gunnery officer, Billy Chandler, up in the main battery director, one deck above.

"We have a solution on the lead ship, Cap'n," Billy said. "They're not quite in range."

"They should be in the battleships' range," Sluff said. Hardly had he said that than a mile behind them the night erupted in red and orange balls of fire as the battleships let go. The thumping roar of their sixteen-inch guns followed a few seconds later, punishing the hot night air. Right behind them, *Walke* began firing.

"What's the range?" Sluff asked Billy.

"Nineteen-five," he said. The effective range of *J. B. King*'s five-inch guns was eighteen thousand yards. "Effective" meant that the chances of hitting the target at nine miles were really good. The guns, however, could shoot out to almost ten miles, or twenty thousand yards.

"Commence firing," Sluff ordered. "Tell your top-side AA gunners to look out for torpedo wakes."

"Control, aye," Billy shouted. Two seconds later, all five of *J. B. King*'s five-inch mounts began blasting away, their barrels trained out to starboard and pointing high, at maximum elevation. The noise was terrific, with clouds of gunsmoke and wadding particles blowing back into the bridge because of that following wind.

Sluff tried to think about what would happen next. Once the heavies started shooting, the Japs would know they'd been ambushed by something a whole lot bigger than cruisers.

What would they do?

Launch a swarm of those terrible Long Lance torpedoes, that's what. He stepped out onto the bridge wing, trying to ignore the ear-numbing blasts from the forward gun mounts. The three mounts back aft were going full tilt as well, and a thousand yards astern he could see *Walke*'s five-inchers pumping yellow flames. The five-inch barrage seemed insignificant compared to the enormous pulses of red-white-orange muzzle blasts from the big guys a mile and a half back. He couldn't imagine what it was like on the receiving end of all that.

"Bridge, Combat," his talker shouted. "Enemy ships are turning around. Control reports we're getting hits on the lead ship, but they're definitely on the run!"

On the run, maybe, Sluff thought. Or, they were turning to present their torpedo tubes, now that they could see the Americans. He just *knew* the torpedoes were coming. The Jap Long Lance was much bigger than *J. B. King*'s torpedoes. Twenty-four inches in diameter instead of twenty-one. They ran at almost sixty miles an hour, with a half-ton warhead, and outranged the American torpedoes by miles. He walked quickly back into the pilothouse.

"Left standard rudder," he called. "All ahead flank, turns for thirty-four knots!"

"*Captain* has the conn," the OOD announced inside the pilothouse. He sounded scared. You ought to be, Sluff thought. He moved quickly over to his chair and punched down the button for the CIC. "Combat, Captain, I'm hauling out of formation to avoid torpedoes. Tell gun control to check fire until we're clear of our own ships. I think there are torpedoes incoming."

"Combat, aye," the exec responded. "Radar shows there are more Japs coming out from around the *west* side of Savo. These look bigger. Cruisers, maybe."

King's guns remained silent as she straightened up and began to run down the column of American ships in the opposite direction. As if to make the exec's point, large waterspouts began to erupt around the destroyers who'd remained in the van. Then another series of shell splashes erupted all around the lead American battleship, *South Dakota.* Sluff could barely see them, but the force of their impact with the water meant that that had to be eight-inch fire from heavy cruisers coming in. He wanted to shout at the other destroyers: Maneuver, do *something* to avoid the incoming shells. Don't just steam in lockstep in a straight line in front of the battleships, whose enormous gun flashes were clearly illuminating the destroyers.

Another round of salvos came out of the night, landing this time on the other side of the column now drifting down their port quarter as *King* accelerated. *South Dakota* was just about abeam, perhaps a mile and half, thundering out nine-gun salvos with clockwork precision as *King* raced by, headed for the rear of the formation so that she could rejoin the shooting. Sluff knew that the Japs were refining their gunnery solution on the steady-as-you-go American formation. Salvos that landed short and then over meant that they just about had the range and the next salvo would be—

There was a bright yellow flash, a massive bang of overpressure, and then the sound of shrapnel flailing *King*'s mast and upper superstructure. A moment later, the bitch-box lit up as huge waterspouts stood up all around them, shaking the ship like a dog with a rag.

"Bridge, Combat, we've lost comms with the task force. Radio says the radio antennas are probably down."

"Okay," Sluff said. "We're coming abeam of *Washington* now, and I'll resume firing when we're clear of her. Looks like *South Dakota* has stopped shooting for some reason. Looks like they're getting hammered by eight-inch."

"Radar shows something really big coming around Savo now."

"Very well," Sluff said. "I'll eyeball us back into formation behind *Washington* as soon as—"

The night lit up behind them as the three destroyers still in the line, *Calhoun*, *Walke*, and *Morgan*, were eaten alive by the arrival of several Long Lance torpedoes. Sluff rushed out to his port bridge wing in time to see pillars of flame rising up from the sea, bright enough that he could actually see the *Washington*, still blasting away with her nine sixteen-inch guns. Ahead of her, *South Dakota*'s guns were still strangely silent, even as she was being straddled again by even larger waterspouts. Damn, he thought. They've got a battleship, too. Up above, on the signal bridge, there were shouts for a corpsman.

"Officer of the deck," Sluff shouted. "Put us astern of *Washington* at one thousand yards. Tell Gun Control to resume firing when arcs are clear."

The TBS, or talk-between-ships, radio blared out a question from Admiral Lee himself: "*J. B. King*: What are you doing?"

Sluff grabbed the radio handset, but the transmit light didn't come on when he pressed the talk button. He dropped the handset into his chair just as the *Walke* blew up from a magazine explosion, showering the front of the formation with pieces of the ship and a million body parts and again lighting up the night. *King*'s guns reached out to starboard and rejoined the gunfight as the OOD adjusted course and speed to position the ship in *Washington*'s tumultuous wake. Compared to the volcanic blasts from *Washington* just ahead, *King*'s guns seemed puny. Sluff stared in horror through the front portholes. *Washington* was still firing, but now her great guns were pointed up at a slightly higher angle, as if she was seeking out a target miles away. Then the *South Dakota* came back into the fight, firing intermittently, but now she was alight with fires in her superstructure and all along her main decks. Only her forward guns appeared to be firing, and then suddenly she heeled to starboard and lurched out of the battle line, or what was left of it. Only *Washington* plowed ahead, punishing the night with her main battery of nine sixteen-inch guns.

Sluff scanned the horizon to the north of them, but he really couldn't see anything because of all the gun flashes. He made sure the OOD had slowed down so *King* wouldn't run up the battle-wagon's stern. The dark gray behemoth continued to send mountainous salvos northwest into the night, still regular as clockwork, the thump of her great guns almost strong enough to hurt his ears.

Behind them the three stricken destroyers, two still burning and one already gone, disappeared into the gloom of the night haze. Then *King*'s guns stopped firing.

"Bridge, Gun Control, no targets in range," the gun boss called over the bitch-box.

"Bridge, aye. Combat, what are the Japs doing?"

"Radar shows two groups to the west of Savo, one turning west, the other coming on. The second group has a really big one, but it's out of range for us."

As he watched *Washington*'s guns blasting into the night, he realized that the big one was probably a Jap battleship and *Washington* intended to kill it. He stared out into the heavy night, but the big guys were duking it out at ranges beyond the night visibility and there was nothing to be seen. He felt useless: his job was to screen the battleship, but the gunfight going on now was way out of *J. B. King*'s league. He was only grateful to have avoided the carnage that had erupted in the van of the formation, the one he'd bailed out on.

Survivors. That was something *King* could do. There had to be survivors from that deadly harvest of the Long Lances. Please God.

"Combat, Bridge, do you have a position for the point where our other tin cans got hit?"

"Wait one." Then: "Affirmative, we have it on the plot."

"Take us there," Sluff ordered. "There'll be people in the water."

"Captain, radar shows there's a Jap line formation coming down from east of Savo. Looks like destroyers. We go back there, they'll be on us."

"Then set up a torpedo solution on that line. We're going back."

"Combat, aye."

Sluff ordered the OOD to haul out from behind *Washington* along her unengaged side and then accelerate to thirty-four knots, leaving the battleship to its long-range duel, and headed back along his own wake to intercept the point where the destroyers behind him had been shredded by the Jap torpedo swarm. He was headed east now, back toward the heart of Ironbottom Sound.

"Bridge, Combat, enemy formation at twenty-four thousand yards, coming straight down towards Cape Esperance. Looks like four DDs."

"If they're on a steady course, set up both torpedo mounts to fire right down their column axis, once they get close enough. Tell Gun Control *not* to shoot until I say so."

"Combat, aye."

Sluff was thinking fast. He had to keep his guns quiet right now, because the approaching Japs would see *King*'s gun flashes and he'd probably never get back to rescue the desperate survivors ahead. The night was dark enough and wet enough that he stood a good chance of remaining invisible. Once the torpedo solution crystallized, he'd launch ten torpedoes right at the approaching Jap column. Once they began to hit, *then* he'd let his gunners go to work while the Japs tried to figure out what was happening.

Wait: If he started shooting, they'd still see him, even if they were dealing with torpedoes. So: No. *Don't* fire. Tear 'em up with his tin fish but keep heading east. Plus, there was a dividend to his maneuvers: Those four Jap tin cans were a distinct threat to *Washington*. A torpedo attack on them would be the one contribution King *could* make to protect the big guy. He looked aft: Where the hell was the *Washington*?

"Where's the *Washington*?" he asked Combat.

"Headed southwest now," the exec replied. "Looks like she's getting out of Dodge. We're on our own."

"Any sign of *South Dakota*?"

"That's a negative. She left earlier."

The relative wind was back up again as *King* headed east at maximum speed. Down below in CIC the torpedo plot was being refined. Up on the bridge it was still hot and dark, and there was nothing to do but wait to see if his gamble would work. The big guys had left the field. Now it was down to *J. B. King* to blunt the oncoming attack and then see if they could rescue anyone from the earlier disaster.

"Range to probable survivor area is eight thousand yards," Combat reported. "Range to Jap column is eighteen thousand yards. Recommend slowing to twenty knots for torpedo release."

Sluff immediately gave the order. He'd forgotten: The torpedoes would go off the port side almost perpendicular to the ship's movement. At thirty-six knots they'd be knocked silly by hitting the water that was rushing by, sideways, at nearly forty-two miles an hour. Even at twenty knots, they'd experience a lot of dynamic stress.

"Tell Gun Control we will *not* fire. Let the torpedoes do their work, but we need to get away. If they keep coming and see us, *then* we'll fight."

"Combat concurs, Combat, aye."

The TBS speakers blurted out a garbled signal. Ching Lee was probably looking for his lone surviving destroyer, Sluff thought, but he wasn't waiting around to make sure we were still operational. Wise move, though. Battleships fought other battleships. Jap destroyers with their Long Lances could overwhelm a battleship like a swarm of army ants could overwhelm a jungle pig. Or a lone destroyer. He wondered why he could hear his boss's queries but not respond. If we make it through this, he thought, there will be plenty of time for queries.

"Bridge, Torpedo Control: Range is twelve thousand yards. Recommend launch at ten thousand yards with this closing geometry."

"Let 'em go when you think it's time, Control," Sluff said. "Report when they're all swimming."

"Torpedo Control, aye."

One minute later he heard the five tubes behind the bridge whooshing their lethal missiles north into the black night. Five more tubes back aft were also punching out their sleek, black loads.

"Bridge, Torpedo Control, all fish away, appear to be hot, straight, and normal."

"Right standard rudder," Sluff ordered. "Steady one eight zero. All ahead flank, turns for thirty-four knots." Then he called Combat. "I'm making a major course change in case they've also launched. Keep track of where the survivors might be and let's see what happens."

"Combat, aye. Teatime in three minutes."

Teatime: actually, T time, when their torpedoes ought to intercept their targets. The ship accelerated as only a tin can could, digging in and thrusting forward in an all-out effort to outrun any Long Lances that might be coming for them. Almost all of the ships hit in the past few months by a Long Lance had been hit in the bows, meaning the Japs always led their targets, assuming they'd maintain course and speed. Turning ninety degrees and running like hell was a pretty good defense. Especially since their best friends in the neighborhood, the battleships, had long since opted for discretion over valor.

No: Wait. The Long Lance could do fifty-five

knots. He didn't have time to do the math, but those fish could possibly overtake the *J. B. King*, even doing thirty-four knots, if they'd been fired early enough. Turn farther. "Right standard rudder, come right to two two zero," he ordered.

Then he waited while the ship steadied up heading southwest. His eyes felt like they had sand in them. He realized he was getting really tired. "Bosun's Mate: I need coffee."

"Coffee, aye," the bosun answered, and then disappeared. There was no eating, drinking, or smoking allowed at general quarters. Bosun's mates, however, always knew where there was coffee. In this case, he climbed the ladders up to the signal bridge, where the signalmen kept a discreet brewer going in the signal shack, hidden under a desk. He was back in three minutes with a cup of oily, black, and definitely aged Navy coffee. Sluff took a sip and tried not to gag.

"Thanks, Boats," he said, his eyes no longer sandy. Just what he needed.

"Teatime in sixty seconds," Combat called over the bitch-box. "This should work—they're still coming. Recommend coming back to the east, though, or we're gonna beach her on Guadalcanal."

Sluff acknowledged and ordered the ship to swing back to the east, finally aware that he'd totally lost track of where the ship actually was in relation to land. He ordered twenty-seven knots to reduce the strain on the main engineering plant. At thirty-six knots, all the machinery would be going Bendix. If anything broke down below, they could lose all power until the snipes regained control.

He went out onto the port bridge wing and stared north into the gloom. He was hoping for a Fourth of July fireworks show.

It was teatime, so where was the sound and light show?

God*dammit!* Ten torpedoes, and—nothing?

And then, *there,* a distant red flare in the night. Then a second one. And then a real crowd-pleaser, a ball of white-yellow-red fire that expanded rapidly even as it dimmed in intensity. He heard the bridge crew grunting out cheers back in the pilothouse as a distant rumble washed over the ship. He stepped back inside and went to the bitch-box.

"Combat, we hit something, maybe even two of 'em. Gimme a course back to the initial datum on the survivors. I think the Japs are busy right now."

"Bridge, Combat, come to course zero eight five to regain track."

Sluff snapped the talk switch twice to acknowledge and then gave the orders, slowing the ship down to twenty knots to give the navigators time to catch up with the plot. He also didn't want to come thundering through the oil-covered clumps of sailors that should be out there, some four miles ahead.

At a thousand yards short of the projected datum

he slowed down to bare steerageway and set the rescue detail. He kept the guns manned in case the Japs recovered from their surprise and came looking for them. There were no more fireworks up by Savo Island and the night remained black as ever. The radar wasn't much help because of all the rainsqualls near the island. Up on the bow the rescue crew was setting up lookouts and rope netting. Sluff ordered the signal bridge to put red filters on the signal searchlights and then to train them out to beacon any survivors.

They found and heard nothing for the first twenty minutes of creeping along in the darkness. Then came the sudden acrid stink of fuel oil, followed by some faint cries out in the water. He stopped the ship and let her drift into the oil slick, which soon produced calls from the signal bridge that they could see men in the water.

"Where are we?" Sluff asked.

"We're ten miles northeast of Cape Esperance," the officer of the deck replied. "Good water, no contacts on the radar."

"How far from Lunga Point?"

"Eighteen miles, sir."

"Okay." He reached for the bitch-box switch. "Combat, Captain, contact Henderson Field on one of those Marine field radios they gave us. Let 'em know we're out here and ask them to get some Mike boats ready to take off survivors."

"Combat, aye," the exec replied. "We've lost

radar contact with *Washington.* Believe she and *South Dakota* have gone south."

"Okay. Could you see what the Japs were doing when our fish got in on them?"

"Their formation broke up, but then a bunch of rain clobbered the screen. We can't see much of anything to the north except Savo itself."

"Keep an eye on that area, XO," Sluff said. "Don't want whoever's left up there to come south looking for a little revenge."

"They're not going to linger, Cap'n," Bob said. "They have to get out of there before first light or the Marine dive-bombers will be on them like stink on shit. I think we're safe right now, unless they have a sub out here."

One of the bridge phone-talkers reported that the deck apes had several survivors alongside but that they needed more people on deck to help them out of the water because of all the fuel oil. Sluff ordered the ship to secure from general quarters except for two gun mounts and their magazine crews. Everyone else was to get top-side to assist getting people out of the water.

By dawn *J. B. King*'s decks were literally covered in oil-soaked survivors from the three lost destroyers. The little battery-operated field radio had worked and the Marines at Henderson Field had sent out five landing craft to begin transferring the badly wounded to the field hospital at the airfield. Sluff realized that *King*

77

would have to get closer to Lunga Point if they were going to get this many people off by the end of the day. The sad pile of body bags on the stern grew steadily. A stream of fighters and bombers flew overhead all morning, headed out into the area of last night's battle, looking for Japs. At ten thirty the daily Jap air raid appeared, but the Marine fighters were ready and none of the bogeys even got close to *J. B. King*, which was fortunate, because she was in no position to defend herself. Sluff remained on the bridge all morning, directing the ship's movements as more and more survivors were sighted.

At noon, the exec came topside and reported that they had long-haul communications back up. Sluff told him to get a message out to the big base at Nouméa, info copy to CTF 64 on the *Washington*, that they had engaged a four-ship Jap formation with torpedoes and were now picking up survivors of the three tin cans. The exec dictated the message to Radio Central, and then took over so that Sluff could get below, clean up, and get something to eat. The entire ship reeked of fuel oil, and the ship's doctor and his two corpsmen were scrambling to attend to all the wounded. A radio messenger caught up with Sluff in his cabin and handed over an urgent message from the task force commander of the previous evening, Rear Admiral Lee, which had been sent to Halsey. Sluff frowned when he read it.

Washington and *South Dakota* were headed back to their carrier group, which was then 150 miles south of Guadalcanal. Lee reported that his force had engaged and sunk a Jap battleship and at least one destroyer, that *South Dakota* had extensive damage, and that he believed three of his own destroyers had been sunk. The fourth, *J. B. King*, had departed formation when the action began, present whereabouts and status unknown.

Sluff swore. That made it sound like *J. B. King* had bugged out when the shooting started, which, technically, he had. As he was changing clothes, the ship's doctor showed up, his uniform covered in equal amounts of fuel oil and blood. He told Sluff that Henderson Field couldn't take all the wounded and that they needed to get to Tulagi or even Nouméa if they were going to save the worst cases.

"What's the count, Doc?" Sluff asked, as he buttoned a fresh uniform shirt.

"We have over four hundred on board, and there's still some more people in the water, although the Mike boats are fishing them out. Twenty-five have died since being hauled aboard. Another eighty to a hundred are serious burn cases. Henderson's field hospital is out of room, and I don't know what they can handle at Tulagi."

"Okay, let's get as many of the able-bodied ashore on the 'Canal as the Mike boats can carry.

Then we'll head for Tulagi, and after that, Nouméa. I'll remind you it's six hundred miles away."

The doc sighed, obviously very tired. "Can we go fast, Skipper?"

"Yes, we can, Doc," Sluff said. "At twenty-seven knots we'll be there in the morning."

"I thought we could do thirty-six," the doc said.

"We can, but that takes four boilers. Twenty-seven takes only two, and that's the best we can do without running out of gas. I'll try to get some fuel in Tulagi."

The doc ran his fingers through his hair, spreading even more oil, and then nodded. "Sorry, sir, I shouldn't have—"

"Forget it, Doc," Sluff said. "Here's a suggestion: Keep some of the able-bodied survivors—chiefs, preferably—on board. Add 'em to your medical teams. That way you guys can get some rest, too."

The doc nodded, and then smiled. His teeth were unnaturally white against the black oil smudges covering his cheeks. "Of course," he said. "I should have thought of that."

"Don't let it happen again, Doc," Sluff said, with a grin of his own. "Now, turn to and quit screwing off."

Once the doc left, Sluff completed dressing and then sat down on the bunk-couch. Big mistake, he thought, as he sat back and relaxed for the first time in almost twelve hours. I should get back topside, he told himself. Okay, maybe five minutes, and then he'd go back up to the bridge. He could hear the shouts and efforts of his people fishing survivors out of the water all along both sides of the ship, as well as the diesel roar of the Mike boat engines as they backed and filled alongside.

He looked at his watch. Almost ten. They'd have to get going pretty soon. He thought about the track back to the base in the New Hebrides Islands. Right through what everybody called Torpedo Alley, where Jap subs lay in wait for a chance to sink something in the endless convoys of transports that were keeping the Marines alive on the 'Canal.

J. B. King left the formation when the engagement began? Someone senior would want to talk about that when they got back to Nouméa. He was glad he'd done it, that maneuver, but he might no longer be in command in a few days.

SIX

Nouméa

Two days later Sluff found himself waiting outside the flag offices on board USS *Argonne*, the submarine tender that had been converted to a support ship for Commander, Southern Pacific

(COMSOPAC). Looking around, Sluff thought these were rather cramped quarters for a vice admiral and his staff. He sat in one of three metal straight-backed chairs lined up against the bulkhead out in the flag passageway, like a truant awaiting a session with the principal. There'd been no offers of coffee and a distinctly chilly reception in the outer office from the assembled yeomen. It was the end of the day, and Sluff wondered if it was the end of his command tour as well.

J. B. King had arrived in the harbor at midday yesterday, her decks crowded with survivors from the *Calhoun*, *Morgan*, and *Walke*. Normally a lowly destroyer would have been sent to anchorage in the beautiful harbor's spacious roads, but because of the wounded, she went pierside. Once everyone had been taken off, they conducted a freshwater washdown, refueled, and took aboard fresh provisions. At noon the port captain discovered that a destroyer was taking up pier space and directed them out to anchorage forthwith. For the rest of the day the ship declared holiday routine, and as many people who could got some much-needed sleep.

Sluff was not one of them. All the message traffic that had been backing up since they'd lost their long-haul communications antennas arrived like an avalanche. Some of it was not friendly. Admiral Lee had sent a more detailed report of the battleship action claiming that the sole Japanese battleship had been so badly damaged by *Washington*'s fire that she'd been scuttled. The *South Dakota*'s damage was extensive, if a bit superficial in terms of her fighting ability. There was a vague reference to the fact that she'd lost all electrical power a few minutes into the engagement. Investigation to follow. The loss of three out of his four van destroyers was cast in the light of a valiant sacrifice, the destroyers eating the Long Lance torpedoes obviously meant for the two battlewagons. Except for USS *J. B. King*, whose maneuvers raised some questions. The fact that *King* had been out of touch since the engagement was described as officially "worrisome."

When he'd read that, Sluff had called the exec and asked him to compile the track sheets from the night of the battleship fight. He had wanted to be ready for the inevitable summons to the headquarters ashore. Normally *J. B. King* would have had a division commander or a squadron commander to answer to, but the formation that night had been a catch team with no unit commander to boss the destroyers.

"Commander Wolf, the chief of staff will see you now," a voice announced from the flag office doorway.

Sluff got up and followed the yeoman into one of the inner offices, where Captain Miles Browning, chief of staff to Vice Admiral Halsey, sat behind his desk like the dragon he very much pretended to resemble. He was partially bald, with a slight mustache and the look of a man who is perpetually fed up with just about everything. Sluff thought the office wasn't very large, considering that this headquarters served the commander of all American forces assigned to the Guadalcanal campaign. There was a conference table in the middle of the room, a steel desk for the chief of staff, behind which was a bank of portholes overlooking the anchorage where the sun was headed for the far, blue horizon. There was a set of wooden batwing doors that led into the inner sanctum, the admiral's office. Three oversized ceiling fans sluggishly stirred the air but did little to cool the room, and the ship's own vents simply irritated the hot, humid air. There was a single chair in front of the desk. Captain Browning indicated with his chin that Sluff was to sit there. Sluff thought it felt a little staged, like a Naval Academy come-around. Sluff decided to be as hard-nosed as this guy seemed to be.

"Commander Wolf," Browning began, "questions have been raised about the performance of *J. B. King* during the engagement off Savo two nights ago. Do you have some answers to that?"

"Probably, sir," Sluff said. "What are the questions?"

Browning frowned. Apparently that wasn't the answer he'd expected. He leafed through some messages on his desk, picked one up, scanned it quickly, and then looked up at Sluff. "Says here you left the battleship formation when the shooting started and then went radio silent. Explain yourself, if you can."

"If I *can?*" Sluff replied. "Is this some kind of court, Captain?"

Browning's face reddened. "Watch yourself, mister," he growled. "I ask the questions, you answer. Why did you leave the formation against orders?"

"There were no orders, for starters," Sluff said. "We received two tactical signals that night. The first was to anticipate night action. The second was to start shooting when the heavies did."

"Bullshit," Browning snapped.

"No, not bullshit, Captain," Sluff said, trying to control his temper. "Those were the only two tactical signals we received before the fight began. We had been assigned a station in the van upon join-up, but other than that, there was no op order, no standard operating procedures, no communications plan or other instruction as to what Admiral Lee wanted us to do."

"He wanted you to screen the heavies, for Chrissakes," Browning said. "That's your job. That's what destroyers do."

"Well, yes," Sluff said. "We assumed that. But he put four tin cans ahead of the battleships and then said nothing further. Once the Japs showed up on radar, all he told us was to start shooting when the big guys did. And that's what we did."

"Then what the hell is this 'departed the formation' business?"

"We tracked the approaching column of Jap ships on our radar. There was one group coming down the east side of Savo. There were more Japs on the other side of Savo, but at that time, we couldn't see them. When the battlewagons opened fire, so did we. All of us, all four destroyers. The range was extreme but the Japs got a pasting, mainly from the two battleships, with us small boys getting our licks in, too. On our radar, it looked like their formation fell apart, but then they regrouped, headed east for about a minute and a half, and *then* turned north. *South Dakota* quit shooting, but *Washington* never stopped."

"Okay, so: Then?"

"That turn to the east got my attention," Sluff said. "If they were just running, they'd have come about a hundred and eighty degrees and bent on the turns. But they didn't—they got broadside to us for ninety seconds, and *then* they turned north. As far as I was concerned, that meant torpedoes were coming. Long Lance torpedoes."

"You saw torpedoes on your *radar* did you?" Browning scoffed.

Sluff stared at him, knowing he was being baited. "No, *Captain,*" he said softly. "We didn't see torpedoes on the radar. You can't see torpedoes on a radar but you can read operational reports. You can study previous engagements. You can learn from those. The Japs aren't chicken. They're street fighters. And when they get sideways to you in a night fight for a minute or so, and only *then* haul ass out of there, it can only mean one thing. The Long Lances are coming. I chose to maneuver out of the torpedo water. That's why I 'departed the formation'—it was doomed."

"You had no *orders* to do that," Browning snapped. "So who the hell—"

"The destroyers were on the sidelines during that fight, Captain," Sluff interrupted. "When battleships duke it out, destroyers take cover. As I said before, we, in fact, had no orders at all, other than to open fire when the heavies did. Which we did. We *all* did. But once I thought the Long Lances were coming, I decided to stay alive to fight another day."

"*You* decided?" Browning said. "Who do you think you are, Wolf? I'll tell you *what* you are: You're a brand-new, untested CO in a brand-new, *un*tested ship. What could you possibly know about a night surface action?"

Fuck it, Sluff thought. This guy was every inch the prick everyone said he was. "More than any aviator," he said, having noted the gold wings on Browning's khaki shirt.

Browning's face went bright red as he rose out of his desk chair. "You listen here, Tonto—"

"All right," a gravelly voice said. "That's enough." Sluff turned to find Halsey himself, all bushy eyebrows and crocodile-faced, standing there in the batwing doors. "Miles, I want to talk to the skipper, here."

"But, Admiral, we can *not* tolerate this kind of insolent—"

"He was there, Miles," Halsey interrupted. "*We* weren't. I want to hear what happened. Captain Wolf, get in here and start from the beginning."

Sluff followed the admiral into the inner office, but not before giving Browning a look that said, See you outside if you think you're man enough. Browning just glared. Halsey sat down behind his desk, lit a cigarette, and then pointed to a decanter of Scotch on a side table. "I take a splash of soda," he said. "Fix one for yourself."

Sluff was a bourbon man, but this was not the time to quibble with Bull Halsey. He fixed the admiral a drink, poured an inch for himself, and then sat down in one of the three chairs in front of Halsey's desk. He was still thinking about going back out there into the other office and pitching Browning through a window.

"Let me set the stage," Halsey said. "Two nights ago, the Japs came down from Rabaul to once and for all smash Henderson Field with a fourteen-inch shelling and then land a convoy's worth of troops, probably fifteen thousand soldiers, to take the airfield and run the Americans into the jungle.

Two nights before that they came for the same purpose, and a force of our cruisers and destroyers drove right into them, literally, right into them, and made them turn back. At great cost, I might add."

"Yes, sir, we saw them, or what was left of them."

"Okay, then," Halsey said. "When Callaghan and Scott went up against two battleships, some cruisers, and a bunch of torpedo destroyers, they got their asses kicked. But: The Japs lost one of their battleships, so they turned back. For one day. To regroup. When it became obvious they were gonna try again, I sent two battleships up there to see if we could stop them. And it worked. The Japs lost a second battleship, and the next morning Marine air on Cactus destroyed most of that convoy. Drowned those sunsabitches. Now the Nips're all back in Rabaul wondering what the hell happened."

Sluff tried the Scotch. Not bad, he thought. "Yes, sir," he said, for want of anything else to say.

"I was eavesdropping when you were talking to my chief of staff," Halsey continued. "I am sympathetic with the fact that you didn't know what was going on and that you had no specific orders. Three of the van destroyers were sub-sequently blown to pieces. *You* managed to avoid getting sunk. Tell me some more about that."

Sluff told him that they were indeed make-

learns out here in the South Pacific, as everyone seemed happy to remind him. So he and his officers had studied the reports of previous battles, talked about what they would do, given certain tactical situations, and then trained to do that. "We were blasting away against that eastern column," he said. "Guns under radar control, shells landing where they were supposed to. Then the Japs opened up and *we* got a taste. One shell exploded overhead and took down all our radio aerials. But it was nothing compared to what the battleships were doing. Every time they fired a salvo we were all blinded. Everybody except our radars, of course." He paused to take a breath. "It was my exec who warned me about what the Japs might be doing."

"Turning to launch torpedoes."

"Yes, sir," Sluff said. "Their five-inch guns— our five-inch guns—they can raise some hell. But nothing like what one of those Long Lance torpedoes can do. *Walke* was right behind us and, by the light of the battleship guns, I saw her get blown in half, both ends jumping into the air and then disappearing in a cloud of fire and steam. Then the other two, *Calhoun* and *Morgan*, blew up. I'm ashamed to say that I was glad—for just an instant—that I'd ordered *King* to turn away, but those three ships never had a chance."

"What happened then?"

"It looked like *South Dakota* stopped shooting

just as she was illuminated by star shells and a ship's searchlight from the west side of Savo. We'd been shooting at the first Japs to show up, but I think the main group was coming down on the west side of Savo, using the island to mask them. She started catching hell. The Japs concentrated on her and she was obviously taking hits. But *Washington* kept going and kept shooting, so I drove down *her* unengaged side to stay out of her way. Our radar showed a big one in the general direction of *Washington*'s fire, and she was shooting back. She was the only one we could see firing, so she may have been a battleship, too."

"She was," Halsey said. "IJN *Kirishima*. Sank later that night."

Sluff grinned. Some good news, for a change. "Anyway, *Washington* finally broke it off and headed southwest. *South Dakota* had already turned south, so suddenly we were alone out there, behind the big guys now, and there were several Jap ships still coming, although they'd slowed down a lot. I turned around and headed back towards where the other three destroyers had gone down."

"Why didn't you stay with the battleships?" Halsey asked.

"We couldn't contribute anything to their withdrawal," Sluff said. "We had no comms with anybody, and there was the matter of three destroyers' worth of survivors in the water. I decided to go back for them."

Halsey looked at him for a long moment and then nodded. "How many did you get?"

"Between four and five hundred," Sluff said. "Some of them went to Guadalcanal, others to Tulagi, the rest we brought here."

Halsey whistled softly. "That's a job well done, Captain," he said. "*Very* well done. And you couldn't tell Ching Lee what you were doing because you'd lost your long-haul antennas."

"Yes, sir," Sluff said. "We rigged a temporary antenna at first light, but our first priority was getting people out of the water. It was bad out there, Admiral. There was so much fuel oil, the guys in the water couldn't see us from fifty feet away. Even the sharks wouldn't come in. We had to use our topside speakers to *call* them in toward the ship. The Marines finally sent out Mike boats for the worst of the injured, and they did a better job getting people out of the water."

Halsey sipped on his Scotch. The setting sun filled the office with an orange glow. Sluff yawned and Halsey saw it. He put down his glass. "Okay, you go get some rest. We're reorganizing the destroyer forces and this time we're going to make sure every ship has a squadron commander. What's your readiness status?"

"We've refueled and reprovisioned. I need some ammo, but they wouldn't bring it pierside. I expect to rearm tomorrow at anchorage."

Halsey nodded approvingly. "We may have

stopped them for the moment, but they'll be back. And so will *J. B. King*. I'll take care of Admiral Lee's concerns. You get rearmed."

"Thank you, sir," Sluff said, standing up. He hadn't finished the Scotch but it had hit him anyway.

"You okay?" Halsey asked.

"Indians and firewater," Sluff said. "I appreciate the hospitality, but I don't drink unless I know there's a night off to recover."

Halsey grinned. "I can guarantee you one night off, Captain," he said. "But after that—"

"Yes, sir, we'll be ready."

"Once again: Good job getting those people out of the water. The battleships couldn't stay there, not with Jap destroyers swarming everywhere, and you were the only tin can left. Good decision."

"Thanks, Admiral," Sluff said.

As he walked through the chief of staff's office, he and Browning exchanged angry looks. "Be seeing you, Commander," Browning said, deliberately not calling Sluff by his proper title of Captain.

"Anytime, *Captain*," Sluff replied. "Call me Tonto again when you come. See what happens. Sir."

Browning glared again, but kept his mouth shut. Sluff wondered if Halsey had overheard their little exchange. Suddenly, he didn't give a damn.

SEVEN

The phone over his head squeaked. Sluff opened both eyes this time, and saw daylight streaming through his lone unbolted porthole. He looked at his watch. Almost nine. As he reached for the phone he realized the exec must have put the word out: Leave the skipper alone until he's had the sleep he needs. "Thanks, Bob," Sluff said. "I better get up and at 'em before the new commodore catches me sleeping in. Appreciate that, by the way. Not sure how you kept the entire ship quiet like that."

"You may not have been the sole late sleeper," Bob said. "I've alerted the signal bridge to be watching for a light from *Gary* and Mose is inbound with coffee and a fat pill."

He'd returned to the ship after his meeting with Halsey and met with the exec and the department heads. Everyone was impressed that he'd actually met Halsey and even had a drink with him. Sluff told them what the admiral had said about their efforts to rescue all those people. He kept his little argument with the chief of staff to himself. After his debrief, he and the exec retired to the inport cabin, where Sluff did tell the exec about Browning, and predicted that there might yet be some fallout from all that.

"Best cure for that noise is to get back to sea and away from all this headquarters crap," Bob had said. "And, in that regard, we finally have a home. We've been assigned to DesDiv Two-Twelve. One Commodore Latham is the division commander, embarked in *Gary*. I don't know if there's a squadron commodore. There's one other ship, the *Westin*, and they'll be arriving in port here tomorrow at noon. We'll chop when they get here and probably head north tomorrow afternoon sometime."

"Perfect timing," Sluff had said. "I'll feel a lot better with a divcom between me and all these flags."

"That depends on the new divcom," Bob had pointed out. "Some of these guys can be real sundowners. And, now, Captain, I have some more message traffic for you."

Two hours later the ship had come fully back to life. The deck divisions were giving the topside another scrubbing to remove the final traces of fuel oil from the survivor-pickup operation. The engineers were completing repairs on one of the main feed pumps in preparation for lighting off the forward plant. Sluff had ordered the signal bridge to send an Able Jig to the commodore, whose flagship had anchored two miles away to receive a fuel barge. ComDesDiv 212 had replied with a curt acknowledgment and a request for a readiness-for-sea report. The ammo barge had come alongside *King* at the appointed time and a conga line of sailors was humping five-inch rounds fore and aft to the pass-down scuttles.

Sluff, sitting in his chair on the bridge, initialed the RFS report and handed it back to the exec. As soon as the ammo was safely stored in the magazines, they'd be ready to get under way on one hour's notice. The three Bs of warship survival: beans, bullets, and black oil. The forward plant was coming back on the line, the aerials had been repaired, and Sluff sensed that the crew was ready to get back to dealing with the Japs.

"Bridge, Signal Bridge."

"Whatcha got, Sigs?" Sluff answered. The officer of the deck watch was set back on the quarterdeck while the ship was at anchor, but the signalmen, the eyes of the ship, always knew where to find the captain.

"Gig approaching, Cap'n," the chief said. "Got a ball. Might be the new commodore. We can't make out a burgee while he's bow-on."

A brass ball on the flagstaff of the approaching boat meant a four-striper on board. "Right," Sluff said. "Make sure the exec and quarterdeck are ready. I'll come back to meet him."

By the time Sluff got back to the quarterdeck, the swallow-tailed red and white pennant on the boat's flagstaff was finally visible. The exec was waiting and ready, the quarterdeck cleared of all the usual stand-arounders, and swabs were being deployed along the main deck to get the last traces of fuel oil off the route to the captain's cabin.

The commodore turned out to be a red-faced man, a bit overweight and shorter than Sluff. He came up the accommodation ladder, saluted the national ensign on the fantail, saluted the officer of the deck, and requested permission to come aboard. The petty officer of the deck rang out four bells on the topside speakers and announced, "Destroyer Division Two-Twelve, arriving."

"Welcome aboard, Commodore," Sluff said, extending a hand. He had to bend a little bit to achieve the handshake. The commodore looked up at him, squinted, and then said, "Harmon Wolf, right?"

"Yes, sir, and this is my exec, Bob Frey."

The commodore shook hands with the exec and then wrinkled his nose. "You have a fuel spill?" he asked. His eyes were darting around, doing a quick inspection.

"No, sir," Sluff said. "We picked up the survivors of *Walke*, *Calhoun*, and *Morgan*. They were pretty much covered in it."

"Oh, right," the commodore said. "Okay, let's go to my cabin."

Sluff glanced at the exec before answering. First little hiccup. "We can go to *my* cabin if you'd like, Commodore," he said. "But the unit commander's cabin on this ship was converted to a Combat Information Center when she was built."

The commodore blinked as if totally surprised by this news. "I had planned to embark, Captain," he said, his almost petulant tone of voice indicating that he was not pleased by this unexpected development.

"You still can, of course," Sluff said. "I'll move into my sea cabin, you take over my inport cabin. We'll fit your staff in wherever we can."

The commodore nodded. This was the standard procedure, but he'd obviously expected that a brand-new destroyer like *J. B. King* would be properly appointed to support a unit commander.

Sluff and the exec escorted the commodore to Sluff's inport cabin. They had to dodge sailors who were reloading ready-service AA ammunition clips along the deck mounts and sponging up little patches of fuel oil. The exec had sent the petty officer of the watch ahead to clear the way, but there was still a lot of activity. The sailors tried not to stare at the diminutive division commander. The commodore's eyes never stopped moving, looking over every detail as he made his way up the main deck. Once they were in the cabin, Mose brought coffee. Sluff sat at his desk, the commodore in the only other chair, and the exec plopped down on the couch.

"Tell me about the battleship fight," the commodore said. "And why *J. B. King* left the formation."

Whoops, Sluff thought. Word do get around. He

nodded and related what he'd told Halsey. When he was finished, the commodore sat there without saying anything. Then he got up and began to pace around the cabin. "That will not happen under my command, Captain," he said. "I want to make sure you understand that."

"Absolutely, Commodore," Sluff said. "Unfortunately we didn't have a unit commander for the destroyers, and Admiral Lee—"

The commodore turned and shook his finger sideways. "Admirals do not normally communicate with individual ship captains," he said. "But when they do, it's incumbent on you to follow the last order given and *not* to take independent action."

"Our last order from Admiral Lee was to open fire when the big guys did."

"Not talking about that," the commodore said. "Talking about your last stationing order. The last order to you was to take station in the van. Absent any other orders, that's where you were supposed to stay."

"And be torn up by the Long Lances that I knew were coming?"

"You could not know that," the commodore pointed out. "You might *suppose* that, but you could not *know* that."

"And, yet, we're here now, and the rest of the van destroyers are on the bottom of Ironbottom Sound."

The commodore stared at him. Sluff realized he might have gone a few words too far, but, on the other hand, he might as well stake out his command philosophy while he could. Or, while you're still in command, he realized.

"XO," the commodore said, softly. "Give us a minute, please."

The exec got up and left the cabin. When the door closed, the commodore sat back down. "You're new to this, Wolf," he said. "Your ship is new, your crew is new, and *you* are new. That's the only reason I'm not going to relieve you of command right here and now. Here's a secret you apparently don't know: When a senior officer gives an order, it just might be that he knows a lot more than you do about the tactical situation. He may or may not have time to bring you into the picture. He may only have time to give you an order. And when the senior officer does that, and the junior officer does something else, it can fuck *everything* up. In your case it didn't, but if you make a habit of obeying some orders and not others, inevitably it will. I have to know, *right now,* that if I give you tactical orders, you will obey them to the letter and you will not 'improvise' according to your instincts, hunches, or superstitions."

"Yes, sir," Sluff said.

"You'd better," the commodore said. "I intend to run a tight division. We're only three ships right now, but more are coming out from Pearl and even LantFleet to make up for our losses out here. We will drill and we will practice and we will drill some more, so that when the Japs come, they'll be facing an enemy as disciplined as they are. I do not care what *you* think about anything, but you'd damned well better care about what I think of you and your ship. Clear?"

"Yes, sir," Sluff said. He felt his face getting red with embarrassment.

"Good," the commodore said. "One last thing: I understand you've been to see Halsey?"

"Yes, sir."

"Don't do that again, ever."

"They summoned me, Commodore," Sluff said. "It's not like I went looking for an audience."

"Bully for you," the commodore said. "But understand this: In the future, they'll summon *me*. And if they summon you, *you* summon me, got it?"

I wonder, Sluff thought. If Halsey wanted the straight skinny, he was reportedly inclined to go directly to the source. "Yes, sir," he said again.

"Now you may call my gig," the commodore said.

"Will you still want to embark, Commodore?" Sluff asked.

"I'll let you know, Captain," the commodore said. Sluff called the exec back in and asked him to escort the commodore back to the quarterdeck.

He should have been the one to do that, but at the moment, he was too angry to be sufficiently respectful. As the commodore left, he did have to ask himself the question: Who you mad at—him or yourself?

Destroyer Division 212 set sail from Nouméa Harbor at four thirty that afternoon. The commodore's flagship, USS *Gary*, a Porter-class, led the column of three, with *Westin*, a Benson-class, second, and *J. B. King* bringing up the rear. The commodore's staff had sent over a copy of the DesDiv 212 standard operating procedures, which Sluff had read and then told the exec to make sure all the officers read as well. As the ships left port and navigated through the minefield channel, the commodore used signal flag hoists for all his tactical signals. The ships were stationed at five-hundred-yard intervals, the traditional distance between destroyer-type ships operating in a column formation.

Sluff was sitting in his captain's chair, watching carefully as the ships turned through the various legs of the swept channel. The quartermasters and the exec were busy taking fixes every three minutes to make sure that they didn't play follow-the-leader into the minefield. When they finally emerged, the formation speed was increased to twenty-seven knots and a course was set for Guadalcanal, nearly six hundred miles distant. The commodore signaled one of the numbered zigzag plans, executed it, and the ships then began to make seemingly random course changes, turning together alternately left and then right of the base course in accordance with a cammed clock mounted on the steering console. The commodore had put them on one hour's notice for thirty-four knots, which meant that the engineers down below had to light off the other two boilers periodically just to keep them hot.

The exec, finished with close navigation, came over to the chair.

"What did I miss?" he asked.

"A C-plus ass-chewing," Sluff said. "Maybe a B, but, I don't know, it lacked a certain finesse."

The exec grinned. "They still mad about our turning away from the Long Lances?"

"Apparently so," Sluff said. "I don't regret it for a moment. I'd still rather be the ship picking up people in the water than be the people in the water. Wasn't like it mattered to those battleships."

"I heard a story when I went over to the repair ship to expedite the antenna jobs," the exec said, glancing around to make sure no one was eavesdropping. "From a guy who said he works at SOPAC headquarters. Intel type. He said the rumor is that Lee put the tin cans up front and then slowed the battleships down once the shooting started. Four destroyers shooting made a pretty good light show so they became the Japs' aiming point. The destroyers soaked up the Long Lances, while the BBs avoided the danger."

Sluff sighed. "Problem is, XO, that could be considered our mission. Everyone says the tin cans are expendable, and this may have been a case in point. Anyway, our new boss was very unhappy with our independent thinking. *My* independent thinking. Brought up the old your-boss-knows-more-than-you-do example. No more of that shit, if you please, Mister Christian."

"Wow," the exec said. "Seriously hidebound." He glanced out the bridge windows. "Kinda like this formation."

"Yeah, we're too close to one another," Sluff said. "Makes good JO training for the ensigns, but one Jap sub could fire a spread, and no matter what the zig or the zag was, a properly fired spread of torpedoes could get us all because we're packed in too close together."

"Perhaps we should send a signal," the exec said with a perfectly straight face. "Make that observation to His Lordship, suggest we widen it out a little."

"Lay below, Bob," Sluff said with a grin. "Before I conclude you're gunning for my job."

"With *this* guy in charge?" the exec said. "No thankee very much."

With the ships running at twenty-seven knots only a quarter mile from each other, Sluff decided to stay on the bridge for a while. His junior officers did not have much experience with close-in formation steaming. He called for Mose to bring him supper whenever it was ready and settled back in his chair. It was going to be a long six hundred miles. He hoped there'd be fuel barges at journey's end. Even with two-boiler ops, they'd burn at least half their fuel.

EIGHT

Twenty-four hours later, the column beheld the green mountains of Guadalcanal on the north-western horizon. The flagship sent out a flashing-light signal: Proceed independently to Tulagi, refuel, report RFS when completed.

That was plain enough, Sluff thought, and asked CIC for a course to Tulagi at twenty-five knots. *J. B. King* was down to just above 50 percent fuel, courtesy of that twenty-seven-knot bell all night. On the other hand, they'd run through Torpedo Alley, the waters between Nouméa and the Solomons used by American ships to get to Guadalcanal, like a dose of salts. Jap submariners were not known for their aggressiveness, and a trio of destroyers zigzagging through the night at high speed made them a poor prospect for torpedo attack from a submerged sub.

Halfway across the sound, CIC reported that they were picking up approaching air contacts.

Sluff sounded GQ and slowed to twenty knots. The raid was still forty miles out, and he didn't want to be trapped in the confines of Tulagi Harbor when torpedo-laden Bettys started diving on him.

"Combat, Bridge, does the commodore hold this raid?"

"They haven't reported it, Captain," the exec said. "We've passed it on, but apparently *Gary*'s radar doesn't hold them."

Sluff put binocs on the other two destroyers, which had already passed them en route to the fuel barges at Tulagi. Both had air-search radars, but they were the older models, not as capable as the one *J. B. King* had. *Westin* was in the lead, headed straight for Tulagi. *Gary* was astern of her by about two miles. Both were drawing away from *J. B. King*.

"Go back to them and confirm the number of bogeys and their course and speed. Any sign of a response from Cactus air?"

"No, sir, they hold the raid as incoming but they have no assets to launch. Recommend starting a big circle in case these are Bettys."

Sluff ordered the officer of the deck to put the rudder over three degrees to starboard and hold it. "Betty" was the navy's aircraft recognition name for the Japanese G4M medium-range bomber, which could deliver either bombs or the airborne version of the Long Lance. Navy fighter pilots also called them Zippos, in honor of the famous cigarette lighter, because the G4Ms' fuel tanks were unprotected and one solid burst usually was enough to flame them. But first you had to hit them, and preferably before they hit you.

Sluff reached for the bitch-box talk switch as the bridge GQ team double-checked that unneeded equipment was stowed, everyone was properly dressed out for battle, and their sound-powered phone circuits were up and ready. "Gun Control, Captain, open fire at maximum radar-controlled range."

"Control, aye, we're locked on the lead bomber right now. Combat says there are fourteen of 'em, constant bearing, decreasing range, now twenty-one miles."

Bad news, Sluff thought. Fourteen bombers against one destroyer equated to really bad odds. Hopefully the other two tin cans would wake up and join the fight. Then a thought struck him: If the other two destroyers couldn't see the raid, they might not even be at general quarters. The sky was a bland, gray haze. He had no idea what the real visibility was. He watched the five-inch guns up forward swing out and point north. The planes were still out of range, but they wouldn't be for long. The guns would commence firing at about ten miles. If they were coming in at three hundred knots, they'd be in range in less than two minutes. As the ship turned in its defensive circle, the guns trained left until they came into the stops, and then whirled off to the other side to pick up the track. Maybe he should steady up? Begin circling again when they got closer? Before he could decide what to do about that, the bitch-box lit up.

"Bridge, Sigs. Signal from the commodore: What are you doing?"

"Reply as follows: Preparing to engage inbound air raid, three four zero, twenty miles."

"Sigs, aye."

God*dammit,* Sluff thought. Fourteen enemy bombers inbound over Ironbottom Sound in broad daylight and he's sending me flashing-light signals? Don't they have radios over there in *Gary*?

"Bridge, Sigs. From the commodore: Proceed Tulagi as directed. Do not hold any air raid."

At that moment, Sluff could not actually see the Bettys, if that was what they were, but he knew from reading the reports from previous engagements out here that they usually started letting down at thirty miles in a slant dive to the surface for a torpedo attack. And this was the time of the morning when they usually came.

He stared into the sky on the reported bearing, but saw only gray. By now, he calculated, they couldn't be more than ten miles from the ship. A second later, *J. B. King*'s five-inch guns opened up in rapid fire, making enough noise that Sluff could no longer think about what to do about the other ships. He had his own fight to deal with. Hopefully the other ships would see what he was shooting at and realize that, yes, old boy, there was an air raid in progress. Then he saw them, black dots, emerging out of the low cloud base, getting bigger by the second.

The swarm of black dots split up, four coming for *J. B. King* and the rest turning left to go after *Gary* and *Westin*, who still appeared to be oblivious, the silhouettes of their five-inch guns clearly still centerlined. Sluff yelled approvingly when he saw the first of "their" Bettys burst into flames and go cartwheeling into the sea. Then a second one did the same as *J. B. King*'s five gun mounts filled the air with variable-time fused projectiles, five-inch rounds that had a tiny radio in their nose. The radio would beam out a signal ahead. If anything reflected the signal back at the nose of the projectile, the fuse sensed it and detonated the round, hopefully right in the plane's face. He kept the ship in that slow turn because that made it really hard for a bomber to set up a torpedo solution.

A third Betty blossomed fire from his left wing and then exploded in a huge fireball, closer now, four miles at best.

There had been four. Where was number four?

He finally found it, turning outbound in a desperate attempt to evade the firestorm of anti-aircraft fire coming up from *King*. The gunners kept after him, even as he fled to the west, and finally a single round burst under his left wing and he turned into a ball of fire that slowly descended to the sea and then went in.

King's guns ceased firing, and Sluff had to shake his head to get the ringing roar out of his ears. He did a quick scan of the horizon north to west, looking for any skulkers, but the sky seemed clear. He swung his binocs right, to the east, and then swore. Eight miles distant, one of their division mates, most likely *Gary*, was stopped in the sea, sagging amidships with a huge bolus of fire, steam, and smoke erupting from her midships.

Torpedoed. No question. There were two Betty bombers still circling the wreck, trying to set up for a kill. More ominously, there was no answering fire from the dying destroyer. He swept his binocs farther right. *Westin* was also smoking from a large fire aft, but she was still shooting at two bombers that were also circling, like wolves, waiting for the wounded destroyer to make a wrong move.

"All ahead flank, make turns for twenty-seven knots," Sluff yelled from the bridge wing. "Steady as you go!"

He jumped into the pilothouse, took a bearing between the two destroyers, and ordered the helmsman to steer that course. He wished he'd had all four on the floor, but it would take an hour to get the other two boilers on the line for thirty-five knots.

"Gun Control, Captain, engage anything within range."

"Control, aye, but I can only use my two forward guns as long as we're headed straight at them."

"Understood," Sluff said. "I'll turn when we close the range, but for right now, shoot at those bastards however you can."

"Control, aye." A moment later the two forward gun mounts, mounts fifty-one and fifty-two, began to blast away at the two Bettys circling *Gary*. There were a few airbursts, but the Japs kept circling, until one made a quick turn, slanted down to five hundred feet, and dropped a stick of bombs on the hapless destroyer. Sluff watched in horror as the bombs went off, erupting from starboard to port, with one, perhaps two making direct hits. Both Bettys then made a run for it as *King* made the air hot for them.

Sluff told Gun Control to shift targets in the direction of the destroyer that was still shooting. He looked back for the *Gary* and saw that she was gone. There was an ugly cloud of steam and black smoke hovering over the sea, which appeared to be covered in small, black dots. The guns opened up again as *J. B. King* raced in, and the two Bettys circling *Westin* maneuvered hard to escape the new barrage of five-inch fire. As he focused his glasses, *Westin* hit one of the jackals still circling her and a large fireball fell into the sea. His brother, the second Betty, pulled away from the scene, apparently saw *J. B. King* approaching, banked hard, and leveled down for a torpedo attack on *King*.

Sluff didn't have to tell the gunnery officer what to do. Mounts fifty-one and fifty-two shifted targets and began rapid fire on the approaching bomber, which was now maybe three miles away. Bursts began to appear alongside it, but then Sluff saw a thin shape drop from her belly.

Long Lance.

"Right *full* rudder," he called, to swerve the ship away from the approaching torpedo. The turn allowed the rest of *King*'s guns to get into it, and they quickly splashed the final bomber. The huge torpedo raced past them down the port quarter, a cloud of steam spitting out of the back end as it went by. Okay, he thought. Enough of going in circles. "Rudder amidships. Make turns for twenty knots. Quartermaster, give me a course for Tulagi."

Suddenly it got quiet as the ship settled down on a new course.

No, wait, Sluff thought: *Westin*'s got problems, but she'd been able to defend herself. But *Gary*? He couldn't go to Tulagi without picking up her survivors.

"Officer of the deck, I need a bearing to the point where *Gary* went down."

"Two niner zero," the OOD called out, after consulting an alidade out on the port bridge wing to get a bearing to the debris cloud astern.

"Steer two niner zero," Sluff ordered.

As the ship came about, it became clear that *Gary* was now just a cloud of dirty steam. That quick. Wow. Welcome to the war, Commodore.

"Bridge, Combat, radar's clear of bogeys. I think we're missing *Gary*."

"That's affirmative," Sluff said. "We're heading that way now. Looks like she took a torpedo and then a stick of bombs from that last Betty. *Westin*'s got a pretty big fire going, but she was still shooting when the Japs finally left. So: The air scope's clear?"

"Yes, sir, no air contacts." Sluff looked at his watch: 1015. The entire attack had lasted, what—six minutes?

"Officer of the deck, secure from GQ and set the recovery detail," he ordered. Then he called Gun Control on the bitch-box. "Keep two five-inch gun mounts and all the forties manned and ready."

He went back to his chair. More fuel oil all over the place, he thought, and then was ashamed of himself. Poor bastards in the water weren't thinking about *J. B. King*'s pretty decks just now.

He wondered why the commodore had ignored *King*'s warnings. *Gary* probably hadn't even been at general quarters when the torpedoes came. He also wondered what he would have done if the commodore had been on board *King* and told him *not* to go to GQ. Could a unit commander do that? Would he have obeyed?

He told the officer of the deck to maneuver the ship to a stop in the middle of all the dots now visible in the water. "You know what to do," he said.

The OOD just nodded.

NINE

The two remaining ships of DesDiv 212 didn't reach Tulagi Harbor until sunset. *J. B. King* had picked up 225 survivors of the *Gary*, and then had had to take *Westin* in tow. She'd been hit by a torpedo just aft of her aftermost gun mount, losing her stern and, thereby, propellers and steering. Because she was down by the stern and not the bow, *J. B. King* could tow her at almost five knots, and they'd made Tulagi before any more air raids showed up. The harbormaster had sent out a crowd of small boats to take off the *Gary* survivors and the worst of the wounded from *Westin*.

The repair facility at Tulagi was by now, sadly, well versed in what had to be done to make *Westin* seaworthy. Soon a fleet tug would be dispatched to bring her back to the floating dry dock in Nouméa. Once a bevy of Mike-6 boats had surrounded the wounded ship and nudged her close to shore, *J. B. King* had gone alongside a fuel barge for some much-needed black oil. Then they anchored about five hundred yards away from *Westin*, whose superstructure was being covered up by camouflage netting strung out from the beach. That's when Sluff found out who the new commodore of DesDiv 212 was.

Gary had been surprised and then hit with a perfectly delivered Long Lance torpedo amidships. A second Betty had dropped a string of six bombs from starboard to port. Five were near misses, although the shock had probably opened seams all along the destroyer's thin hull and hastened her sinking. It turned out that the sixth had hit just below the bridge and taken out everyone there, including the ship's captain and the commodore. When they got into Tulagi, *Westin*'s CO, who turned out to be one of Sluff's classmates, had sent *J. B. King* a visual signal informing Sluff that, since he, CO *Westin*, was fifteen lineal numbers junior to Sluff, Commander Harmon Wolf was now acting ComDesDiv 212.

Sluff invited the CO of *Westin* for a meeting over in his cabin. He sent *King*'s boat so that the damaged destroyer didn't have to launch one of her own. His name was Tom Miller. Although Sluff didn't remember him from the academy, he did remember the name. He greeted Miller on the quarterdeck and took him up to his inport cabin. Miller looked exhausted and more than a bit sad. He'd lost twenty-six men in the attack and the fire back aft had come very close to mount fifty-five's magazine, requiring that it be flooded. His uniform was still wet from the fire-fighting efforts, and there were bloodstains on his cuffs. Sluff sat him down, opened up his safe, extracted a bottle of Old Grand-Dad, poured a measure into his personal coffee mug, and offered it to the shaken CO, who downed it in one grateful pop. Sluff restored Grand-Dad to the security of his safe and then asked if Miller could figure out why in the hell the commodore hadn't acted on *King*'s radio warnings.

"We heard you loud and clear and went to GQ, although our radar didn't hold any contacts. I knew you had the new SG model so I figured you weren't making shit up." He paused, inhaled, and let out a long whiskey-tinged sigh. "Latham is— was, I guess—a bit of a strange duck. Always on the lookout for slights, real or imagined, to his authority. Larry Goddard, CO *Gary*, told me one time that he had to hold school-call on the wardroom on how to talk to the commodore, lest he take offense at the way something was said. Personally, I think he had a bad case of short man's disease. You couldn't tell him anything, unless you first set it up so that it came out sounding like *he'd* thought of it first. He was also a screamer, and you know how the troops love that shit. I was awfully glad he was in *Gary* and not riding me."

"I don't think *Gary* was even at GQ," Sluff said. "At least you were shooting."

"Well, Commodore," Miller said with a weary grin, "I sure as shit hope you tell it that way in your report."

"Oh, hell, Tom, I'm not the commodore of anything. I'm just senior surviving skipper. Trust me, there'll be a new four-striper coming up from Nouméa in just a couple days. Now: How the hell they gonna get you going again?"

Miller shook his head. "That torpedo took off the final fifty feet of my ship," he said. "Broke both shafts in several places, *removed* the entire stern along with the rudders . . ." He stopped and shook his head. "That torpedo whiplashed the entire ship," he continued. "Bent watertight doors, knocked machinery off its foundations. I've still got people shoring bulkheads in the entire after part of the ship. We got the big fire out pretty quick, but I still don't have a clear picture of all the damage."

"Can they make you seaworthy here in Tulagi?" Sluff asked.

"Barely," Miller said. "Either way, we're eventually gonna have to be towed back to the States, or at least to Pearl, which means we're talking four thousand miles at five knots, tops. I don't know if Halsey has the assets to do that. He may just decide to scuttle her."

Sluff had no response to that possibility. It was that real. *Westin* was a Benson-class destroyer, and, although not exactly obsolete, in comparison with the new Fletcher class she was far less capable. The big bosses might very well decide to cut their losses, send the crew back to the States to man up a new Fletcher, strip her for parts, and then consign the old girl to Davy Jones's locker.

The radio messenger knocked on the door and brought in the message board. "Oboe from COMSOPAC," he announced. Sluff had sent out a brief report on the air raid, the sinking of *Gary*, the loss of Commodore Latham, and the fact that *Westin* had no back end anymore. This must be the reply. He scanned the message.

The date-time group was less than an hour ago. It was an operational immediate precedence, known in radio central parlance as an "Oboe." It was addressed for action to *J. B. King*, information to the other four ships involved. He read the text aloud. "CO *J. B. King* assume duties as ComDesDiv Two-Twelve. Tow *Westin* from Tulagi ASAP. Rendezvous with USS *Bobolink*, USS *Carter*, USS *Evans*, currently en route Cactus. Once handover of *Westin* complete, *Carter*, *Evans*, *King* return Cactus for NGFS duties. CDD Two-Twelve acknowledge."

Sluff showed the message to Miller. "Well,there

you go, *Commodore,*" Miller said. "Congratulations. I think."

Sluff shook his head. "Temporary," he said. "Like I said, there'll be some eager-beaver four-striper here by tomorrow, probably. But: That said, how soon can you set up to take a towline? I'd like to transit Torpedo Alley in the dark if we can."

"Give me an hour to get a final damage assessment, make sure we're safe to go to sea. I'll send you a light as soon as I can."

Sluff nodded. Miller got up, thanked him for the shot of Dutch courage. "Take a good hard look at your hull," Sluff said. "If you think she's *not* ready for sea, we won't go."

Two hours later, as *King* remained at anchor awaiting word from *Westin,* a message came in from COMSOPAC changing the plan, confirming what the old destroyer saw: If you don't like the plan, just wait a minute—it'll change. The two destroyers coming northwest from Nouméa had been detached from the slow-moving fleet tug and told to proceed at best speed to Guadalcanal, there to rendezvous with *J. B. King,* chop to ComDesDiv 212, and await further orders. The fleet tug, USS *Bobolink,* would keep chugging toward Tulagi at twelve knots and get there when she got there. The two destroyers, however, would arrive in Ironbottom Sound waters by dawn tomorrow.

Sluff called the exec to his cabin and told him what was going on. They'd decided to shut down one boiler room for the night while steaming auxiliary on the other until sunrise. That would give the engineers some much-needed rest. The ship had been refueled and the gun boss had managed to cadge a few hundred more rounds of five-inch ammo from the base magazines. The exec said he would tell radio central to take the communications guard for ComDesDiv 212. Sluff agreed while reiterating that his "appointment" was going to be short-lived, but he recognized that, since the commodore and most of his small staff had been killed aboard *Gary*, any messages addressed for DesDiv 212 needed somewhere to land.

While they were speculating on what the "further orders" might be, Chief Hawkins on the signal bridge called down.

"Cap'n, we're getting a light in from *Westin.* They're experiencing progressive flooding and they're putting all their people ashore as a precaution. There's more but we're still taking in the message."

Sluff thanked him for the heads-up and told the exec. They both headed topside to the bridge. There was nothing *King* could do other than come alongside and add her pumping capacity to that of the damaged destroyer, but if *Westin* was truly experiencing progressive flooding, that would only delay the inevitable. Apparently that torpedo had done a whole lot more damage than tearing off the ship's stern.

It was a peculiarity of Tulagi Harbor that the water depth along the shore fell off steeply to a depth of hundreds of feet. That meant damaged ships could be brought right up to the shoreline, literally moored to palm trees along the beach, and then covered with camouflage netting so as to appear to be part of the island to visiting Betty bombers. *Westin* was now no more than fifty feet offshore and was using her boat and some landing craft from the harbormaster to ferry the crew from the sinking ship to the shore. Sluff offered *J. B. King*'s launch to the CO of *Westin* by flashing light, but he said he had enough help.

"What's left of her stern is damned near awash now," the exec said. "I'm surprised they can't get flooding boundaries set." The scene in front of them was beginning to look like a movie set, with work lights on deck illuminating the desperate effort to keep the pumps running even as a muted evacuation was under way from the forward end of the ship.

"She's not that old, XO," Sluff said, feeling helpless. "But that torpedo probably opened her seams from end to end. Those damned things hit you amidships, they break you in half, like *Gary*. If they hit you on one end or the other, the explosion torques the hull so bad that suddenly

121

you're fighting hundreds of small leaks. *Dammit!*"

They watched for another thirty minutes as the small landing craft surrounded the dying ship, their hulls barely visible in all the diesel smoke and spotlights as they bumped up against the destroyer's sides to get people off. Then came the sound Sluff had been waiting for: a loud crack, as the first of the mooring lines holding her to the shore parted like a gunshot. Then came another. Suddenly he could see her main deck tilting toward him. *Westin* was beginning to capsize.

"Hope to Christ they safed their depth charges," Sluff muttered. By now several of the *King*'s officers were lining the bridge wing, watching the evolving spectacle. There was no talking. Everyone knew that there, but for the grace of God . . .

Three more mooring lines parted in quick succession and, like an exhausted whale, *Westin* rolled slowly to starboard until her mast reluctantly touched the water, and then she subsided in a tumult of boiling water, steam, dust, and smoke, all made surreal by the small searchlights mounted on the harbor boats as they backed out of harm's way. The doomed destroyer turned turtle, her back half well down in the water, her stumpy sonar dome visible now just behind the bow, and then she slid out of sight in a rumble of escaping air and the sudden bright stink of fuel oil. There was a moment of silence, and then the diesel engines of the various boats assaulted the night air as they pushed into the foaming patch of black water, looking for any people who might have made it off in her last moments.

Sluff waited anxiously for a series of thunderous explosions to erupt from *Westin*'s depth charges as she sank past set-point depth, but nothing happened. Then he remembered: The torpedo had taken her stern off. Including the depth-charge racks. At this moment, while there were all those boats circling in there and possibly even sailors struggling in the water, that was very good thing.

"Bring me a message blank," he said. COMSOPAC needed to know what had just happened. He stared back out over the dark waters of Tulagi Harbor. Of the *Westin*, nothing remained but a three-hundred-foot-long patch of foaming bubbles, as sixteen hundred tons of steel tumbled soundlessly down the drowned flanks of Florida Island into the abyss below.

TEN

At 2200 that night, two high-priority messages came in from COMSOPAC. Both were addressed to ComDesDiv 212. The first acknowledged Sluff's report about the loss of *Westin*, and instructed him to pass on to the CO of *Westin* that air transport would be dispatched to remove him and his crew to Nouméa.

The second message revealed what that term "further orders" was all about. According to coast watchers, six Jap destroyers were preparing to make a high-speed run down the Slot to land reinforcements for the Jap garrison on Guadalcanal. They were expected to arrive at or around midnight of the next day. Since there were no cruisers available following the debacle of the Savo engagement, DesDiv 212 was ordered to intercept and break up the resupply effort. Sluff called the exec and asked him to get all the officers not on watch to assemble in the wardroom.

When the exec knocked on his door to tell him that everyone was assembled, Sluff showed him the second message. The exec whistled softly. "Two-to-one odds in a night fight against the masters of that game," he said.

"Well, yes," Sluff said. "But now that we know how they do it, I plan to hand it right back to them."

When they came into the wardroom all the officers stood up as custom required. Sluff went to the head of the table, sat down, looked around the room, and said, "Okay, seats."

Everyone sat down.

"It's late," Sluff began. "It's also hot and dark, and everyone's tired, so I'll keep this short." He paused for effect. "Tonight we watched a destroyer succumb to her damage. That was not a pleasant sight. Fortunately, we're pretty sure all her people got off safely ashore. The people in *Gary* were not so lucky. You saw the survivors today. They have my sympathy, but we did warn them that an attack was coming and somebody pretty senior dropped the ball. There will be an investigation of her loss, so I want each of you who were on the bridge or in CIC to write down what you remember about the minutes leading up to the actual attack and hand it in to the XO.

"Now: You may have heard that I've been designated as ComDesDiv Two-Twelve. That is a temporary expediency. The system needed a landing place for all of the division's message traffic."

That produced some tired smiles.

"The operational reason for that expediency is that six Jap destroyers are going to show up off Cape Esperance tomorrow night to land supplies and reinforcements for the Nips over on Cactus. We've been told to break that up."

"Who's 'we,' Captain?" Billy Chandler, the gunnery officer, asked.

Sluff smiled. "Yeah, Billy," he said. "We started out as a three-ship division, but now we're down to one. Actually, two more tin cans, the *Carter* and the *Evans*, are showing up tomorrow morning to join the fight. I plan to meet with their skippers as soon as they get in and refuel, and then we'll go out there tomorrow at sundown and kick some Jap ass. I need you to get the word out to your people that another night fight's coming. Once we have a plan of attack, we'll meet again so everyone's up to speed. Now: Go write down what you remember in your wheel books and then get some rest."

Sluff was up on the bridge by sunrise as the harbor waited for the morning air raid from Rabaul. This time the Cactus fighters had been able to get up to intercept the raid, and nothing much came of it. The casualties of yesterday appeared to have taken the fight out of today's Betty squadron. The destroyers *Carter* and *Evans*, both Benson-classes, came steaming into Tulagi at 0830 and were assigned anchorages near *J. B. King*. They were both fairly new, sporting five single five-inch guns and ten torpedo tubes. Tugs pushing fuel barges came chugging out shortly thereafter, and then each ship launched a boat to bring its captain aboard *J. B. King*. The day had opened as every other day in the Solomons, hot, humid, with growing squall lines already assembling to the west over Savo Island. The oil slick from the late departed *Westin* was no longer in evidence.

Each of the captains had brought along his navigation officer, who in some destroyers were beginning to be called the operations officer. Sluff was waiting for them in *King*'s wardroom with the exec and his own navigation/operations officer, Lieutenant Tim McCarthy. The two skippers were both from the class one year behind Sluff, and both called him commodore. Sluff went through his usual disclaimer about that, sat everyone down, and then laid out what he planned to do that night. As he began talking he was struck by the fact that both of the other COs had immediately assumed their roles as his tactical subordinates. He was the senior CO, and they were here to learn the plan and then go execute it. It was one of the Navy's better aspects: Lay out who's who, and then everyone falls in line and gets to work. They were all three-stripers and commanding officers of a destroyer. Sluff Harmon was the senior officer, and therefore the boss. No hurt feelings, no quibbling, no discussion. He found it heartening.

Sluff began with a question. "Have either of you fought a surface action with the Japs?" he asked.

They both shook their heads. Both of them had done carrier escort duty and had been through some air attacks, but that was it.

"There's six of them and three of us," he said. "But: They're going to be loaded with troops and supplies, and we are going to be loaded for bear. Doesn't mean they can't fight, but they'll be encumbered by their mission, which is to get into coastal waters along Cape Esperance and get all those soldiers and rice bags ashore.

"My plan's fairly simple: We're going to set up

a patrol line athwart their most likely course into Guadalcanal. *King* here has a really good SG radar suite, so we should be able to detect them before they even know we're there. When they're in range, I want all three of us to fire five torpedoes each. That's fifteen fish. We'll shoot straight up the bearing of the lead Jap. When the torpedoes start going off, we will open fire with everything we've got—for one full minute. Then we'll cease fire, turn diagonally to the northwest or northeast, depending on which way we were headed when it started, run for two minutes at best speed, and then slow and open fire again. For one minute."

He paused for a moment. "The reason for this is that they'll shoot Long Lance at our gun flashes. It'll take 'em a minute to figure out the attack geometry, and that's when we douse our gun flashes and maneuver so as to *not* be there when the Long Lances arrive. We'll do this for as long as it takes: maneuver at high speed in a great big circle around their formation, opening fire for one minute, cease firing, maneuver again, resume firing. With luck they'll think they're surrounded by an entire posse of American ships. Even if they don't, they'll be getting hit from a continuously varying sector. Now: This means four-boiler ops, because we need to move, and I mean, *move*, like they do. As you know, their tin cans routinely go thirty-six knots."

"What happens if it all falls apart?" the CO of *Evans* asked. "Do you intend to control the formation like the cruiser guys do?"

"Before it starts, I'll use flashing-light signals as much as possible, and I'd like you two guys to remain radio-silent. I'll use TBS radio once the shooting starts. *King* will lead the column, and we'll pass you range and bearing data. If your radars can see them, great. If they can't, use our data. If it all turns to crap, then Nelson rules, okay?"

Both skippers nodded. "Oughta work," the CO of *Carter* said.

"With any luck," Sluff said. "Now, why don't all you ops people go up to CIC and work out the charts and formations. Plot out a dry run on a chart. See how it shapes up; look for holes in the plan, and whether or not we need any more comms or special signals. Oh, and the standard distance between ships will be a thousand yards."

"Why so long?" the CO of *Evans* asked.

"Because they're used to our being only five hundred yards apart. That makes us a more compact target for their torpedoes. This way, we're hopefully outside their spread calculations."

The two COs nodded. The meeting broke up and Sluff took them to his cabin. He asked them to brief him on their ships' capabilities, since they were both the class that had preceded the Fletchers. He was especially interested in whether

129

or not they had a CIC and the new surface SG search radars. *King* was a brand-new ship. *Carter* and *Evans* were two years older. *Carter* had a CIC kludged together in the captain's sea cabin and the older SC radar. *Evans* had the earlier-version radar, but no CIC.

"Okay, then we will probably be sending you targeting data," Sluff said. "I don't want another melee like Callaghan fought. I'd like to set the fish to run out to their max ranges at the low speed setting. Oh, and I want torpedo target depth set at five feet."

"*Five* feet?" the *Carter*'s CO asked. "They'll broach."

"I talked to some sub COs when we came through Pearl," Sluff said. "They're all up in arms about their torpedoes not working. They're being forced to use the magnetic exploder, but they're convinced the fish are running too deep. One CO told me to set the depth back to the first pin, five feet, and you might hit something."

"I hadn't heard that, but I've read a lot of after-action reports full of torpedo complaints."

"The Japs don't have that problem, do they," Sluff said. "And the only fix for the Long Lance is to guess when they shoot 'em and then maneuver boldly to get out of their way. I said we'd turn after every firing run, but I want you to know I'll be playing that by ear. If I see them steady up, even under fire, then I figure they're turning the big dogs loose, and we're gonna do something. We may even slow way down. Okay?"

The *Carter*'s CO asked Sluff about the battleship action. Sluff asked what they'd heard down in Nouméa.

"The SOPAC staffers are saying the *South Dakota* screwed the pooch right in the middle of it and had to withdraw."

"What else?" Sluff asked. The *Carter*'s CO cleared his throat. "They said you bailed out of the destroyer line when the big boys started shooting and the Japs started shooting back. That the only reason you weren't hit was because you weren't there."

"That's exactly correct," Sluff said. "I wasn't there—especially when the Long Lances arrived."

The two captains looked at him with incredulous expressions.

"Look," Sluff said. "Ching Lee put all four of his tin cans in a line in front of the two battleships. He issued no plan and there was no SOP. He told us to start shooting when they started shooting, and that's what we did. My CIC reported that the Japs were getting hammered, but then they turned east, steadied up for about a minute, and then turned north. That told me they'd just launched a swarm of torpedoes against our line, and the operational reports from the Savo fights all said the same thing: They aim for the front of the formation, for the van. Basically, I felt like I knew what was coming, and so, yes, I turned out of the formation."

"Um," the *Evans* CO began, but Sluff held up a hand.

"Consider this, okay?" he said. "There were eighteen guns of sixteen-inch caliber behind us firing at the Japs. The range was down to ten thousand yards—five miles—and those two battle-wagons were throwing eighteen *tons* of metal at that Jap formation every forty-five seconds. The four destroyers in the van were throwing one *half*-ton of metal at the same formation. Now I'll admit that it felt good to light up the night with five-gun salvos, but our contribution to what was happening was insignificant. In my view, that's the problem with tying destroyers to the main body of heavy-caliber ships. Look: We all keep thinking—guns. But our main battery ought to more properly be the ten torpedoes we can each set loose into the equation. Admittedly, our fish are nowhere near as good as theirs, but ten torpedoes fired from a destroyer equals eight thousand pounds of joy juice, or four tons versus one-half ton from our guns. Basically, when the elephants got into it that night, we became Long Lance sponges. That's why I bailed, and why *King* was the ship picking up survivors after the battleships left us all behind to fend for ourselves."

The two COs stared down at the deck and said nothing.

Sluff grinned. "Heresy, yes?"

Carter's CO shook his head. "Tomorrow night

it's gonna be just us chickens, so what you're proposing makes a lot of sense. But if I'm part of a cruiser or even a battleship-cruiser formation, I'm inclined to do what I'm told."

Sluff nodded. "I understand that," he said. "But here's the thing: Tonight I think *King* will have the best radar picture, so I'll want you to do what I tell you to do, even if that sounds a lot like 'Do as I say, not as I do.' Or did, I guess. We're gonna be outnumbered by some ships that are pretty damned good at this night-fighting stuff. Our only chance will be to surprise them before they even know we're there."

They nodded again, but Sluff had the feeling he hadn't convinced them. He knew what the problem was: Admiral Lee had put four destroyers in a column formation ahead of his battleships. He'd had every right to expect them to stay there, perhaps, and this was hard for Sluff to swallow, to soak up the initial salvo of Long Lance torpedoes. Now Sluff was demanding that these two skippers do what *he* told them to do in the upcoming fight. As he had not. He tried to think of some argument to make that would show why his situation was different from that of the battleship action. He couldn't.

Considering further discussion pointless, he stood up, indicating that their meeting was over. The two skippers headed up one level to join their ops people in *King*'s tiny CIC.

ELEVEN

Savo Island

A half hour after midnight the three destroyers were quietly steaming at fifteen knots on an east-west line across the most likely approach route for the Japanese formation. They were just east of Savo Island, cutting the line between the Slot and the Japanese army sector east of Cape Esperance. The night was dark and steaming hot with not the slightest hint of a cooling breeze. Every time they turned around, the sulfurous gas from their smokestacks hung over each ship like some kind of evil miasma until they steadied back up. *J. B. King* was in the lead, then *Carter*, then *Evans*, all spaced at a distance of half a mile. There was a low overcast and the occasional rainsquall line, but for some reason that seemed to make the talk-between-ships radio circuit even clearer. Sluff had used it sparingly, depending mostly on red-cloaked flashing-light signals to maneuver the formation.

He'd spent the last half hour down in the CIC room. The radar picture was just about perfect. The fringes of Savo Island were visible to the south, and his three-ship formation was clear as a bell. He'd begun to wonder if he shouldn't take station down here in CIC instead of on the bridge. It was traditional for the captain to be on the bridge to maneuver the ship, especially once an action started and the possibility of collision increased. But now he was, technically, at least, a unit commander. He needed to see the entire picture, not just what was appearing right out in front of the ship. Because he was still the skipper of *J. B. King*, he'd reluctantly returned to the bridge. He would just have to depend on his exec to translate the radar picture.

He was also aware of the fact that he was disobeying the standard destroyer rule about *where* the exec manned up for his battle station. Traditionally, and also by the regulations, the exec was supposed to be stationed at what was called secondary conn, a small and totally exposed GQ station back aft, behind the ship's second stack. It had a steering console and an engine order telegraph, plus access to all the major sound-powered phone circuits. That way, if the forward half of the ship was disabled and the captain killed, the exec should be able to take command. The advent of radar and the Combat Information Center, however small, had forced COs equipped with the new surface-search radar to make a choice: the second senior officer standing out in the wind and the dark, not to mention exposed to the effects of near misses, shrapnel, or actual hits, or one deck below the bridge overseeing the tracing table and the radar scopes. As far as Sluff was concerned, the technology had clearly out-paced the regulations.

"Bridge, Combat, radar contact, bearing zero one zero, range thirty thousand yards, composition four to six. Initiating track."

Sluff reached forward for the bitch-box talk switch. "Bridge, aye, and alert the other ships by TBS. Keep it short."

"Combat, aye."

"Officer of the deck," Sluff called softly. "Alert all GQ stations that the enemy has arrived."

The ship had gone to GQ at 2200. Sluff had previously put out the word that everyone was to stand easy on station until contact was made. That meant that even though the entire crew was at their GQ stations, the ones manning guns and torpedo stations or damage-control parties could open hatches, untie their kapok life jackets, lean back against a bulkhead, and nod off until something actually happened. This did not apply, of course, to the engineers down in the four main spaces or the CIC and bridge teams. The hammers could doze off, but the power and the eyes had to stay awake. Sluff could hear hatches closing and power amplidynes lighting off all over the ship as the five gun mounts came to life. Three minutes later, Combat had developed a radar track.

"Bridge, Combat, enemy formation appears to be on course one seven zero, speed three-five."

Wow, Sluff thought. Those Jap destroyers could move out when they wanted to. He did the math in his head: they'd be in range of American torpedoes pretty damned quick. He acknowledged the information from CIC and then listened to Bob Frey down in Combat going out over the TBS radio circuit with position, course, and speed data for the enemy formation. The other two destroyers might actually hold the Japs on radar, but they had been ordered to maintain radio silence. Then he heard the torpedo mounts training out to starboard. The American column was driving west on its ambush line. He wondered if he should increase speed, but for launching torpedoes, fifteen knots put much less strain on the weapons when they hit the water sideways than thirty knots would.

"Bridge, Combat, coming up on time to fire," Combat said over the bitch-box.

"XO, you take control of the torpedo mounts," Sluff ordered. "I'll keep control of the guns unless I lose the picture. Make sure the other ships are ready to launch when we do."

Combat acknowledged. Sluff felt a shiver of concern, now that he'd given control of the torpedo attack to the CIC. Then he rationalized it: A torpedo firing solution was a simple math problem, but it depended on knowing where the target was and where he was headed at the moment of launch. Up here on the darkened bridge, he was relatively blind; CIC was not. The gun director's radar was being cued onto the oncoming targets by the ship's search radar until *King*'s fire-control radar picked them up. Those cues came from CIC. Once the little white spikes of video danced in the range gate of an oscilloscope down in gun plot, the gunnery officer would know when to open fire long before Sluff would. The only rule binding them was that the torpedoes had to start hitting before the Americans revealed themselves to the enemy by opening fire with fifteen guns. He'd still have fifteen torpedoes in reserve if another attack opportunity presented itself.

The night seemed to get even darker as the heavy, humid air pressed in on all the topside watch standers. Steel helmets, a lumpy hot kapok life jacket wrapped around everyone's torso, shirts buttoned up to the neck, trouser cuffs stuffed into their socks, the officers wearing gun belts with a heavy .45, extra clips of ammo, a medical kit with the morphine syringes, a flashlight, and a big knife. Sluff thought about increasing speed just to generate a breeze, but then the torpedoes began to launch into the black waters around them. A whoosh, a big splash, and then silence. Five fish went off the ship in quick succession, burrowing down into the sea and then rising to the preset depth, then screaming away at the onrushing Japanese ships at nearly thirty miles an hour. The Mark XV fish could go forty-five knots, but at the slower speed its range increased to almost seven miles. Sluff wanted the torpedoes to hit them way out there to give his little band time to then shoot them up with five-inch. Five away, five left.

The Japs were coming straight at them at thirty-five knots. Combined with the speed of twenty-six knots for his own torpedoes, Sluff calculated a closing speed of almost seventy miles an hour.

"Time on target?" Sluff asked Combat.

"Eighty seconds," the exec answered.

"Officer of the deck, inform the snipes to stand by for thirty knots."

His plan was to stay at fifteen knots so that the gun computers would have a stable speed input for the initial minute of firing. Then they were going to kick her in the ass and run like hell northwest to get on the enemy's starboard bow before the next round of gunfire.

"Main Control says they're ready-teddy," the OOD announced. Sluff grinned. Apparently his chief engineer was sensitive about having to be *told* to be ready for a sudden high-speed dash. And yet he knew that, down in four main holes, two boiler rooms and two engine rooms, the snipes would be dumping their coffee cups into the bilge and getting up close to their giant steam machines, making sure that all the critical temperatures and pressures were in range, the steam leaks reduced to a bare minimum, and the boilers ready for a huge temperature transient.

"Twenty seconds," Combat called. Everyone on the bridge held his breath. Sluff was tempted to go out on the bridge wing to see what happened, but in a few seconds he'd be ordering the whole formation to open fire, and then the noise of the guns would overwhelm conscious thought if he went outside.

"Mark intercept," Combat called. "They didn't change course, so—"

At that moment flares of red and white explosions lit up the horizon to the north. Sluff picked up the TBS handset and ordered the other two ships to open fire with guns. Then he looked at his watch, as the two five-inch on the bow opened up with a satisfying pair of ear-squeezing blams. He could feel the other three guns aft doing the same as the ship performed its full-salvo wiggle from bow to stern. Then another salvo. Then a third. When the fourth salvo let go he ordered the division to increase speed to thirty knots.

J. B. King palpably jumped when the snipes opened the throttles and hit the turbines with a bolus of steam for fifty thousand horsepower. The forced-draft blowers screamed as they spooled up to feed the boiler furnaces with enough air to atomize the sudden gouts of fuel oil going into the fireboxes. *King* was the lead ship, so if the other two didn't get the message, there was no danger of *King* driving over the top of a destroyer still loafing along at fifteen knots. They'd better be paying attention, he thought. If we don't all move out now, the Japs will soon be sending us a lethal message.

As the ship accelerated, a welcome breeze blew through the pilothouse, which happily pushed the gunsmoke out of everyone's eyes and noses. The guns stopped firing on command from CIC. He went out to the bridge wing to see if the other two had also stopped shooting. He saw one last full salvo come off the third ship in line, but then they, too, went dark. He went back to the bitch-box.

"Combat, Captain, turn in two minutes or whatever it takes to keep the range at about eight thousand yards. Once all three ships have steadied up, open fire again for one minute. *You* give the commence-firing order and keep passing our range and bearing data to the other two ships."

"Combat, aye," the exec said. Sluff trained his glasses out on the dull glow of several fires four to five miles away. It would take Combat a few minutes to sort out how many ships had been hit or at least stopped, and if there were still any of them pressing on toward Guadalcanal. If nothing else, he thought, we sure as hell achieved surprise.

He got back up into his chair and waited. It was so dark that his eyes were having trouble readjusting after the flashes of the forward gun mounts. He swiveled the chair around to the right, where he could still see the dull glow of fires on what looked like the horizon. Suddenly there was a massive explosion, bright enough to reveal three Jap destroyers in silhouette. They appeared to be milling about in the vicinity of the torpedo intercept point. The TBS transmissions were just about constant now, as the exec's team in CIC fed the other two ships range and bearing data. Then he heard the words he'd been waiting for, the order to turn the column to the north. The ship heeled smartly at thirty knots, tilting enough to make the bridge team grab something to stay upright. The relative wind changed suddenly and a blast of air ruffled all the charts on the chart table behind him, sending the quartermaster scrambling after them. Ninety seconds later, the command went out: Commence firing.

Sluff remained in his chair as the two forward guns spat fire and steel into the night. On the third salvo, he heard something else: incoming. The Japs, fully alerted now, had opened fire on their tormentors. They were off in range, judging by the shell splashes and explosions in the water around *King*, but they were right on in bearing. That meant they had guessed correctly that the American column was running fast. If they think they know our course and speed, Sluff thought, they'll get a torpedo solution. Four large waterspouts rose close enough to the ship that everyone could hear metal splinters humming through the night air. Then the guns fell silent.

"Combat, Bridge, immediate execute over TBS: Speed fifteen."

"Combat, aye, speed fifteen."

The Americans might have stopped shooting, but the Japs were now in full cry. He could no longer see the ships themselves, but their gun flashes were rapid, disciplined, whole-ship salvos. Damn, he thought, admiringly: they're good. They're really good. But as his column slowed down to half the previous speed, the incoming shells began to walk ahead, still all over the place in range, but definitely still being computed as if the Americans were still blasting through the night at thirty-something knots, just as the Japanese would have been. Sluff hoped they wouldn't fire star shell, because then the plan would have to change.

"Combat, Captain. Immediate execute: speed ten."

"Combat, aye," the exec said, but his voice sounded doubtful.

"Based on their shell splashes, they still think we're going thirty knots," Sluff said. "I want their torpedoes ahead of us, not amongst us."

"Combat, aye," the exec replied, as the ship began slowing even more. Ten knots in a running gunfight was unheard of, but as long as the Japs didn't have radar, Sluff thought, this ought to work.

"Bridge, Combat, sonar detecting high-speed screws, up Doppler."

And? Sluff thought.

"Passing ahead," the exec called. "Multiple screws. Good call, Captain."

This time, Sluff thought, but now we have to finish this somehow. "Combat, Captain. First, alert the division: Stand by for second torpedo attack. Second: Order up thirty-three knots, and turn us to the northeast, to whatever it takes to get back into torpedo range. We'll run for four minutes, slow down, and let loose."

"Combat, aye."

Sluff heard the orders going out to resume thirty-three knots speed, and then a course change order to 040, farther right than he had expected. Then the warning to stand by for a torpedo attack. He relaxed in his chair as they sped up and then executed the turn. The Japs had quit firing once they'd dispatched torpedoes, probably because they couldn't find the Americans.

"Combat, Captain: Any idea of what we've accomplished?"

"There are three contacts milling about in one location," the exec replied. "There's one intermittent contact, but no sign of the other two. The good news is that they're all bunched together."

"And not moving south?"

"No, sir, probably rescuing survivors. Recommend we slow down early and send the fish in, before they realize what's happening."

XO was right, Sluff thought. "Concur, set it up.

And once our fish arrive, we open fire again, and this time we keep it up until they stop shooting back."

"Combat, aye."

Two down, four to go, he thought. Maybe only three if that fuzzy contact was low in the water due to battle damage. It was a strange feeling to sit here in his chair on the bridge and listen to his exec issuing formation orders. But there was no getting around it: The exec and his team down there had a plotting table that showed where everyone was and which way they were moving, friendlies and enemy alike. They had a radar picture, which meant that they could assign search radar contacts to the gun director's radar directly, converting them from contacts into targets.

Another course change went out, this time to 060, as the exec adjusted their direction of attack to ensure their torpedoes would be within range. Then a speed change, followed by a final stand-by for launching torpedoes. The fires on the local horizon were muted now. Hopefully the Japs thought the Americans had gone into the night. When that ship blew up and lit up the sea, they'd have been able to see there were only three American destroyers out there opposing them, not cruisers or something even bigger.

The ship plowed into the sea as she slowed and her own wake caught up with her, the bow pushing a mass of water to either side as the guns came out to the surface-action starboard position, pointing south. He watched the pitometer needle as it wound down to the left to indicate fifteen knots. When it stopped moving, the order went out to let them go. This time it was *King*'s after torpedo mount firing, with none of the recoil and hammering blasts of the five-inch. Just muffled thumps as five torpedoes leapt into the black water and drove away into the darkness. Behind *King* the other ships were also launching, and soon a swarm of fifteen torpedoes would be streaking toward that dull glow on the horizon only four miles away.

He waited. He wanted to ask Combat how long it would take, but he didn't want to disturb their concentration. As the fish ran toward the cluster of Jap ships, the gun director and main battery plot were honing their solution, getting ready to take control of the gun mounts and begin rapid continuous fire. As soon as the first shells started landing, the team in CIC would see the splashes showing up as small pips among the bigger ship targets. They could then call main battery plot and apply spots, small adjustments in range and bearing to merge those little contacts with the actual Jap ships.

"Bridge, Combat, mark intercept time."

Nothing happened.

Five seconds, ten seconds. Fifteen. Had every one of those fish missed? *Nothing* out of fifteen fired?

Then came a single large explosion in the general direction of the Jap formation. A yellow-white ball boiled upward, and then another one, both explosions turning red and then into a profusion of what looked like tracer fire erupting into the night in all directions. A magazine hit, he thought.

Okay. Three to go. He reached for the bitch-box to order commence-firing, opened his mouth to say the words, but the forward gun mounts beat him to it with satisfying blasts. He jumped out of his chair and went out onto the starboard bridge wing to make sure the entire formation was shooting. It was, with fifteen five-inch guns flashing yellow gouts of fire to the southwest. There was enough light from the gun flashes for him to see his other two ships, *his* other two ships, their images blinking like a slow-motion film as their guns fired, the red-hot shells arcing away, rising at first and then descending in a lethal arc, ending in a red flash as they either hit something substantial or tore into the sea and then went off underwater.

The Japs started shooting back, but the volume of fire was nothing like the first time. He thrilled to the knowledge that they were battering their blinded and confused enemy. Then he remembered: Once they can see you, they'll send the big dogs.

"Combat, Captain," he called, shouting over the noise of the forward guns. "Speed three three. *Now.*"

"Combat, aye," the exec replied. "We're killing them. Can't tell the shell splashes from the targets anymore."

The order went out on an immediate execute. Speed thirty knots. Move. Jump out of the way of any incoming fans of Long Lance. We saved some fish—they would have, too. *J. B. King* settled for a moment in the froth of her suddenly accelerating propellers and then lunged ahead.

We did this before, he thought. Vary the speed. Now we need a course change, too. He called Combat and told the exec to order a thirty-degree change of course to the right. The range no longer mattered: the American guns could shoot out to eighteen thousand yards, but he was still wary of giving the Japs a steady fire-control solution.

"Tango, this is Tango Baker. Immediate execute: Corpen zero niner zero, I say again, corpen zero niner zero, stand by—execute!"

The ship heeled to port as she came around, still accelerating from fifteen to thirty knots. Sluff had a blinking memory of a Western movie, with the Indians riding around the wagon train in a big circle, shooting everything up. He heard a ripping sound above the ship as a salvo of Japanese fire passed right overhead. He fought off a sudden urge to turn right into the Japanese formation, to take it down to point-blank range and kill them all.

Reason prevailed. From eight thousand yards

out in the darkness and executing a huge circle around the cluster of Jap destroyers, they should be able to pound them into submission with relative impunity.

"Captain, Combat, *Carter*'s been hit in her after engine room. Can't sustain thirty knots."

"Slow down to twenty, then," Sluff said, "relative" obviously being the correct term of art. More shells passed overhead, a little lower now as the Japs searched for the correct range. He went out to the bridge wing to see if *Carter* was burning and thus more visible, but all he could see were the flashes of gunfire from both ships behind him. He put his binoculars out in the direction that his own guns were pointing, trying to hold them steady as blast after blast of fire and smoke cracked the night air, almost right in his face. There was still a red glow in that direction, but it was now punctuated by the flashes of their own shells going in.

"Combat, Captain, how many of them still afloat?"

"Two for sure, possibly three, but there's so much shell-splash return over there we can't be sure."

"Cease firing, and *turn* the formation back to the northeast, zero six zero, speed two-zero. I'm declaring victory before they find the range."

"Combat, aye, ceasing fire, zero six zero, speed two-zero, by turn movement. Going out now."

A turn movement meant that the ships would turn together instead of following the guide ship in a column, as in a corpen movement. The sooner they turned, the sooner they'd be running away from the Long Lances while presenting the smallest possible target to those dreaded torpedoes.

The sudden silence brought palpable relief. His ears still rang from the five-inch salvos, and the inside of the pilothouse looked like a seedy pool hall with all the smoke. He could hear the clink and clank of brass powder cases rolling all over the forecastle deck. As long as they outran any torpedoes coming their way, they could indeed declare victory. It looked like they'd sunk half the Jap resupply force, if not two-thirds. He looked at his watch by the light of his red-lens flashlight: 0215. The Japs would have to retire now because they needed to be well out of range of the Cactus air forces by daylight. His orders had been to break up the resupply effort. As soon as they turned north back toward Rabaul, it would be mission accomplished.

"Combat, Captain: Get me an update on *Carter*'s damage. I plan to run northeast for twenty minutes, then turn down in the direction of Tulagi. What's the range to the Japs now?"

"Range is thirteen thousand and opening. Radar shows two contacts now; the third one is no longer onscreen. Looks like we maybe got four of them."

"Four out of six ain't bad," Sluff said. "And if those other two are damaged, Cactus'll be after them by daybreak. Get a report off to the flyboys with their position and probable course and speed. Tell 'em they were carrying Jap soldiers, so there may be some work to do in the morning."

He shone the light on his watch again. If they ran for twenty minutes at twenty knots, they'd be almost twelve miles away from the Japs and any pursuing torpedoes. It was still darker than a well digger's ass out there, so the Japs *should* not be able to target them, much less pursue. That was one of the big differences between Jap and American destroyers: The Japs carried reloads for their torpedo tubes. The Americans did not.

Combat came back five minutes later with a report on *Carter*'s damage. A shell that went off right on the deckplates had wrecked her number two engine room. The entire engine-room crew had been killed by the explosion and subsequent superheated steam leaks. The space had been isolated, but *Carter* was starting to fall behind. Sluff ordered up eighteen knots to keep his formation together.

"You still hold those two ships?"

"Yes, sir, and they appear to be headed back up the Slot. We're still developing a track on them."

"Good," Sluff said. "Pass it on to Cactus once you compute it. In the meantime we're gonna keep heading northeast and then swing south. Get the quartermasters to make sure we're not running into dangerous ground ahead."

"Combat, aye."

Sluff went back to his captain's chair, took off his steel helmet, and crushed the urge to bum a cigarette from someone. He'd quit smoking years ago, but in times like these . . . "Bosun's Mate," he called.

"Bosun's Mate, aye," came a voice from behind his chair.

"Make some damn coffee, if you please," Sluff said.

"Damn coffee, aye."

TWELVE

Purvis Bay

By midafternoon the three ships of DesDiv 212 were anchored in the anchorage at Purvis Bay, next to the Tulagi base. All three had rearmed and refueled upon return to the Tulagi complex. *Carter*'s after engine room was a total loss, so it was likely she was bound for Pearl or even all the way back to the States. She had been able to maintain eighteen knots on the trip back to the anchorage, but a single-screw destroyer wasn't worth much in a fight. They'd buried their dead at sea on the way back, and now they were simply awaiting orders while mourning their shipmates who'd joined the almost three thousand other American seamen already asleep in the deeps of Ironbottom Sound. The single, small hole low on her starboard side belied the devastation in the engine room.

Sluff had sent off an abbreviated operational report of the night's action to COMSOPAC, but there had been no reaction as yet. He'd issued an order to the division to let their people stand down and get some rest now that all three were back to a full ammo allowance and fuel load. If *Carter* ended up being sent back, Sluff had ordered her to off-load some of her VT-Frag five-inch ammo before leaving the forward area.

Sluff had met with the other two COs at noon. The captain of *Evans* had been delighted with the apparent results of the night's running gunfight. The captain of *Carter* had been subdued and obviously saddened by the loss of an entire engine-room crew. The Japs had achieved only one hit on the division, but it had been a costly one. *Carter* was probably out of the war for some time, and with all the newer destroyers coming on line, she might actually never come back. Sluff had asked the other two skippers to send over their track charts for the engagement so that he could prepare a more detailed report. He was proud of what they'd accomplished and how it had been done, but he kept those sentiments to himself at his meeting with the other two skippers out of respect for *Carter*'s losses.

After lunch with the other two captains, he'd met with his own wardroom and praised them for a job well done. They'd achieved a total surprise attack on that Jap formation, and the survivors had gone back to Rabaul instead of on to Guadalcanal with their troops and supplies. Or some of them, anyway.

"Right now, we're the only ships here that can go after these bastards," he'd told them. "All the original heavy cruisers have either been sunk or are back in Pearl getting major repairs. The battleship fight the other night took the wind out of their sails, but they *will* be back, and I, for one, am anxiously awaiting the arrival of some more cruisers, even light cruisers. And yet: We showed what can be done if the tin cans are allowed to go first with torpedoes. Even *our* torpedoes."

The officers had laughed at that, but it was a bitter laugh. Everyone knew that their torpedoes were vastly inferior to what the Japs were launching at them.

"Last night," he'd said, "we ran rings around them, stopping their forward advance with a torpedo attack out of nowhere, and then shooting at them from all the way around the compass. If we get some more cruisers up here in the near future, *we're* going to be the ones circling them with torpedo attacks while the big guys do the gunnery work. So stay loose: the best way to beat these guys is to change our tactics every time we fight them. They hate that. Again, well done: I think we won this one."

He'd taken a much-needed hot shower and then a nap after meeting with the officers. He called the exec and asked him to bring up whatever paperwork and message traffic had accumulated in the past two days. The exec had asked which in-box he wanted: DesDiv212 or *J. B. King.*

"Oh, Lord," Sluff sighed. "I guess it's both."

The exec brought up the response from COMSOPAC an hour later, and it was most positive, even congratulatory. It was addressed to ComDesDiv 212 and the three ships by name. Back-channel intel had revealed three enemy destroyers sunk in the engagement, one so badly damaged that the Cactus air force had caught up with her forty miles north of Guadalcanal and sent her down. The other two had escaped, but none of the relief supplies and reinforcements for the Jap garrison on Guadalcanal had made it through. Mission accomplished, and then some.

Carter was ordered to return to Nouméa for further transit back to Pearl. Halsey was sending two light cruisers, USS *Wichita* and USS *Providence*, plus a flag officer to Guadalcanal to form a new task group. A replacement destroyer would be sent up when one became available to fill out DesDiv 212, hopefully within the week.

"Does it say who the flag is?" Sluff asked.

"No, sir, it doesn't. But they sure liked what we pulled off last night."

"It'll be interesting to see if we get to do it again, or just get pasted onto the cruiser column as the duty 'screen.'"

The exec nodded. "I still think that's what Admiral Lee was doing that night when the battlewagons met up," he said. Sluff realized that a lot of his officers still resented being offered up as some kind of sacrificial lamb by the battleship admiral.

"Well," Sluff said. "It worked, didn't it? Listen, I've got a question for you. Last night we set all the fish at minimum running depth. Obviously more of them worked than ever before, but that setting directly violated SOP for torpedo attacks. Should I put that in my detailed report?"

Bob rubbed the side of his face as he thought about that. "I think you should, Captain," he said. "If we'd done that and made no hits, then maybe I'd finesse that little detail. But we did *hit* them, and hard, too, based on that magazine explosion."

"But somebody, some staffer, back in San Diego at DESPAC or even Pearl is going to second-guess that 'little detail' and fang us for it."

The exec shrugged, then yawned. "Excuse me," he said. "But screw 'em if they can't take a joke."

Sluff snorted. Easy for the XO to say, but he agreed. What was the point of having unit command if you couldn't take some chances. If some of those staffies back at Commander Destroyers Pacific wanted to try it for themselves, there certainly were some vacancies out here. The worst that would happen would be that he'd be relieved as the division commander and revert back to being CO of *J. B. King*. He still expected a four-striper to hitch a ride on one of those cruisers and arrive by boat to take over. The XO yawned again and Sluff did the same.

"Okay," he said. "I've had as much fun paper-work as I can stand. So far, we're on Halsey's attaboy list. Remind *Carter* to hand back some VT-Frag to the harbormaster. Dawn GQ as per usual, and make sure you get some sleep tonight. Tell Mose I'll have filet mignon, a baked potato, and a Caesar salad for dinner tonight."

"Um," the exec said. "I think it's meat loaf again. There may even be a wee bit of SPAM in it."

"Thought that's what I just said."

At dawn the following morning the Japs came seeking revenge for the mistreatment of their destroyers, but the Cactus air force was up to the job and flamed a dozen of the attacking Bettys twenty miles out from Purvis Bay. The remaining bombers elected to flee the scene, pursued by Cactus fighters to the limit of their avgas. The three destroyers, who'd gotten under way from anchor to meet the air raid, secured from general quarters and went to breakfast but remained in a loose antiaircraft defense formation at ten knots.

During the night a message had come in from Commander Task Group 64.2, Rear Admiral Francis M. Tyree, directing Commander DesDiv 212, minus USS *Carter*, to chop to Task Group 64.2 and to be ready for sea by 1800 local time. Action was anticipated.

"Action anticipated," Sluff muttered to himself. "What a surprise."

He called the exec and told him to make sure *Evans* had the message, and then to prepare the chop message. "Chop" was Navy slang for change of operational command. A ship ordered to "chop to" a senior commander sent that commander a message, which included her operational readiness, fuel and ammo status, and any mechanical problems affecting her ability to perform her mission. Sending the chop message meant that ComDesDiv 212 now worked for Commander Task Group 64.2, and while Sluff knew that his brief taste of independent unit command was over, he also took some comfort in having a flag officer, and some heavier guns, overseeing whatever was shaping up for the evening's entertainment.

Evans and *J. B. King* got under way at 1730, *King* leading, and stood out from Purvis Bay to meet the two cruisers coming up through Sealark Channel. Sluff had ordered the two ships to be at condition II, which meant that half the ship's weapons and GQ stations were manned up, while the other half of the crew got some chow and rest. Using ComDesDiv 212's visual call sign, Sluff flashed an Able Jig message to the flagship, *Providence.* The two letters, AJ, meant "reporting for duty." CTG 64.2 came back with a signal directing the two destroyers to take station ahead of the lead cruiser at one-thousand-yard intervals. No further information was forthcoming.

Shades of Ching Lee, Sluff thought, but then he turned to the business of stationing his now very small division ahead of the oncoming cruisers at half-mile intervals. The admiral didn't make it easy: CIC's plot showed that the cruisers were going twenty-five knots, which meant the two destroyers had to hustle.

The problem was that the destroyers only had two boilers on the line, which meant they could go twenty-seven knots. If the task group commander wanted more speed than that, then the tin cans would have to light off two more boilers to get them to their top speed. That took about an hour. Sluff cracked out a visual signal to *Evans* to prepare for four-boiler ops and then set a course to intercept the approaching cruisers' track line at twenty-seven knots. If nothing changed, they'd be on station in about a half hour. As it became obvious that the two destroyers did not have the speed available to dash into station, the admiral sent out another flashing-light signal. The chief brought the visual message board down with an embarrassed expression on his face.

Whoops, Sluff thought. Now what. He read the signal: RFS means full power available. Advise when you are actually RFS.

Sluff felt his face turning red. By destroyer doctrine, ready for sea did *not* mean all four boilers on the line. Four boilers consumed prodigious amounts of fuel, and Sluff did not see any oilers accompanying the cruisers. Two-boiler ops were standard until specifically ordered otherwise. Francis Marion Tyree was acting like a jerk. He grabbed a pencil and drafted a hot reply. The chief looked at it, nodded silently, and left the cabin. Two minutes later the exec appeared on the bridge with the visual message board.

"Captain, you can't send this," Bob said.

"Why the hell not?" Sluff said. "We drive around with four on the floor and we're out of fuel in twelve hours. He ought to·know that. Since he obviously doesn't, somebody needs to tell him."

The exec took a deep breath. "The right answer is to respond to his question, not his opinions," Bob said. "We'll be ready for full power in about fifty minutes. That's the correct answer." He looked at his watch. "Eighteen thirty."

Sluff gave his exec a sideways look. Obviously the chief had read Sluff's intemperate reply and called the exec, who was now here to save Sluff from himself.

"All right," he grumbled. "Make it so."

It was nineteen hundred before *Evans* reported ready for full power, at which point Sluff sent a light to the flagship that they had thirty-five knots available. He was not familiar with the new Cleveland-class light cruisers, other than that they sported twelve six-inch guns. He wondered if *they* could make thirty-five knots. The Japs' cruisers could all do that or better. His signal was followed by an order from CTG 64.2 to change course by column movement to the northwest and increase speed to thirty-two knots.

"Where we going in such a hurry?" the exec asked, bringing Sluff a fresh mug of coffee.

"Beats me," Sluff said. "We're still in mushroom mode right now, but maybe we should set up the GQ team in CIC at least."

"Bridge, Sigs, signal has been executed."

As lead ship in the column, *King* turned first and steadied up on the new course. At the same time the OOD rang up flank speed, turns for thirty-two knots. It had always fascinated Sluff that two of the ship's boilers could push her at twenty-seven knots, but it took two more to go just five knots faster. The exec said he was going down to CIC.

"Watch your station-keeping, Mister Conklin," Sluff called to the officer of the deck. "Those cruisers will take a little longer to get up to thirty-two knots than we do."

As darkness fell, the bridge would have to rely on CIC's radar to tell them their range and bearing on the flagship, *Providence*, the third ship in the column. Because she was the guide of the formation, everyone else had to keep station on her, no matter what she did. Sluff got out of his chair to go out to the port bridge wing to see how the column was shaping up. It was almost fully dark now, but he could still make out the ghostly gray shapes of the two light cruisers astern, *Providence* swinging through her turn now, and *Wichita* behind her, still a half mile from the turning point. He wondered if the admiral was up on the flag bridge of *Providence*, staring out into the darkness to see what his two destroyers were doing. He came back in and took a look at the chart. They were east-northeast of Savo Island and obviously headed for the Slot.

"Captain, Combat, we have a message in from the flag. Says we're headed to intercept a Jap force of one heavy, two light cruisers, and four destroyers coming down from Rabaul. Intentions are to set up an east-west barrier line between the Russells and Malaita. *King* and *Evans* will be detached when enemy detected on radar to conduct a flanking torpedo attack from the *west* side of the Slot, after which cruisers will engage with guns. Intercept time is estimated to be zero one hundred. All ships set condition one by twenty-three hundred. Maneuvering signals by flashing light until action commences, then TBS. Acknowledge by light."

"Okay, got it," Sluff said. "Get a light off to *Evans*, make sure she has this message."

"Combat, aye."

Interesting, Sluff thought. The admiral wasn't going to let the Japs get down into Ironbottom Sound, where they'd have room to maneuver. He was going to hit them in the more constrained waters of the Slot. Most important, he was going to let his destroyers get off a torpedo ambush to start the evening's bloody business.

He studied the chart again. It was almost 2000. At thirty-two knots they could be as far as 120 miles up the Slot by midnight. All the engagements prior to this had been in the vicinity of Savo and Guadalcanal, with the American forces waiting defensively for the Japs to arrive. The enemy would not be expecting to be hit by an American surface force so far up into the Slot, especially since the Americans would be at the limit of their own air protection from Cactus. On the other hand, at night, Cactus could not provide *any* air cover, so that probably didn't matter.

Interesting indeed. Tyree might be a jerk, but he appeared to be thinking like a fighter. Sluff told the exec to summon the gunnery officer and the navigation officer for a meeting on the bridge. He wanted to make damn sure they knew what was being planned. They'd also have to be much more careful with navigation. Their charts were old, some of them from the days of HMS *Bounty*, and the farther up the Slot they went, the more uncharted reefs they could encounter.

They broke out the charts all along the route to the possible rendezvous with the enemy formation. The gunnery officer had brought along the torpedo officer as well. On each chart the navigator plotted out boundary lines up the western side of the interisland channel, beyond which they could not safely venture. The official effective range of their torpedoes was six thousand yards, or three miles. If the Japs came down the center of the channel, Sluff's two destroyers had to be within three miles of their projected line of advance.

"This will happen fast," Sluff told his department heads. "They'll be coming at thirty-five knots, so we'll have to fire our fish in plenty of time for them to intercept and not end up chasing their targets. No more slow-speed attacks like last night."

"We gonna shoot 'em all?" LTJG Karenski, the torpedo officer, asked.

"I think we should hold back two fish," Bob Frey, the exec, offered. "I'm assuming the admiral wants us to join in once our fish hit something and the cruisers open fire. If it turns into a melee, a couple of torpedoes in reserve might come in handy."

"Good idea," Sluff said. "And I think once we're detached and get up on the western flank of their line of advance, we slow down. Way down—like fifteen knots. We'll be able to see them on radar, but they'll be depending on visual. A thirty-two-knot bow wave is visible at night."

Once they were finished, the exec went below to CIC to duplicate the lines of attack geometry they'd laid out on the bridge's charts. An hour later, as usual, the plan changed.

"Bridge, Sigs, signal from the flag: Immediate execute: Speed fifteen."

"Sigs, Bridge, understood."

"Execute," the chief called, and the OOD rang up standard bell for fifteen knots. A moment later the after stack popped a boiler safety, scaring the hell out of everyone on their topside GQ stations. With four boilers on the line, fifteen knots wasn't much of a steam demand.

Once the column had settled into the new cruising speed, a second signal came out, addressed this time to ComDesDiv 212. The chief wrote this one down and brought it to the bridge. "Destroyers detached, proceed north up western side of Slot. Take up torpedo ambush position ten miles north of cruiser line. Launch at will. Open gunfire once cruisers fire. Intend to skedaddle after fifteen minutes. Destroyers do likewise."

"What in the world is 'skedaddle'?" Sluff asked.

Billy Chandler, the gunnery officer, was from Birmingham, Alabama, although his accent had mostly disappeared. "That's a Confederate cavalry term, Cap'n," he said. "Means to run like hell."

"Francis Marion Tyree," the exec said. "Not from Massachusetts, I'll wager." The gunnery officer laughed.

Sluff smiled in the darkness. He might have to revise his first impression of the new admiral. "I think he's being realistic," he said. "He's facing two light cruisers and one heavy. We're the only ones who can hurt the heavy cruiser, which means we'll have to try hard to ID her on the radar. If we can do that, she's our primary target. Share this with *Evans*."

The meeting broke up. He called the chief. "Signal from ComDesDiv Two-Twelve to DesDiv Two-Twelve collective: Execute to follow, corpen three three zero, speed three zero."

The chief read it back to him, and then had his boys get on the signal light to the *Evans*. Sluff asked Combat if they'd copied. They had.

A minute later, the chief was back: Signal understood on the *Evans*.

"Execute," Sluff ordered. "Officer of the deck, course three three zero, speed three-zero."

Sluff sat down in his bridge chair to think. Why had the admiral cut short the run north? Was he worried about having air cover in the morning?

Or had the Japs made more ground than they'd expected? The original signal said set condition I at 2300. It was now just past 2100, two hours and sixty miles short of the original order to go to GQ. He decided not to take chances.

"Sigs, Captain, tell *Evans* to set condition one."

"Sigs, aye."

He called the exec on one of the admin phones. He had to be careful of the bitch-box, because there were twelve stations on that circuit in different parts of the ship. All they had to do was press the button for Bridge and they could eavesdrop on everything said by the bridge.

"Bob, I think we should go to GQ now. I get the feeling that they know something we don't, or they don't know enough. Either way, let's us be ready."

"Aye, aye, sir," Bob said. Sluff told the OOD to sound general quarters. Five minutes later, after all the manned and ready reports were in, he got on the ship's general announcing system, called universally the 1MC. He told the crew what was going on, what the plan was, what they knew—the composition of the enemy task group—and what they *didn't* know: when they'd show up.

"We have the advantage of radar," he concluded. "We should see and be able to attack them before they know we're here. But once our cruisers start shooting, the Japs will launch a swarm of torpedoes at them—and at us. We'll commence firing at slow speed so they can't see our wakes. Once *we* start shooting guns, we're gonna dance around, high speed and big course changes, so be ready. Here's the good news: The task group is going to wait for us to fire our torpedoes, wait for them to hit, and then open up with guns for fifteen minutes. After that, the admiral has ordered us to, um, skedaddle. If you don't know what that means, ask a Southerner on your GQ station. That is all."

THIRTEEN

The Slot

Sluff awoke with a start in his captain's chair. He hadn't meant to doze off, but he surely had. The air in the pilothouse was still heavy and wet. The ships were doing only fifteen knots and the tropical heat bore down on everyone, even this late at night. He thought he'd heard a rainsquall come pounding on the steel skin of the ship. That's probably what had put him to sleep. He looked at his watch in the red light of the bitch-box power button. 0115. Where were the Japs? Had they turned around? Had they gone another way? That was possible, especially after the ambush of the destroyer relief column the other night. They could have left the Slot way above where *King* was waiting and slashed south along the outside of the Solomon island chain. Their ships were fast enough to be able to do that and still get down to Guadalcanal, if that was their mission, and escape before dawn and the inevitable Cactus air force reprisals.

He got up and went back to his sea cabin, the tiny steel box behind the bridge where there was a bunk, a sink, and a steel toilet. He tried to wash his face but the fresh water had been shut off for GQ. The fewer water lines charged throughout the ship, the less the flooding in case of damage. The spring-loaded water tap sucked air, almost as if mocking him. He used the commode and then went back out onto the bridge. He could literally smell the bridge team: every man sweating in his bulky kapok life jacket and closed-up shirts and trousers. He momentarily envied the XO, whose GQ station in CIC had air-conditioning because of all the electronics.

He called the exec on the admin phone. "Anything?" he asked.

"Not a sign of them," Bob said. "Our cruisers are loitering on an east-west track ten miles south of us."

"They wait much longer, they'll have an interesting morning."

The exec started to reply, but then a report came in over TBS, from *Evans*. "Contact report," a voice announced. "Bearing zero one zero, range thirteen miles, composition, many. Solid radar return."

The destroyers had been told to maintain radio silence on the TBS, except for initial contact reports. *Evans* had a first-generation Sugar Charlie radar, known to be unreliable, especially out at ranges approaching the visible horizon. *Evans* had directed the report at ComDesDiv 212, but the admiral down on the cruiser line would also have heard it.

"XO—we see anything on that bearing?"

"That's a negative, sir. There's a rainsquall line just south of there, but no contacts."

Sluff thought fast. Thirteen miles was out of *King*'s gun range, but if *Evans*'s radar was in fact seeing something out there, they had very little time to set up the torpedo attack. He'd pulled *Evans* in to 250 yards astern precisely because he'd expected to be sending her ranges and bearings to the Jap column. That way she could shoot on *King*'s solution.

Evans spoke again: Enemy formation on course one eight five, speed three-six. Damn, Sluff thought, as he tried to piece together the relative positions of his two destroyers and the enemy formation. They needed to come right and close in on the enemy's track right now—assuming *Evans* had a real contact.

"Captain, Combat, let's assign the gunfire-control radar to that bearing and range, see if it detects some metal."

"Concur, do it," Sluff snapped. "In the meantime, set up a course and speed to get to torpedo launch position before they run right past us."

"Combat, aye."

Sluff turned to his JA sound-powered phone circuit talker, who happened to be the chief yeoman, Chief Meyers, the ship's administrative officer. "Tell all stations, stand by. We think they're here."

He heard the chief pass the word. What the hell was wrong with our radar, he asked himself. He'd just assumed the *Evans*'s radar couldn't see anything as well as *King*'s, and yet . . .

"Captain, Combat, come to course zero eight zero, speed twenty-five, to get within attack range of the enemy's line of advance."

Sluff waved his hand at the OOD, who started to call the new course and speed orders to the helmsmen. Then Sluff remembered: Stop. You have to order your two-ship formation to do that. Otherwise, *Evans* would be left in the dust as *King* accelerated to the east. The exec caught the error, too.

Sluff heard the TBS radio circuit light up with a signal, from ComDesDiv 212 to DesDiv 212, all two of them, to bolt east at twenty-five knots. Stand by, execute.

"Okay, *now!*" Sluff shouted at the OOD, and

sixty seconds later *King* was accelerating to twenty-five knots and coming right to 080 true. The plan for a low-wake approach had evaporated.

"Captain, Combat, we see 'em. We *see* 'em! Fire-control radar holds, and now our search radar holds."

"Aim at the biggest one in the group," Sluff replied. "And tell the admiral: attacking with torpedoes."

As the ship pushed forward through the black night, Sluff heard the reports going out from CIC to the waiting cruisers. To his dismay, he heard the cruisers report *no* contacts on their radars. How could the cruisers start shooting if they didn't hold the enemy formation?

He called down to CIC and told the exec to tell the flag that *J. B. King* held enemy contacts on both fire-control and search radars. In other words, look harder! Use your gunnery radars. Obviously the search radar performance had turned to shit.

As his two ships charged through the hot, black night to their launch position, Sluff took a moment to think. Okay: We launch. Then what? Turn around? Turn south to parallel our targets and start shooting? Wouldn't that put us in the frame along with the enemy ships when twenty-four six-inch guns open up? Nope. Not gonna do that.

"Combat, Captain: Once we launch, turn our

formation away to the north-northwest. I want to go *behind* the enemy column before we open up *and* stay out of range of the cruisers once they get going."

"Combat, aye. We're three thousand yards from launch position."

"Then slow down. Come to fifteen knots. Come right if you have to for relative motion, but let's smother that bow wave."

The order went out over TBS a few seconds later, and *J. B. King* relaxed in the water as she slowed down. Sluff went out on the port bridge wing and looked aft. The torpedo tube mounts were trained out at about a forty-five-degree angle. He swept ahead with his binoculars and saw precisely nothing. The Jap formation was still pretty far out but coming fast. If CIC had done the numbers correctly, *King* and *Evans* would launch a spread of sixteen torpedoes into the darkness on an intercept course that should cover the first half of the Jap column. Assuming the American cruisers were awake and alert, a single torpedo hit would bring a salvo of twenty-four six-inch shells down on the Jap ships.

Sluff heard the phone-talkers down on the torpedo deck shouting out: Stand by! And then came the first whoosh of a torpedo going over the side. Then the second one. Sluff went back inside and told the OOD to get ready for a course change back to the northwest to get out of the way of the cruisers' fire. He called Combat and reminded the exec to use a turn movement to get away, not a column. That way both *Evans* and *King* would pivot in place and hustle off to the north-northwest, away from any friendly fire.

"Captain, Combat, torpedoes away. Recommend coming to three three zero, speed two-zero when the signal is executed."

"Let her go, XO," Sluff said. "We need to clear tails and get out of here."

The signal went out over TBS and was executed ten seconds afterward. The OOD gave the orders and *King* turned to port as she increased speed to twenty knots. Somewhere out there in the night sixteen torpedoes, containing 13,200 pounds of HBX explosive, were hurtling toward the computed intersection of the Japanese formation and the destroyers' firing bearing.

"Time to intercept?"

"One hundred seconds."

Sluff went back outside to make sure he could see *Evans* paralleling *King*'s movements and not running by behind them. It was too dark, even as close in as she was. He realized again that he was at a big disadvantage standing out here on the bridge wing. The tactical picture *was* available, but not on the bridge. He figured the exec would have called him had *Evans* not made the turn, but if he'd been down in CIC, he'd have known within thirty seconds that there was a problem. He told Combat to open *Evans* back out to one thousand yards.

"Mark teatime," the exec called over the bitch-box.

Nothing.

Goddammit, he thought. If we missed the whole formation, the cruisers waiting to the south would lose their range advantage if they waited—

The sky on their starboard quarter flared up into a mini-sunrise that began white but then quickly turned to yellow and then red. As it subsided there were two more, and then a fourth. Finally, the sounds of explosions came rolling across the black waters of the Slot like distant thunder. Then, hull down on the southern horizon, lightning flashed, illuminating the bottoms of low clouds over the sound.

"Combat, Captain, I think we just did some good work for Jesus," Sluff called. "Ships are blowing up out there. Now: Give me a formation course to take us north of the Jap formation and just out of range of our own cruisers."

"Combat, aye, and the flag reports they are in contact and have opened fire."

Sluff hoped the admiral knew that the two cruisers couldn't just sit there, plugging along at the same course and speed. Whichever Jap ships evaded the American torpedo attack would launch many torpedoes at all those gun flashes to the south.

"Combat recommends a formation course of three five five, speed two-seven."

"Transmit the order. Once we're on the new course and speed, order commence-firing."

"Combat, aye. Order going out now. On the plot it looks like our cruisers are reversing course to the west."

Good, Sluff thought. Fire a bunch of salvos, then reverse course. Without radar, the Japs would aim their Long Lances on a course to intercept all those east-headed muzzle flashes from twenty-four six-inch guns.

Standing in the starboard bridge-wing door, he trained his binocs out to the southeast. He felt *King* crouch for a moment as her twin screws bit down, and then she began accelerating up to twenty-seven knots. The night air was so humid he saw only blurred images in his glasses, but there was obviously a storm of six-inch fire landing on the Jap formation. Then he heard *King*'s forward five-inch guns swing out. He stepped away from the open doorway just as the first salvos went out. This time the relative wind was from the port beam, so all the smoke and wadding particles were blowing clear of the bridge. The noise, however, came right on in.

Okay, think. Now they can see *us*. They'll start shooting back, and then one or two of them will launch torpedoes. He didn't want to maneuver just yet: a steady course and speed made for far more accurate gunfire than when the ship was twisting and turning.

"Combat, Captain, what's the range?"

"Fourteen thousand, five, and four of their ships have come to a stop on the plot."

"Okay: Continue firing on this course and speed for one minute, then order cease-firing, and then a *turn* one eight zero, same speed."

"Combat, aye."

Sluff stood by his chair and mentally counted down from sixty. He wanted to execute the turn maneuver *right now,* but ten five-inch guns were happily sending hundreds of pounds of steel and explosive into the disordered Japanese formation. They would soon start firing back. The two cruisers to the south were presumably still hammering away. The resulting cross fire must be hell on earth right about now.

A blast of light and sound off the starboard bow, followed by six large columns of erupting water, concentrated his mind. They might be catching hell over there, but someone *was* shooting back, and doing a pretty good job of it. His own gun crews seemed to up their rate of fire when they felt the near misses. That had to be cruiser fire— too big for destroyer guns. He realized he'd lost count of the remaining seconds. A second salvo came screaming overhead, landing beyond them but not that far away. He could actually feel the thump of those shells exploding underwater through his feet and legs.

Damn! They'd been bracketed. Fire short. Fire over. Halve the range. Fire again—keep doing that until you start hitting.

Then he heard the radio order to cease firing, followed by the 180-degree turn. They were half-way though that turn when a third salvo came in, erupting in *J. B. King*'s wake, halfway between *King* and *Evans*.

Thank you, God, Sluff thought. Now: Steady up on the new course, head due south, and then start shooting again. He wondered if he should fire some star shells to illuminate what was left of the Jap formation for the cruisers. No. We all have radar. Star shells will just illuminate *us*.

Another six-gun salvo landed astern of them, again raising huge waterspouts of seawater and smoke. Shit, Sluff thought. That's eight-inch stuff. We didn't get the big boy, but at least his salvos are trending behind us now.

"Captain, Combat, our cruiser formation is reversing course again. Two of the Jap ships have turned north. The rest are presenting a pretty confused plot."

"Combat, Captain: Once we steady up, open fire again—but only for ninety seconds. Then slow down to fifteen knots. Are they within our torpedo range?"

"On this course, they'd be a marginal shot, using

178

slow-speed fish—come left ten degrees and the picture gets better."

"Okay, we'll do this: Resume firing for ninety seconds, then cease fire and come left and head straight at them, speed fifteen. When we get into ten thousand yards, launch our remaining torpedoes, reverse course, and get out of there."

"We stand a chance of crossing our own cruisers' line of fire—wait one—flag says they're withdrawing to the south, and for us to follow them out."

Damn, Sluff thought. He hated to go back to base with unexpended torpedoes, but an order was an order. "Okay, immediate execute, speed thirty-five knots, course southwest to open the range on any pursuing torpedoes."

"Resume firing?"

"Negative. If the cruisers are leaving, *we're* leaving. No reason to give the Japs an aim point."

The signal went out a few seconds later, and *King* came right to the southwest, 230, speed thirty-five. Sluff went out onto the starboard bridge wing to see if the *Evans* was following. He couldn't make her out in the darkness, but her bow wave made a bright white V in the water on *King*'s port quarter. He saw another six-gun salvo land off in the distance, six simultaneous red pulses of fire followed by thumping great waterspouts. He went back into the pilothouse and climbed up into his chair, suddenly very tired. The fight seemed like it had lasted for hours. He looked at his watch: 0210. They'd made first contact at about 0130. The whole thing had taken just forty minutes. Time passes fast when you're having fun, he thought.

"Bosun's Mate."

"Goddamn coffee coming right up, Cap'n," the bosun responded. Sluff smiled in the darkness.

FOURTEEN

The following morning the admiral convened an after-action conference aboard the flagship, USS *Providence.* He'd requested Sluff plus the COs and XOs of both cruisers and the CO of *Evans* to attend. The four ships had returned to Purvis Bay at 0530 and anchored. The fuel barges had appeared after sunrise GQ to top everyone back off; the Japs had not come down from Rabaul. Torpedo and gun ammo barges were laid on for noon, so the admiral called his meeting for 1030.

Sluff had offered to pick up the CO of *Evans* in his boat for the trip over to *Providence,* about a mile distant from where the destroyers had anchored. When they arrived, there was some momentary confusion on the cruiser's quarterdeck when two three-stripers arrived at the top of the sea ladder. The somewhat flustered OOD asked which one of them was ComDesDiv 212.

"I'm DesDiv Two-Twelve," Sluff replied. "This is *Evans*."

The requisite number of bells was sounded for each of them. A moment later, the exec of *Providence* popped out of a hatch to escort them up to the wardroom. He, too, was a full commander, and senior to both the captain of *Evans* and Sluff. He seemed to be somewhat surprised to see the "commodore" wearing silver oak leaves on his collar instead of silver eagles. They walked up the port side of the cruiser's main deck, past the quarter-mounted twin-barreled five-inch mount, underneath the forty-millimeter gun tubs, and then through a hatch and down one deck to the wardroom. There they were introduced to the COs of *Providence* and *Wichita*, both captains, and the admiral's chief of staff, another captain. The skipper of the *Wichita* had bandages on both forearms and looked as if he was in pain.

Sluff felt uncomfortable at being addressed as commodore by all these four-stripers, but if they thought the situation strange, they gave no indication of it. If he'd been just a lieutenant in command of a squadron of minesweepers, he'd have still been called commodore.

Finally the CO of *Providence* called a quiet attention-on-deck as Admiral Tyree came into the wardroom, followed by his aide and a tall, thin commander. The admiral looked a lot like the pictures Sluff had seen of Robert E. Lee, with the

181

same wide forehead and piercing dark eyes, missing only the gray beard and mustache. He was about one inch shorter than Sluff, but carried himself with quiet dignity and a visible command presence.

"Gentlemen, good morning," the admiral said. He spoke with a wide Southern drawl, confirming Bob Frey's guess that he was indeed not from Massachusetts. The admiral nodded to both of the cruiser captains and introduced himself to Sluff.

"Commodore Wolf, Caw Tyree. A pleasure, suh. Nice work last night. Nice work indeed."

"Thank you, sir," Sluff said. "This is Commander Brian Hopkins, CO *Evans*."

The admiral greeted Hopkins warmly and then indicated for everyone to take seats. The admiral sat in the middle of the main wardroom table, apparently unconcerned with rank by just choosing the nearest seat. The other officers followed suit while the commander set up an easel board and arranged some papers and a message board on the table in front of him. He raised his eyebrows at the admiral, who nodded.

"Gentlemen, I'm Tom Reese, Admiral Tyree's operations officer," he began. "The admiral has asked me to tell you what we know about the results of last night's match. This info comes from our own track analysis and a back-channel message from COMSOPAC.

"The enemy formation actually consisted of four

destroyers, a light cruiser, and a heavy cruiser, six ships in all. DesDiv Two-Twelve's initial torpedo attack sank one destroyer, damaged a second one, and damaged the light cruiser, *Niitaka*. The heavy cruiser, the *Kako*, was not hit. In the subsequent gun engagement, the *Niitaka* was hit repeatedly and probably scuttled. The damaged destroyer was also sunk, probably by a combination of five-inch and six-inch gunfire. A third destroyer was damaged and withdrew, apparently to escort *Kako* out of the engagement, along with an undamaged destroyer. *Kako* was hit repeatedly with six-inch gunfire, but her armor held and she was still able to make thirty knots out of the engagement area. The admiral aboard *Kako* was killed during the engagement."

Jesus, Sluff thought. How in the hell do they know that?

"The better news is that at sunrise this morning, *Kako* was sunk by one of our submarines on the way back to Rabaul. So, box score: We accounted for one light cruiser and two destroyers. Our sub took down the heavy cruiser, and whatever their mission was last night, it did not happen. A very good night's work."

"Amen to that, gentlemen," the admiral said. "Commodore Wolf, a question: I had some plotters last night tracking all my ships on the DRT. I noticed that after you launched torpedoes and then began firing when we did, you fired for only about ninety seconds and then made some, shall I say, dramatic course changes and even speed changes, if my plot can be believed."

"Yes, sir, we did," Sluff said. "It was all about avoiding Jap torpedoes."

"This is a tactic you've developed to deal with the Long Lance?"

"Yes, sir. Their Type Ninety-Three torpedoes are vastly superior to ours. They can shoot them going thirty-six knots because they weigh almost three tons. If we did that with ours, they'd probably break up hitting the water."

"Go on."

"We assume that once they can see us, they will fire torpedoes at us after about a minute of visual tracking. They can see us when we start shooting. Muzzle flashes show them where we are. A minute of bearing analysis will tell them whether, on a relative basis, we're going the same way they are or the other way. It will also tell them if we're going fast, medium, or slow. That's all they need for an initial salvo.

"So: We shoot for ninety seconds, and then we do something—reverse course, speed up, slow down, something dramatically different with respect to the relative motion picture—*and* we stop giving them an aim point by turning off the muzzle flashes. Their Type Ninety-Threes go almost sixty knots. We can compute when the danger should be past. Then we reopen fire. Same thing again—ninety seconds, then a bold course and speed change and a cease firing. When we open up again it can look like a new set of ships is firing at them. At least that's what we hope they think, but, either way, they're shooting on visual bearings and an educated guess as to which way we're going and how fast. If we deny them a visual bearing and add a bold maneuver, we have a good chance of avoiding the Long Lance."

"But your total rounds fired at the enemy formation is reduced by only firing for ninety seconds, yes?"

"We had ten guns between us, firing fifteen rounds per minute. That's two hundred rounds in ninety seconds. Five tons of metal on target. With radar direction, so most of those are going to be at least close to if not hitting. Your two cruisers were firing twenty-four six-inch guns, firing ten rounds a minute each: Three hundred sixty rounds in the same ninety seconds. Twenty-three tons of metal on target."

"You're saying that, proportionately, the destroyer's gunnery contribution was only one-quarter of the total weight of our metal on target."

"Yes, sir, and thus it didn't much matter if we only shot for ninety-second intervals. By maneuvering, we knew we could stay alive, even when *Kako* started in on us, by wide course changes and even slowing down, at one point, to fifteen knots. When we're in a cruiser formation our important contribution is a salvo of torpedoes. Our five-inch fire is window dressing compared to the cruisers' six- or eight-inch fire."

The admiral was silent for a moment. Then he changed the subject to talk about logistics, fuel and ammo supplies, and asked for updated reports on equipment problems. He also wanted each ship to provide its track charts from the previous night's work. He said that they didn't have any information on what the Japs might do next, but that they were expecting an update shortly. Then he stood up and concluded the meeting.

Sluff was talking to the CO of *Providence* when the admiral's aide came back into the wardroom. He approached and told Sluff that the admiral would like to see him for a minute up in the flag cabin.

"Yes, sir?" Sluff said, once seated.

"When you were throwing numbers around down there, had you rehearsed that?"

"Um, no, sir. I was kind of computing as I went along."

The admiral nodded. "That's pretty impressive. Look: There's something about what you were saying, this business of shooting for ninety seconds and then going dark, that's bothering me."

"Yes, sir?"

"I don't know, dammit," the admiral said with a wry grin. "I understand the tactical logic, but . . ."

"It's undestroyer-like, maybe?"

The admiral nodded again. "Something like that, I suppose. I guess I'm used to the proposition that once the shooting starts, we all shoot back until we're either chased away or we've sunk 'em all."

"I understand, Admiral, and if they'd put up star shells or turned on their searchlights, then continuous shooting would have been the only response. But last night, if *Kako*, for instance, had opened up a searchlight, looking for us, the Japs knew she'd have become the focus for every American gun out there, like our cruisers were at the first Savo fight. I don't think they grasp that *we* don't need star shells or searchlights to 'see' them for gunnery purposes. The only way they could see us was by our muzzle flashes; you and the cruisers were literally over the horizon."

"Because we opened fire at twenty-two thousand yards," the admiral said.

"Yes, sir, and the local horizon for us, anyway, is twenty-four thousand yards. Your gunfire probably looked like heat lightning. Ours looked like muzzle flashes, which is why I think the heavy cruiser opened on us, or in our general direction, anyway, rather than on you."

"Interesting," the admiral said, leaning back in his desk chair. "I need to think about this," he said, finally.

"Yes, sir, I know it sounds like heresy to stop

shooting, but it must be damned confusing to the Japs to have us blink on, then blink off and reappear somewhere else."

"It's the use of radar that's brand new, to me, anyway," the admiral said. "I'd seen it before, of course, but this new Sugar George set changes the whole ballgame. Look: Let me give you some advice. Be careful with innovative tactics. Discuss that sort of thing with your boss, preferably before the shooting starts."

Sluff just looked at him. The admiral grinned again.

"Yes, okay, that wasn't possible last night, was it? But try: I'm willing to listen if you think there's a hole in my plans. I want your ideas. These Japs aren't little bucktoothed monkeys we see in the propaganda posters: they're really good, and their ships are really good. If anything's going to save us, it will be technology, so I want to exploit that."

"Taken to its logical conclusion, Admiral," Sluff said. "The idea of a freewheeling destroyer squadron or division might mean that the destroyers become the main bang, with cruisers in support once our torpedoes have gone in."

"I recognize that, young man. I may not love it, but I do recognize that possibility. By the way, do you have an SOP for your division?"

"Um, no, sir, I didn't think I'd still be a unit commander. I view myself as a stand-in. I've been expecting a four-striper to be inbound to put the 'captain' back in ComDesDiv Two-Twelve."

The admiral grunted. "Actually," he said, "what's inbound are two more destroyers who will chop to DesDiv Two-Twelve sometime in the morning." He eyed Sluff's surprised face. "Commodore."

Sluff was at a loss for words.

"Check with my ops boss, Commander Reese, before you leave. Get a copy of our cruiser division standard operating procedures, use that as a guide, and write one up for your ships. It's really helpful when new ships show up."

"Aye, aye, sir," Sluff said, getting up. "Thanks for that."

"I'll put the word out when we find out what's next," the admiral said. "If the coast watchers don't report Japs in motion, I'll send you out to make a destroyer sweep of Savo and the bottom of the Slot. Be a good way to see if your brand-new SOP works."

As in, Commodore, get one written up this afternoon, Sluff realized.

FIFTEEN

Purvis Bay

As Sluff and Commander Hopkins rode back toward the *Evans*, Hopkins wanted to know what the admiral had wanted. Sluff told him that he'd wanted to discuss tactics.

Hopkins snorted. "You should have seen how those four-stripers were looking at you when you went through that business about avoiding torpedoes."

"Like they were seeing some plebe being awfully ratey?"

"*Just* like that," Hopkins said. "As in, who the hell does this upstart think he is, telling Caw Tyree how to run a surface action."

"You might be surprised to learn that the admiral agreed with me," Sluff said. "He's trying to figure out how to formalize that tactic. By the way, we get two more ships tomorrow, and I have some homework to do—a divisional SOP"

"Damn, Sluff, you're gonna turn into a real commodore yet. Sir."

Sluff laughed. "You did good last night, Brian. Caught every signal, maneuvered like an expert. Didn't break down, even though I know you're holding some parts of that plant together with marline. Just so you know, I've got a list of matériel problems of my own in *J. B. King*, like any other tin can. I'm still learning how to divide my time between my two hats: CO *J. B. King* and ComDesDiv Two-Twelve."

"That's going to get harder, I suspect," Hopkins said. "You're going to have to load up Bob Frey even more."

"Well, I know," Sluff said, as the launch came alongside the *Evans*'s pipe ladder. "Okay, I'll be in touch. When the new ships show up, I'll be calling a confab over in *King*."

Hopkins stood up in the rocking launch as the coxswain gunned the engine back and forth to hold steady alongside the *Evans*. Then he put his gold-braided cap back on, saluted, and climbed out of the boat.

"Coxswain," Sluff called, "make the *J. B. King*."

The rest of the day was spent at anchorage, with all four ships doing maintenance, writing up reports, trading repair parts and other supplies among the task group, rebuilding freshwater reserves, and, where possible, getting some sleep. Sluff called in Bob Frey and handed over the cruiser division SOP.

"Get with the appropriate department heads, see if you can gen something up between now and sundown. Keep it simple and short—for now, anyway. Readiness—ammo, fuel, water.

Communications. Maneuvering rules. GQ policy, dawn and dusk. Like that."

"Yes, sir, we'll get right on it."

"Bob, I know you've got many other things to do, so get the department heads to help, really help with this. Call me when you have an outline and I'll help flesh it out, but I think we're going hunting tonight, and it'd be good to try it out. Especially with new ships arriving."

The daily air raid had failed to materialize, causing some unease in the task group, so Sluff made sure both *King* and *Evans* had at least two mounts ready to go to work on a moment's notice. He assigned *King* to maintain an air-search radar watch over the Tulagi area. He was pretty sure the cruisers were doing the same thing, but, if they weren't, he wanted someone looking at all times. Then he realized that this was the sort of thing that ought to go into the new SOP.

At 1630, two new Fletcher-class destroyers hove over the horizon and established visual communications with *Providence*. A half hour later, as they nosed into the anchorage, they both sent AJ signals by flashing light as they reported for duty to ComDesDiv 212. Sluff's division was now officially a four-pack. He called a COs-plus-one conference for 1800 aboard *King* and then went to meet with the exec and the department heads to look at their first draft of the SOP.

The two new ships were USS *Malone* and USS

Stayers, fresh out of new construction by way of three months of training with LantFleet and a staff in-brief at Nouméa. Their skippers were both out of the class of 1928, two years behind Sluff. Each brought his navigation officer, as did Brian Hopkins, CO *Evans*. Introductions were made all around, and then each of the new COs handed in a readiness-for-sea report and a list of his equipment problems. Both of the ships were refueling from a barge as the meeting opened. Sluff sat at the head of the table and began by saying: This is what we did last night.

He told them about the engagement up the Slot, the initial reports of enemy losses, and the tactical plan that had been devised mostly on the fly.

"DesDiv Two-Twelve came out here as a four-ship division, lost two and the commodore right away in the first fight, which is how I ended up as commodore. Unlike a real squad dog, I have no staff, so my exec and department heads are also double-hatted. We're coming up with a division SOP by plagiarizing CruDiv Six SOP as much as we can. The original commodore, Captain Latham, had one but it had little relevance to how things go out here, with 'here' being called Ironbottom Sound for reasons known sadly to all of us.

"Basically, I want your ships ready to go out and fight on about thirty minutes' notice unless I tell you to stand down, which still means two gun mounts, the director, and two boilers ready to go into action. You refuel and rearm when you come in, and then, and only then, relax a little now that you're back in port. We use flashing light and keep radio silence until the shooting starts, and then *I* am in control of TBS. I'll try to let you know in advance when we'll need four boilers, but you should assume if the group is going out against a *known* threat, we'll need four boilers.

"I've been talking to the admiral about letting the destroyers go in first with our torpedoes before anyone starts shooting guns. We did that last night and had some success. But let me warn you: The Japs are far more experienced at night surface actions than we are, and they have a weapon that is truly a ship-killer, *and* both their cruisers and destroyers carry it, *and* they can reload. *And* did I mention that their fish work damn near every time?"

He paused to take a breath. "Now, there's a 'but,' and it's a huge 'but.' We have radar, and that can even things up a lot, in my opinion. No more of these opposing formations blundering into each other in the dark. Last night the cruisers opened fire at eleven miles instead of two miles like at the first Savo. They didn't start shooting until our fish had started blowing ships up. I suspect it confused the hell out of the Japs. They knew there were American destroyers within five miles of them, but then six-inch started landing on them from over the visible horizon. This is not to say that they're not up there tonight in Rabaul analyzing what happened, which means, next time, we'll have to innovate again. It's that kind of war out here. You will see that the one thing my SOP does not talk about is tactics. In my opinion, that will be a work in progress until we're anchored in Tokyo Bay."

He looked around the table. "Okay—there endeth the lesson. Go back to your ships and get ready to go out sometime tonight. No specific threat, but the admiral wants his destroyers out there on the prowl in case the coast watchers have missed something. Welcome to the South Pacific."

After the meeting, Sluff had Old Mose bring him dinner in his cabin, after which he lay down for a few minutes. An hour later someone was knocking on the cabin door, and then the exec came in.

"Commodore," he began. Sluff groaned theatrically.

"The division has been directed to conduct a radar sweep of Ironbottom Sound commencing at twenty-two hundred. No specific threat or coast-watcher reports."

"The cruisers staying in?"

"Yes, sir. Apparently they need their beauty sleep."

Sluff grinned. "Okay, good, this will give us a chance to shake out the new guys, see how they

195

do. And, listen: Silence on the coast-watcher nets can mean everything from the Japs taking a rope yarn Sunday to an undetected battleship formation coming to tear up Cactus. We'll up anchor at twenty-one thirty."

"Twenty-one thirty, aye," Bob said. "Operational speed?"

"Twenty-seven knots until midnight. Then I want four boilers available."

Bob grinned. "You think they're coming, don't you."

"Actually," Sluff said, "I do."

By midnight they were in a column formation, thousand-yard intervals, and headed north up into the Slot. All four ships had been brought to general quarters. It was a typical Solomons night: a low overcast, scattered rainsqualls, humid to the point of fogged-up binoculars, darker than the familiar well digger's ass, and hot. The radar picture was extremely good, as the microwave signals were ducted along the surface by the wet blanket of clouds above. Down below in the four main holes, the engineering plant was almost unbearably hot with all four boilers on the line. Sluff had the formation steaming at twenty-five knots, if nothing else but to generate some relative wind to cool the topside GQ stations, where everyone was encased in kapok life jackets, steel helmets, and, for the gunners, flash-proof gauntlets and hoods. General quarters, my ass,

Sluff thought. Sauna quarters was more like it. It felt like his helmet was sweating.

He'd brought the division to condition I at midnight. It was a bit ludicrous, Sluff thought. If the Japs wanted to run a mission on Guadalcanal, they had this small window of operational opportunity dictated by simple geography. It amazed him how every aspect of this surface war already was subsiding into almost predictable routine. The red light on the bitch-box snapped on.

"Captain, Combat, radar contact, bearing three three zero, range twenty-five thousand yards, composition two large, six small, course one six zero, speed thirty-two. Looks like three destroyers ahead, two cruisers, then three destroyers astern."

Well, well, well, Sluff thought. "Combat, Commodore: Alert the division by TBS, get a radar confirmation from one other ship, then set us up on a course to cross their T, reduce speed to twenty knots, and prepare for a torpedo attack."

"Combat, aye."

Crossing the T: the tactic by which one force aligned itself perpendicular to the approaching enemy column, the theory being that the force crossing the T could bring all weapons, guns or torpedoes, to bear on the enemy column, while the enemy could only bring the weapons of the first ship in the column to bear against the other force.

"Commodore, Combat, *Malone* and *Evans* confirm the contact. *Stayers* does not hold yet.

Ordering course zero seven zero, speed two-zero now."

"Very well," Sluff said. "Intercept range is to be at six thousand yards, torpedoes running on high speed, shallow depth. Tell all ships to fire a pattern of eight torpedoes."

"Combat, aye, and we'll have to slow down even more to make that geometry work—the Japs are going too fast."

"Order what you need, Bob. And get an oboe out to Sixty-Four Point Two that we're engaging and what our posit is. Then tell the division to start shooting when they see our torpedoes hitting."

Sluff heard the formation-maneuvering orders going out over the TBS speaker above his head. It took an effort not to get out of his chair as he felt the ship slowing down, but there was nothing to see. He had to trust the ship behind *King* to get the message and not run over the top of them. He was totally dependent on the exec and his plotting team to compute the setup and then pass firing orders to the torpedo mounts. Six thousand yards was the maximum effective range of the Mark 15 destroyer torpedo. That was closer than he wanted to be when the fish went off, but he didn't want to take a chance by firing the torpedoes at their slow speed and have the damned Japs change course while the fish were en route. This way, the fish would be going almost fifty miles an hour against targets that were going forty miles an hour right at them. Once fired, they'd collide in just less than 120 seconds.

Then what, he thought. Guns for ninety seconds, then bolt straight ahead at thirty-two knots on the current course to get out of torpedo water? Reverse course and accelerate? Don't shoot at all, and thus stay dark, turn together to the south and run like hell? Two cruisers, six destroyers; those were tough odds. Thirty-two torpedoes might thin them out some, assuming the fish worked, but still, two cruisers were a handful.

There was one final option: Launch the fish, wait for them to start hitting, and then turn left down the torpedo-firing bearing and run right at the Japs at maximum speed. Or almost right at them—offset to one side or the other, scream past them at two thousand yards, and open with all twenty guns. They'd never expect that, and his four tin cans would be going by them so fast that their torpedoes would be useless. After that, assess the damage done, and either "skedaddle" as the admiral called it, or circle around the damaged ships like a bunch of Comanches and shoot 'em up until things got too hot.

"Commodore, Combat, launching now on bearing three one zero, current range eight thousand five hundred, intercept range five thousand eight hundred."

"Okay, here's what I want," Sluff said. "Put out an execute to follow. Three one zero corpen, speed three-two. Open fire on my command."

Bob repeated the orders back. The corpen signal meant that the lead ship, *King*, would turn left to the new course when the signal was executed, and each following ship would turn in succession in an accelerating follow-the-leader formation. Sluff vaguely heard torpedoes going over the side to port, but his mind was concentrating on the tactical geometry. He'd ordered a ten-degree offset because he did not want to lead his column directly *into* the Japanese formation, if nothing else to avoid the risk of collision with undamaged Jap ships going thirty-plus knots. The TBS came to life with the execute-to-follow signal.

"Intercept time, fifty seconds."

Sluff turned to the OOD. "Mister Heimbach, alert main control we'll need thirty-two knots in about one minute." Then he called Gun Control to confirm that his director was locked on the enemy column. Billy Chandler reported that they were locked on to the fourth ship in the column. He waited a few seconds and then ordered Combat to execute the formation course and speed change. He heard the forced-draft blowers spooling up almost immediately, and *King* began her squirming rumble as she gathered speed.

The fourth ship—that should be the first cruiser, Sluff thought. That would leave the three Jap destroyers leading the cruisers out of the gunnery barrage. On the other hand, they would be the first to face the torpedo barrage coming at them right about—

The night sky lit up in a series of four large explosions, followed by a twenty-second pause and then two more fireballs. The explosions were close enough to white out his night vision, but he could still see that his column was going to pass within about two thousand yards of the enemy formation. He couldn't make out which types of ships had absorbed torpedo hits, but there were definitely four distinct fires out there. He also saw that the bearing rate was accelerating as his division sped up. Time to do it.

He picked up the TBS handset next to his chair and, using his ComDesDiv 212 call sign, ordered all ships to commence firing. *King*'s own guns jumped into action with what looked like oversized muzzle flashes, followed by the usual cloud of burnt wadding and gunsmoke whipping through the bridge portholes. He jumped out of his chair, went out to the port bridge wing, and looked aft. Behind *King* he could see a line of five-inch muzzle flashes banging away into the night. He swung his binocs to the right and observed a stream of red-hot projectiles arcing flat over the water and crashing down into black objects a mile away. It looked like the Jap formation had fallen apart, but with the two columns passing each other in opposite directions, *King*'s forward two guns were inexorably training aft to keep on target. Time for a course change.

He went back inside the pilothouse, where the smoke and debris from the two forward mounts was creating a minor fog, and hit the bitch-box, ordering Combat to bring the formation to the left thirty degrees. Once the immediate-execute signal went out and *King* began to turn left, he picked up the TBS handset and ordered an all-ships cease-firing. Right about now the Japs would be training out their own torpedo mounts and guns, aiming at the line of gun flashes created by twenty five-inch guns in rapid-continuous-fire mode. So: This should work, he thought. A high-speed course change to the left, maintain high speed, maximize the change in bearing to the enemy formation.

"Commodore, Combat, recommend a second course change to the left, to two four zero, to keep the Japs in torpedo range."

"Great minds think alike, Bob. Let's run on this for two minutes, then do that and set up to shoot the remaining torpedoes."

"Combat, aye, and reopen fire once the fish go in?"

"That's affirmative."

He closed his eyes to frame the tactical plot in his mind as the relative wind from their high speed cleared the fog out of the pilothouse. They'd raced by the Jap formation going just a bit north of east, firing as they went. Then they'd changed course to due north, ceased firing to make themselves invisible again while opening the range and fouling the Japs' torpedo calculations. Now they should swing left again, this time to the southwest, and make a firing pass down the Japs' western flank, all at ranges between three thousand and five thousand yards. As soon as they steadied on the new course, he'd order the guns to go back to work and then let each of his four ships fire off their remaining two torpedoes at whatever targets they chose.

He heard the immediate-execute course change go out over TBS and felt *King* heel sharply as she came about and headed down a line behind what was left of the Japanese formation. There were now five distinct fires burning out there in the darkness, but without being able to actually look at the radarscope picture, he had no idea of how many Jap ships were still operational. As *King* settled back upright, steady on 240, he found out that at least one Jap cruiser was still in the game as nine waterspouts boomed into the air about five hundred yards on their port beam.

Somehow, the Japs knew where they were. He grabbed the TBS again and ordered the division to resume firing. He told his gunnery officer to concentrate on whatever ship was firing six-inch shells at *King* if he could. He went back out to the port bridge wing to see if he could make out the cruiser, which should be about two miles away on their port beam. Once again he was enveloped in gunsmoke, clouds of burnt wadding, and the hammering blasts of his own five-inch guns working overtime. At thirty-two knots, they'd be past the enemy formation very soon, and either firing over their shoulders or executing another turn in the Comanche circle.

Another nine-pack of six-inch ripped overhead and landed on *King*'s starboard side, closer than the first salvo. He clearly saw the cruiser's gun flashes this time, as well as several others out there in the darkness.

They're getting the range, he thought. Next salvo will split the difference and maybe also *King*'s paper-thin steel sides. Not to mention the Long Lances that were probably coming.

Maneuver, *now.*

He ran back into the pilothouse, grabbed the TBS handset, and ordered a simultaneous turn to port to a course that would take them directly at the Japs. As the ship swung around in another tight arc to the left, the constellation of distant gun flashes began to move across the night horizon in the opposite direction. A moment later all four ships of his division were racing directly at the Jap formation, which now seemed to cover an arc of almost ninety degrees directly ahead based on the gun flashes. The maneuver meant that the Americans could only use their forward two guns against the Japs, but it also meant a much better launch angle for the division's torpedoes. As he was about to tell Combat to let them go, he felt the percussion thumps back down on the 01 level as *King*'s last two fish whooshed off into the night. He picked up the TBS handset again.

"All ships maneuver independently to go *through* the Jap formation. Fire at will. Once we clear their formation, I plan to skeee-daddle to the southeast."

By now he could see three separate ships dead in the water ahead on fire from stem to stern. One looked like one of the cruisers. The other cruiser let go a nine-gun salvo right at the *King* but all the shells racketed overhead. With *King* and the other ships racing right at them at thirty-two knots, the Japs' fire control couldn't correct for the rapidly decreasing range. Sluff realized that, in a moment, the division would be *inside* the Jap formation, making it impossible for the Japs to shoot without hitting their own ships, while at the same time the Americans could shoot in all directions. He yelled at the OOD to steer directly astern of the cruiser that was firing at them while watching *King*'s own projectiles crashing into her midsection, sending red-hot shrapnel and other objects flying off the cruiser in all directions.

Another nine-gun salvo bloomed right in their faces, and this time something hit mount fifty-one with an ear-hammering clang, visibly knocking the mount sideways. Mount fifty-two kept on firing, its barrel swinging rapidly to the left as

King passed no more than a few hundred yards from the outraged cruiser, at which point all of *King*'s guns could be brought to bear. Sluff tried to think about what his next order should be, but the chaos of a close-in gunfight mesmerized him. The cruiser's secondary armament, five-inchers like *King*'s, was shooting at them now, and Sluff felt two more hits somewhere aft. Hits, but not explosions—they were too close in now and the Japs' shells hadn't had time to arm. The same was true of *King*'s own guns, and he could actually see his own ship's shells bounce off the cruiser's armored side and go spinning off into the darkness like frustrated red hornets.

And then the night exploded into a sunrise of white fire, followed by a tremendous noise and a sudden hot pressure wave that enveloped the bridge. Sluff was flung back against the director barbette's foundation. He was vaguely aware that three of the bridge GQ team had been punched back into the pilothouse like rag dolls, their wide eyes clear evidence of the shock of the explosion. He sat down suddenly as his legs failed him, aware that the ship was still going ahead. He could feel the deck vibrating with the thrust of two propellers thrashing at full power. He dimly heard Combat calling him on the bitch-box from inside the pilothouse, and then hands were reaching for him and pulling him to his feet.

He grabbed the bull rail on the port bridge wing

and looked aft. The cruiser was gone, replaced by a stub of a bow literally bobbing up and down in a maelstrom of flaming fuel oil, steam, and red smoke. He realized she had blown up, disintegrating right in their faces. They must have penetrated one of her Long Lance magazines.

He stumbled into the pilothouse, grabbing various stationary objects to keep himself upright, and barely got to his captain's chair. He tried to get up into the chair but it swiveled away from him and a quartermaster had to help him up.

"Combat, Commodore," he said, his voice a raspy squawk. "Give me the picture."

"Combat, aye, and we're clearing the Jap formation. What happened out there?"

"Cruiser blew up. Magazine explosion. She's gone. Where's the division?"

"Forming behind us as we open the range. Our radar track shows all our ships are still making thirty-two knots, so it looks like we pulled it off."

"Okay, immediate-execute a column movement to the southeast, back towards Tulagi. Advise if you think the Japs are coming after us. Make a major course change to the east two minutes after we settle on the escape course. Maintain thirty-two knots: I sense Long Lances are coming after *us* right now."

"Combat, aye. DC Central has damage reports when you're ready. Gun Control has lost comms with mount fifty-one, and fifty-two is reporting bodies out on the forecastle."

Sluff sighed as he felt the adrenaline in his system beginning to subside. He put his head back in the chair and closed his eyes, but then a voice told him to wake up: This isn't over until we're clear of pursuing torpedoes. Then he had an idea.

"Combat, Commodore: Who's the last ship in the column?"

"*Evans*, sir."

"Direct *Evans* to begin dropping depth charges, set for fifty feet, one every thirty seconds."

"Combat, aye, and, be advised, no Jap ships are headed our way. I think they've had enough fun for one night."

"Good, because I sure as hell have."

The last ship in his column would be the first one the Long Lances might overtake. If *Evans* dropped five-hundred-pound shallow-set depth charges in their faces, it would surely disrupt a torpedo attack from astern. One could hope, anyway.

His JA talker, Chief Meyers, turned to him with the initial damage reports coming up from Damage Control Central. A damage control party had reached the forecastle. They reported that mount fifty-one had been knocked off its roller path by a direct hit on its left front shield and had suffered three dead and eight seriously wounded with burns. Sluff swallowed hard. He knew that only by the grace of God had that six-inch round not exploded *inside* the mount, which could have led to a catastrophic magazine explosion, like the holocaust that had torn that Jap cruiser to pieces.

He called the exec down in Combat and asked for damage reports from the division. As he was talking he heard a thumping roar from astern, followed thirty seconds later by another and then another. Depth charges. He hoped.

He went forward a few minutes later to inspect the damage to mount fifty-one, the forwardmost five-inch gun. He saw that the mount had indeed been blown off its roller path. It was now canted to one side with its gun barrel pointing off at an odd angle, knocked completely out of line. The left front side of the mount was dished in and blackened, with bright steel striations emanating radially from the point of impact. The doc and two of his corpsmen were attending to the wounded out on the forecastle deck, while a firefighting team was hosing down the smoking interior of the mount. The smell of burned flesh was everywhere, along with the stink of high explosive and hydraulic oil, which was bleeding out from the gun mount in several streams. He stopped short of going to look inside the mount. He would have been in the way, and he had no desire to see the charred corpses, which he knew were still inside. Based on what the wounded looked like, he knew the KIA count was going to go up.

Bob Frey joined him on the darkened forecastle. He'd brought some notes on the damage and casualty reports from the other ships in the division, but he'd forgotten his red-lens flashlight.

"Anything major?" Sluff asked.

"Not that I recall," Bob said, with a yawn. "My sense of it is that they're all ready to fight."

"Good," Sluff said. "Let's take a walk."

SIXTEEN

When the Jap ships faded off the radar screen, Sluff set the division up on a fifteen-knot patrol line between where their fight had taken place and the Guadalcanal-Tulagi axis. He'd originally planned to run right for the harbor but then realized the Japs were still out there. They should leave before daylight or the Cactus air force would have a field day, but until then his job was to make sure they didn't regroup and pursue. He then called for readiness reports from the other three ships by flashing light so as to restore radio silence, ordered condition II in the formation, and then went to his cabin to make a head call and clean up. He then went back to Combat and supervised the preparation of the after-action report and the track charts. Finally he was able to lie down in his cabin for a quick nap before they all went to GQ at dawn for the run into Tulagi.

As they lined up to make the harbor approach lanes, Combat reported enemy aircraft inbound. The bridge lookouts reported that the cruisers appeared to be getting under way, so Sluff turned the division around and ran for the open sea at thirty knots to get some maneuvering room. It turned out to be a small raid, perhaps ten bombers, most of whom were either shot down or run off by fighters launched from Cactus. None of the destroyers got to even shoot, but the cruisers put up an impressive AA barrage, which unfortunately bagged one of the Marine fighters from Cactus. Sluff sent *Evans* to pick up the pilot.

He reported aboard the flagship at 0930. His eyes were sticky with fatigue, having been up all night. He'd been dozing in his chair as they made landfall on Tulagi, but then had come wide-awake when the Jap bombers had shown up. The admiral's operations officer met Sluff on the quarterdeck and escorted him to the flag cabin. On the way he asked Sluff if he'd had breakfast.

Sluff had to think about that for a moment. "No," he said. "Coffee, yes, but breakfast? No."

The staffer knocked on the admiral's door, went in, and beckoned Sluff to follow him.

Damn, Sluff thought. I am bushed. The admiral came out of his bedroom with a broad smile on his face. He looked freshly showered and had on clean, pressed khakis. Sluff felt like a tramp at a church social.

"Commodore Wolf, you look like you got rode hard and put away wet, if I may say so, sir."

"Busy night, Admiral," Sluff replied. "Sorry for my appearance." He eyed one of the conference table chairs with visible longing.

"Do sit down, please." The admiral asked if he'd eaten and then nodded at his ops officer, who left the cabin to roust one of the admiral's stewards. "Tell me all about it. I ordered a sortie when your contact report came in, but by the time we were ready to go, you were already on the way back. I have some work to do with my cruiser division, I do believe. So: Let's hear it."

Sluff laid it out, from the initial contact to the torpedo ambush, the first gunnery run, going quiet and getting north of the Jap formation, turning southwest, being surprised by being taken under fire by the cruiser, and then turning directly into the Jap formation, where each ship fired off two more torpedoes plus as much five-inch as they could cram through their barrels.

"Then we skedaddled," Sluff finished. "Before we pissed them off."

The admiral shook his head. "Damn," he said. "I'd like to have seen that. Any ideas as to a score?"

"Four distinct fires after the first torpedo launch. I think we really hurt one cruiser, and either that one or the other one blew up in our faces as we were going toe-to-toe. He shot my forward mount off and then something happened and he simply disappeared in a tower of fire. Definitely a magazine explosion. Beyond that, I don't *know* anything factual, but we probably got a destroyer or two. I do know that they did not pursue us once we headed back southeast. They may have gone on down to Cape Esperance and unloaded some troops." He paused to deal with a large yawn. "It all happened pretty fast, Admiral. We do have battle damage and casualties, but all four ships made it out of there by the grace of God."

There was a knock on the door and then a steward came in bearing a tray of scrambled eggs, bacon, toast, and coffee. The admiral joined him in making short work of what Sluff considered real food. And no SPAM, either.

"We'll have a proper report in to you later this morning," Sluff said when he'd finished, feeling much better. "Plotting charts, damage reports, personnel casualties, and a summary RFS report. The harbormaster is refueling us right about now, but he says he has no torpedoes, so we're somewhat defanged."

The admiral nodded. "We have an ammo ship due in from Nouméa today," he said. "Mostly ammo for General Vandergrift, but they'll have torpedoes, too. Now: The Japs have had their noses bloodied twice. I would suspect they won't be back tonight."

"But we *will* go back out tonight, correct, sir?"

"Absolutely, and all of us this time. They've taken some losses, but one thing we've learned about the Japs: They do not give up. And: *They* learn, too. They've been ambushed twice, so the next time they're going to do something different. What, I don't know. Maybe come down outside the Slot, or bring battleships again—they have a fair number of them and they know they've sunk most of our heavy cruisers."

"What's their objective now, then?" Sluff asked.

"What I'm hearing from General Vandergrift is that the Jap army on Guadalcanal is in trouble—out of food, lots of disease, plus some very bad tactical decisions that have decimated their numbers. Their troops are apparently calling Guadalcanal Starvation Island."

"Great," Sluff said. "They started it as I remember."

"Well, the thing is, Navy intelligence reports that they're starting to use their warships as fast supply carriers. That's probably what that mob you tangled with the other night were up to."

"Cruisers and destroyers as troop carriers?"

"Thirty-six-knot cruisers and destroyers," the admiral pointed out. "They can get in and get out before the Cactus air force can get at them, so if you indeed did sink some of those guys, you helped Vandergrift out, too."

"I think we did," Sluff said. "But it's all radar

plots, except for the cruiser that blew up in our faces."

"Got a little close, did you?"

Sluff smiled. "A little bird, actually a big bird, told me that I was getting a rep for running from a fight. Thinking too much about preserving my ships. Thought it might be time to correct that impression."

The admiral nodded but did not smile back. "More advice," he said finally. "Thoughts about your professional reputation should *not* play a part in tactical decisions. Now, that's easy to say and very hard to do, but as a unit commander, you have to focus down on the task at hand and not *ever* factor in what other people might think of you afterwards. The ability to do that is what separates the pro from the amateur, okay?"

"Yes, sir. Sorry, sir."

"No, no, that's entirely natural. After thirty years of peacetime, we all have to overcome the tendency to worry about our careers, but now it's time for the cold-eyed killers amongst us to advance. Don't get me wrong: What you did last night, running right through that Jap formation, must have flabbergasted them, which is probably why your division survived taking on a force like that. I am delighted. Halsey will be delighted as well."

Sluff held up a hand. "Maybe we should wait to see what, if anything, we accomplished," he said.

The admiral smiled. "Get me my reports," he said. "As you well know, the fight's not over until all the paperwork is in. In the meantime, refuel, patch up what damage you can, and have your division ready for sea by sundown."

"Four boilers or two, sir?"

"Two on the line, two on the boil, young man."

On the boat ride back to *King*, Sluff thought about what the admiral had said about allowing careerism to influence his decisions last night. Had he done that? Maybe not consciously, but . . . subconsciously? He shouldn't have made that crack about correcting bad impressions. The truth was, he'd gone directly at the Japs because, somehow, they'd figured out his Comanche ride tactic, found the range, and were getting ready to tear up his little force with six-inch gunfire and torpedoes.

He stood up in the cockpit of the motor launch as it approached *King*'s rust-streaked side. There was a fat black barge alongside forward, pumping black oil into *King*'s thirsty tanks. Mount fifty-one, still askew after taking that hit, had its barrel pointed almost straight up in order to allow men inside to clean up the remains of the gun crew. He could see hoses playing through the open hatches, and some of the cleanup crew were wearing face masks. They'd already transferred the most badly wounded ashore to the field hospital on Tulagi, and tonight they would be doing a burial at sea on the way out into Ironbottom Sound. Yet another sad offering, he thought, to those bloodthirsty gods keeping watch over the waters off Guadalcanal.

In the distance he saw the gray shape of two Navy freighters inching into the harbor. He reminded himself to find out which one had torpedoes. As he climbed the pipe ladder, he heard the announcing system come on, four bells being rung, and then: "DesDiv Two-One-Two, arriving." He thought back fondly to the days when it would have been: "*King*, arriving." This commodore business was making his ass tired. Then he saw the exec waiting on the quarterdeck, with the by-now-familiar *two* message boards. He resisted a groan.

SEVENTEEN

Guadalcanal

The group sortied from Purvis Bay at sunset, headed not up the Slot but over to Guadalcanal, where General Vandergrift was anticipating a major push by the Japanese army against Henderson Field. He had asked for shore-bombardment support and Admiral Tyree was more than willing to oblige. He had set up two bombardment units, each with one light cruiser and two destroyers.

Wichita would cover the mouth of the Tenaru River, where ground patrols reported the enemy was massing troops under the cover of the jungle. *Providence* was to go four miles northwest up the coast, where coast watchers had reported a second staging area for artillery two miles inland, cleverly hidden from the Cactus air force in an abandoned copra plantation. The Japs had strung netting laced with palm fronds across the tops of the coconut groves and then set up a large artillery park to support the big push against the Marines at Henderson Field. Both units had been ordered to stand off the coast until full dark and then move in to two miles offshore, there to await the call for fire from Marine spotters on the ground.

Sluff's ships were operating as individual destroyers this time, mobile gun platforms, rather than as a tactical unit. Each ship was assigned to a specific radio frequency, on the other end of which was a Marine second lieutenant sweating it out in a foxhole much too close to the murmuring jungle across the river, where thousands of banzai-minded Japanese soldiers were gathering to make the emperor proud.

Sluff called the exec and the gunnery officer to the bridge once they'd made their creep into the beach and turned to parallel the shoreline.

"The jungle bunnies want us to wait until the Japs actually attack," he told them. "They say it will be obvious when they do—they fire flares, blow trumpets, and yell a lot. They've sent us preplanned area fire targets—where they *think* the Japs are gathering. When it starts, our spotter will call for area fire. The idea is to saturate the Japs' jump-off lines with naval gunfire. The group north of here will simultaneously open on the artillery park that's supposed to support the infantry attack."

"Why not start it now?" LTJG Chandler asked.

"The Japs are probably still moving up to their jump-off line along the river. The Marines want them all present for duty when *we* join the game. That's why we have a spotter. For right now, we're going to set up in our fire-support area and get the navigation track stabilized. We don't have mount one, and, of course, our cruiser will be the main punch. We're joining in because the Japs are supposedly bringing up four *thousand* troops, and they'll take up a lot of real estate."

"This sounds like a slaughter in the making," the exec said.

"Which is what the Japs are intending to do to the Marines," Sluff pointed out. "Bob, I want you in charge in Combat. The biggest thing is not to fire into friendly front lines. Use spots-away any time you're unsure of where the good guys are and then let the spotter bring you back into the target."

"Won't our spotter know where the Marines are from the git-go?" LTJG Chandler asked.

"Let me tell you about spotters, Billy. An artillery or naval gunfire spotter's life expectancy on the front line is about one hour. That's why they send second lieutenants, because the first lieutenants simply won't go. The Japs know who and what they are. They have special teams who go in with the sole mission of hunting down the spotters—the scared-looking kid with the 'different' field radio and a set of tripod-mounted binocs. So the first thirty minutes will be the most effective. We lose our spotter, we stop shooting until we get another one, okay?"

"Who's guarding Ironbottom Sound?" the exec asked.

"Right now, nobody," Sluff said. "The coast watchers have reported no ship movements up or down the Slot or even around Rabaul. So, once this little affair is over, the group will probably head north up above Savo, just to make sure."

"Hope they're right," Chandler said. "Those coast-watcher guys."

The Japanese attacked just before midnight and there was no mistaking when the Jap army jumped off. The air over the river lit up with several flares, and then came the racket of Jap rifles and Marine fifty-caliber machine guns trading arcs of tracers across the shallow flats of the river. *King*'s area-fire initial aim point was right into the river itself, and then extending north, back into the jungle on the Japs' side of the river. The river's wide mouth erupted into a continuous flashing roar of incoming shells, punctuated by the even larger rounds coming from *Wichita*, which was stationed behind the two destroyers and offset ten degrees so as not to be firing right over the tin cans. Then all three ships began to move the barrage to the right, degree by degree, hopefully covering the area where several thousand soldiers were formed up to run forward when the command came. *King*'s spotter wasn't much help. All they heard from him was: Goddamn! God*damn!* Yeah. Keep it coming. For the moment, it sounded like their spotter had become their cheerleader.

After three minutes, the preplanned fire mission was over. Now it was time for the spotters to bring the individual ships' guns onto urgent targets—infantry coming in from an unexpected direction or tanks emerging from the muddy jungle, grinding right over the hundreds of bodies that lay before them and then lurching into the shallow water of the Tenaru River. The entire mission was being conducted from Combat, so Sluff occupied himself as senior spectator, watching the annihilation of an entire Jap army from the port bridge wing. Mount fifty-one remained silent, as if in honor of the ghosts of its gun crew who were now laid out in a row of rubber bags on the ship's reefer decks, the compartment where the refrigerated and frozen food was stored. Mount fifty-two blasted away in ten-round increments,

221

pausing to let the spotter refine his calls for fire. Sluff could smell the paint burning off its barrel.

A few miles to seaward a rainsquall was marching across the sea. The muzzle flashes from *Wichita* made it look like a slow-moving thunderstorm. She was running a three-knot track beyond the destroyers but not by much, blasting away with her fifteen six-inch guns in majestic salvos, each rippling blast coming almost as fast as the destroyer guns. Fifteen balls of fire, followed by a simultaneous shock-wave thump to the ears and then the roar of the guns themselves.

He looked up to the north and saw similar lightning flashes as *Providence* and her two destroyers worked over the massed artillery park. As he watched he saw what had to be an ammo dump go up in a pulsing ball of fire, accompanied by a fountain of hot shells falling into the jungle in every direction. Ten seconds later he heard the thump of the primary explosion, followed by a series of smaller thumps as the shells fell back to earth and into the Japanese lines.

Five minutes later, Combat reported that the spotter had called a cease-fire order. He reported that it looked like everyone and everything anywhere near the banks of the river had been obliterated. The jungle on the Japanese side, reaching back for five hundred yards, had been reduced to flaming tree trunks, mangled piles of shattered mangrove, and mounds of wet, black mud covered in body parts.

"Captain, Combat."

Sluff smiled in the darkness, glad for the cessation of mount fifty-two's ear-crushing noise. Captain now, he thought. We're just a destroyer again.

"Go ahead."

"Marines are saying the attack is over. Our spotter is actually hysterical right now, but he's happy. Looks like we're done here for tonight. Waiting for orders from CTG Sixty-Four Point Two."

"Okay, we'll stay at GQ for now. Have the gun crews police the brass. Ask the galley if they can get some chow moving out to the GQ stations."

He went out to the port bridge wing again and surveyed the scene ashore. Everything within about a twenty-degree arc was burning. He looked north. The ammo dump was still pumping out red-hot projectiles, although at a lesser rate.

An hour later the ships were steaming in column formation at a stately fifteen knots five miles north of Savo Island, scene of the Navy's worst defeat at sea. Somewhere below them, two thousand or more feet down, lay the shattered remains of heavy cruisers *Quincy*, *Vincennes*, *Astoria*, and the Australian cruiser *Canberra*, all sunk during their very first encounter with the Imperial Japanese Navy, whose sleek heavy cruisers, loaded to the gills with Long Lance torpedoes and trained for years in night surface-action tactics, had slashed through the weary and inexperienced American formation like a samurai sword through butter. No American sailor could look at Savo Island and not remember that night.

The admiral's night orders said they would patrol north of Savo on an east-west line until daylight. Sluff told the OOD on the bridge to secure from GQ and set condition II so that half the crew at a time could get some rest for a few hours before relieving the other half on station. But then he remembered: First they needed to bury their dead.

They'd lost six men killed outright in the forward gun mount. All hands not actually on watch were called to the fantail, where Sluff read the committal prayers as six weighted bags, one after another, were slipped down a plank into the sea to join the thousands of dead already asleep on the bottom of Ironbottom Sound. It was cold comfort to know that there were also a few thousand Japanese sailors down there now, too. Sluff was pretty sure that every man standing at attention in ragged ranks on the fantail and the 01 level just above it was wondering if he, too, would one day make that deepest of all dives.

After the service, he found the exec down in the wardroom, where some of the officers were having a quick cup of soup and a sandwich before they went on watch. Everyone stood when he came into the wardroom. He told them to carry on and then went to the sideboard for a sandwich. He sat down at the head of the wardroom table for a few minutes and chatted with the officers. LTJG Chandler was there and Sluff asked him to prepare letters of condolences for his signature. LTJG Bob Warren, the supply officer, asked him if they were expecting more shooting tonight.

"I don't think so, Bob, but we're at condition two for a reason. The Japs have a lot more ships than we do right now, so they *could* come at any time, and from any direction, for that matter. The coast watchers usually give us warning, though."

"Who *are* the coast watchers, Cap'n—er—Commodore?"

Yeah, Sluff thought with a mental smile—which is it?

"The system was started by Australian naval intelligence a few years before the war broke out last December," he replied. "They used the colonial administrators already in place. Then they sent out naval officers to set up camps all through these islands to keep watch on what the Japs were doing in the Solomons. Gave 'em a radio and let them hire some of the natives to act as bearers for the equipment. They sit up on mountain ridges and call in warship sightings to the Marines on Guadalcanal."

"The Japs know about them?"

"I think they do. They reportedly captured one of them in the Shortland Islands, right below Rabaul."

"What happened to him?"

"They cut his head off, actually."

That brought a moment of silence to the table. Sluff reached for his plate as it began to slide across the green felt tablecloth to one side of the table. The ship was turning, and then the sound-powered phone mounted under the table squeaked.

"Captain," Sluff said.

"Formation is coming about to two seven zero," the OOD reported. "Still speed fifteen."

"Very well," Sluff said. He gave the exec a signal and then got up, passed his plate to the steward in the wardroom pantry, and went into his cabin. The exec came in after him.

"I'm hoping we'll get the night off," Sluff said, easing into his desk chair. The exec leaned against the doorframe. His face was drawn and there were dark circles under his eyes. "In that regard, I want *you* to hit the rack. Now would be a good time."

"But I've got—"

"No, not tonight," Sluff said. "Hit the rack, get a solid four, five hours of sleep. We'll go to GQ just before dawn for the morning air raids. You've been doing a hell of job, running just about everything from Combat, both for the ship and the division. You've made it possible for me to be both CO and unit commander. I hope that will soon be over, but some things the admiral said make me wonder. Anyway, get some sleep. That's an order, Bub."

The exec grinned. "Thanks for the kind words, and, aye, aye, sir."

Once the exec left he called Radio Central and asked for the message boards. Both of them. Then he sent for Mose and asked for a small carafe of coffee and a fat pill if there was one to be found. Their cruiser-destroyer column was settling into a watchful night-steaming formation. He planned to get through as much of the fleet broadcast message backlog as he could and then get some sleep himself. Sleep was becoming a rare commodity out here in the Solomon Islands. For everyone.

EIGHTEEN

Savo Island

Two hours later his phone squeaked. He heard it, ignored it. It squeaked again, harder.

"Captain."

"Captain, this is Lieutenant McCarthy in Combat. *Wichita* and *Providence* both are reporting air contacts inbound from the north. *Wichita* says they look like multiple heavy bombers. Right now they're forty-eight miles out and closing at a hundred sixty knots."

"What time is it?" Sluff asked.

"Zero two thirty, sir."

"GQ," Sluff said, and rolled out of bed.

In the passageway outside he heard the bosun piping all-hands over the ship's announcing system, followed by the words "General quarters, general quarters, all hands man your battle stations." Then came the familiar gonging noise. He dressed quickly and scrambled up to the bridge, accompanied by everyone else headed for a topside GQ station.

He didn't get a chance to look at his watch until he made it to his chair. It was 0235, which meant that the Japs had now thrown night-capable bombers into the Solomons campaign, maybe even equipped with radar. He looked out the bridge windows and saw only the typical Solomon Islands darkness. No visible moon, the air heavy, wet, and still in the low nineties, even at this early hour. Then he heard the radio speaker above his chair come to life. The task group commander ordered the formation to execute an immediate-execute turn together to the north and head right for the approaching bomber formation, speed twenty-seven knots. Then he executed it, and all the ships swung left and began to accelerate.

The Japs wouldn't be trying to drop bombs at night. This would be a torpedo attack, and by presenting their narrow bows to the oncoming bombers, the admiral had much reduced the target aspect of the American column. Sluff called Combat and asked if *King*'s radars held the approaching planes.

"In and out, Captain," the exec said. "I think they're just now descending to drop level. I'm guessing Bettys. As soon as we get a solid contact, I'll designate to director one."

"But on this course, we can only bring one gun to bear," Sluff said.

At that moment both cruisers opened fire. Each of them could bring six barrels to bear on the descending aircraft. Their radar-controlled dual-purpose six-inch guns were designed to fill the air in front of an approaching bomber formation with white-hot shards of steel at a range of ten miles. The destroyers would have to wait until the bogeys got into seven or eight miles before they could even reach them, depending on their altitude.

"Captain, Combat, we've got 'em on the surface-search radar now, which means they're down on the deck for a torpedo run. Fifty-two will open up in about forty seconds."

Sluff didn't like this setup, but there really was no alternative. If they turned perpendicular to the attacking waves, each destroyer except *King* could bring five guns to bear, and the cruisers fifteen. But he knew the reason they were turning into the attack. Come right or left and the torpedoes would have six hundred feet of cruiser to collide with; this way, they had fifty-five. He stared out the front portholes. Mount fifty-two was in automatic, its barrel raised and quivering in response to the delicate servomotor commands coming up from the main gunnery computer.

B-Blam! Fifty-two finally got into it. Between muzzle blasts, Sluff could see the northern sky filling with brilliant flashes as the light cruisers laid into the first wave of bombers. Then he saw flaming contrails light up in the near distance and then descend into the sea, where they were snuffed out in an invisible crash. Fifty-two was going strong, blasting away at some invisible radar contact flying right at them at close to 160 miles an hour. Sluff felt absolutely helpless. Either they would steam right through the swarm of approaching torpedoes, or they'd take one on the chin and the front half of the ship would disappear in a magazine explosion. And all *King* could do was shoot one damned five-inch at them.

The sky ahead was now looking like the Fourth of July, with flaming contrails going every which way, shell bursts stabbing the night sky in groups of three and sometimes six, and then he heard the bombers as they roared overhead, chased now by *King*'s forty-millimeter and even twenty-millimeter guns in a quick swinging arc of fire. Then the after two mounts opened fire, finally able to bear on the outgoing Japs. Fifty-two went silent, and then Sluff saw the hatches open and a few men jump out to begin wrangling the brass powder cases out of the way of the mount's training circle. The relative wind caused by the twenty-seven-knot ordered speed quickly blew all the smoke out of the pilothouse.

Had the torpedoes passed? He was about to call down to Sonar to see if they'd heard anything, but at twenty-seven knots, the ship's sonar was effectively deaf. And then off to port, at some distance, a bright white light bloomed into a yellow and then red ball of fire, reaching for the sky.

Shit, Sluff thought. Somebody caught one. Then the speaker came to life again as the admiral ordered a reversal of course, 180 degrees, speed still twenty-seven knots, to head back in the direction of the outbound bombers. There was nothing to say that the Japs, too, wouldn't turn around and have another go. Halfway through the turn, with the ship heeling hard to port as the rudders forced the stern to go sideways into the sea, *King* was directed to go to the assistance of *Wichita*. Sluff picked up the handset and rogered for the order.

"Combat, Captain—where's the *Wichita*?"

Combat came back with a range and bearing to *Wichita*'s last known position, and Sluff ordered the OOD to come to that course. Once the ship steadied up, *Wichita* became visible fine off the port bow, illuminated by a glowing fire that seemed to be consuming her forward super-structure from the inside out. Sluff studied the wounded cruiser through his binocs as *King* closed in and then figured out what was wrong. *Wichita* was missing her bow and forwardmost gun turret. She was down by the head and making no way through the sea. He ordered the OOD to slow down and approach the cruiser from astern and then had the bosun call away the rescue and assistance team. Then he remembered the Jap bombers.

"Combat, Captain—what are those Bettys doing?"

"We no longer hold radar contact, Cap'n," the exec replied. "The rest of the formation is still headed south but the air-raid reporting net has gone quiet."

"Keep an eye peeled, Bob," Sluff said. "Nothing to say those bastards can't make a wide swing around Savo and then come back up here to finish off the *Wichita*. Looks like she's lost everything forward of turret two. There's also a nasty fire at the base of her bridge. I want to go alongside so we can put some hoses on that."

"Combat, aye."

Sluff then took the conn and maneuvered the ship in a wide arc so that she could then turn and come up alongside *Wichita*'s starboard side. He had his talker tell DC Central to set up fire hose parties along the port side. He then slowed to bare steerageway and came alongside the darkened cruiser. He could see several men up on the starboard bridge wing, illuminated by the fire that seemed to be eating its way upward toward them. He backed *King* gently and then *King*'s damage-control parties began to play two-and-a-half-inch fire hoses on the glowing steel above them, creating huge clouds of steam. He had to back and fill several times, maneuvering gently so that the two ships wouldn't bump up against each other in these close quarters. The streams of seawater coming from *King* had the desired effect, dousing the visible, external fires. Several portholes along the cruiser's starboard main deck exploded when hit by the relatively cold seawater, and *King*'s damage-control men trained their hoses to inject high-pressure streams directly into the interior of the badly damaged ship. Amidships, the bosun's mates passed over a four-inch hose to the cruiser's damage-control teams. They connected it to their own fire main, and then *King* was able to augment the damaged ship's two operational fire pumps.

After twenty minutes, Sluff was getting nervous about being so close in alongside the *Wichita*, which, having lost almost two hundred feet of her hull forward, was now in danger of becoming unstable and capsizing—onto USS *King*. He kept an eye on her forward mast, which was rocking gently in what little seaway there was, but also hanging for a few seconds at the end of each roll. That was a bad sign. He was too close to determine how far down by the bow she was.

"Captain, Combat. From the flag: *Providence* holding intermittent air contacts to the west. The Japs might be coming back. Flag says they are turning around and will attempt to get between *Wichita* and the Bettys' attack line."

"Focus on your surface-search radar, Bob," Sluff said. "They'll be low on the deck. We're on the wrong side of *Wichita* to shoot, so I'm going to back down and come up the other side. You have comms with *Wichita*?"

"Negative, Captain. Maybe use the 1MC topside speakers?"

Great idea, Sluff thought. He asked the bosun to bring him the announcing system's microphone.

"Ahoy, *Wichita*: The Japs are making another run, from the west. I'm going to back down and come up your port side to provide AA fire. Are your guns operational?"

Sluff's amplified words echoed strangely in the steel canyon formed between the two ships' hulls. There was no reply for a long thirty seconds, and then the CO of the cruiser came up on his announcing system. "The torpedo dismounted our turbogenerators," he said. "We're on emergency diesels, all boilers off the line. Trying to get steam up. After turrets can shoot in local control, but we can't see right now. Radar's down, main battery plot has electrical fires and smoke. Appreciate any AA help you can give us."

"I'll stay on your port quarter, then, Captain," Sluff said.

Sluff waited for the midships crew to disconnect the fire-main hose and then ordered a slow astern bell and eased *King* back down the cruiser's starboard side, maneuvering the rudder so as not to rake the cruiser with his port anchor. Once he was clear astern, he came left and then stopped, perpendicular to the cruiser's stern. He noticed that an awful lot of her black waterline across the transom was exposed. He could also see that she had about a ten-degree list to starboard.

"Captain, Combat, three bogeys inbound on the surface-search radar, range fifteen miles. Coming straight in. Director one is on the lead plane and we'll open fire when they're at nine miles."

"Open fire when they're at *ten* miles," Sluff ordered. "Maybe we can spook 'em out of here if we happen to hit one."

"Combat, aye, ten miles."

Sluff heard mount fifty-two train out to port and ordered up ten knots. There was no point in high speed right now, not until he thought Long Lances were coming. The Bettys were known to be flying fire hazards; flame one, the other two might bolt. Otherwise, and especially if they had radar, they had a sitting duck in the stationary light cruiser.

The five-inch erupted into their familiar symphony and Sluff went out onto the port bridge wing to watch the show. He was proud that his officers and crew were pretty much in automatic when it came to fighting. He visualized the fire-control problem, which, on a direct attack, was simple. The computer would be aiming the shells at a point in space in front of and slightly above the approaching bombers, steady bearing, decreasing range.

There. An orange flare blossomed out in the distance as one of the Bettys suffered a gas-tank hit. He put his binocs up and could see that the plane was still coming at them, but losing lift and descending toward the black sea. He could actually see the other two, flying in close formation on either side of the burning plane. He wondered if they could see the cruiser. With her stern pointed at them, maybe not. They sure as hell *could* see *King*, with four five-inch guns blasting away at them, joined now by the forty-millimeter batteries with their double-thump gunfire and red tracers arcing out at the incoming planes, initially too low but then rising and, finally, someone connected with the Betty on the right. The plane literally blew up, sending a fountain of fiery wreckage in all directions. The third Betty jinked left, away from the exploding plane, just as the first bomber hit the sea in a sheet of flame.

They were close now. Sluff decided it was time to maneuver.

"All ahead flank, come *left* to"—he glanced down at the pelorus on the bridge wing—"three *two* zero."

"Three two zero, all ahead flank, aye," cried the helmsman and lee helmsman.

King jumped to it, squatting briefly before surging ahead and then left into a hard turn. Sluff watched the sea surface intently by the light of his guns' muzzle blast, looking for the telltale signs of approaching torpedoes. His five-inch followed the third Betty as it made its escape. Sluff thought he saw a thin trail of smoke coming from its left engine, but then it disappeared into the darkness. A moment later all the guns went silent, leaving only the ringing silence of the air all around the ship, smashed into nothingness by all those guns, broken soon by the sounds of brass powder cases rolling around on the deck.

Sluff ordered the ship to slow down and told the OOD to take her back to the *Wichita*, which apparently had escaped any torpedoes launched in her direction. Or, the pilots had panicked, just dumped their fish, and turned away into the safety of darkness and opening range from the decidedly unfriendly welcome provided by *J. B. King*. Way out on the port quarter, Sluff could see a fire on the water, the remains of the first Betty still burning.

"Combat, Captain, two out of three ain't bad.

We'll go back to *Wichita*, see what we can do for her. May have to rig a tow, although with no bow . . ."

"Combat, aye, and the scope is clear for the moment. No contact on the rest of the formation."

"Tell the flag what happened and that we're assisting *Wichita*."

NINETEEN

Wichita managed to get steam up two hours after the night torpedo-bomber raid, but then had to back down all the way over to Tulagi, accompanied by *Providence* and two destroyers in case the Japs came back at sunrise. *J. B. King* and *Evans* went ahead to refuel and take on ammo and provisions. Once *Wichita* had been taken into the harbor, *Providence*, *Malone*, and *Stayers* joined the morning operation pit stop. At ten thirty the admiral summoned Sluff to the flagship for a meeting and lunch. As he was riding over to the cruiser he saw what looked like two Fletcher-class destroyers in the distance heading into the harbor from the southeast.

Providence's exec led Sluff directly to the admiral's cabin, where he found a small crowd assembling. The flag quarters consisted of an office/conference room, a bedroom, and a bathroom. The meeting was going to take place in the office area. The CO of *Wichita* was there, looking exhausted, along with his exec. Commander Reese, the admiral's ops boss, his aide, and three other Cruiser Division Six staffers were standing around as if waiting for a ceremony of some kind to begin.

"Commodore, welcome," the admiral said when Sluff entered. "Good work last night."

"Amen," said the CO of *Wichita*. "And I really mean that. I thought we were toast when those torpedo bombers came back."

"We got lucky, Captain," Sluff said.

The admiral asked everyone to sit down, and then said, "Not so fast, Commodore."

Sluff blinked. The admiral and his aide came over. The aide handed a small cardboard box to the admiral, who instructed Sluff to remove his silver oak leaf collar devices. He then pinned on silver eagles, stood back, and offered a hand of hearty congratulations. "Admiral Halsey is extremely pleased with what DesDiv Two-Twelve has accomplished the last few times out," he said. "He has spot-promoted you to Captain, and ordered you to take command of Des*Ron* Twenty-One, which will consist of the ships of DesDiv Two-Twelve two plus two more Fletcher-class destroyers, *Barrett* and *Cannon*, who are arriving right about now. As a squadron commander you will have a staff, which is currently embarked in *Barrett*. That's the good news."

Sluff was thunderstruck. Then that "good news" comment penetrated.

"You will be relieved of command of *J. B. King* by Commander Tom Reese," the admiral continued. "Most recently my excellent operations officer. I want the change of command to be executed by eighteen hundred today. You will then break your burgee in *Barrett* and have your squadron ready to sail by twenty-three hundred tonight. We will have business to attend to—the Japs are sending down another resupply run. Lunch, anyone?"

By the time Sluff got back to *J. B. King* his brain had finally settled down. Lunch had been necessarily a quick affair, as he had a destroyer squadron to organize, including two new ships to meet, not to mention a change of command. As he climbed the pipe ladder to *King*'s quarterdeck, he smiled at the exec's startled expression when he saw those silver eagles.

"Things have changed," Sluff announced.

At one thirty the next morning the task group was steaming east at a sedate twelve knots on the familiar east-west line drawn across the approaches to Guadalcanal. Savo Island was ten miles astern, a bright green blob on the radar-scopes but otherwise invisible in the near-total, hot, and desperately humid darkness. The only advantage they had over the Marines back on the island was that there were no mosquitoes.

Providence steamed alone on a separate east-west line, three miles south of the destroyers.

Commander Destroyer Squadron 21, Captain Harmon "Sluff" Wolf, occupied the port-side captain's chair in the pilothouse of USS *Barrett*, sweating in full battle gear along with everyone else, and marveling at all that had happened the previous day. Commander Reese had come aboard an hour after Sluff returned to *King*, where he was taken in tow by the exec and given a tour of his new ship. A change of command aboard a destroyer normally took at least a week, with inspections, departmental briefings, change-of-matériel-custody meetings, a day or two at sea while the officers and crew demonstrated their professional abilities, and then, finally, a personnel inspection and the change-of-command ceremony itself. With an 1800 deadline, all of this had been condensed into a two-hour meeting in the wardroom, during which *King*'s department heads briefed the new CO on the matériel and personnel status of their departments.

Sluff then took him on a tour of the ship from stem to stern, before departing to embark in USS *Barrett*, another new-construction Fletcher-class destroyer and now his flagship. There he met with his new staff of four officers and six enlisted men and found out what had happened to open this particular unit commander billet. The previous commodore had suffered a heart attack on his first night ashore in Nouméa, having just completed the long transit from Pearl to the islands of New Caledonia. Halsey had broken up the headless six-ship squadron, assigning two to Sluff's collection of four destroyers for a total of six, and the rest to one of the carrier groups. Sluff had assumed command of the squadron number of 21, and thus now had *King*, *Evans*, *Malone*, *Stayers*, *Cannon*, and *Barrett* under his command.

With *Wichita* out of action, *Providence* had become the sole heavy left in the Guadalcanal striking force. The admiral had said at lunch that there were two more cruisers coming but he did not know when. Before Sluff had left the flagship, the admiral called him in for a quick one-on-one conference. The coast watchers had reported six Jap destroyers headed south into the Slot. He'd told Sluff that they'd go out after dark that night to block what he thought was a resupply mission to bring supplies and reinforcements to the Jap garrison on Guadalcanal.

"I want you to conduct a torpedo ambush and then shoot the bastards up," he'd said. "*Providence* will join the fun once we see torpedoes exploding north of us."

Sluff hesitated. "Yes, sir, but we'll execute a high-speed maneuver right after the torpedoes start hitting. *Then* we'll start shooting, just like last time. But if *Providence* opens up, she'll become the target for however many Jap cans are still able to shoot torpedoes, while we're still dark."

"What, you're suggesting we're just gonna watch?"

"No, sir, but let us start it with torpedoes, then do our Comanche circle around them, shooting, going dark, shooting some more, take their focus north as we run around the clock, and then *Providence* joins in."

"*Providence*, in support of the destroyers."

"Well, Admiral, if there were more cruisers . . ."

"Bite your tongue, Commodore." He paused. "I'll think about it."

"Thank you, sir."

He'd gone back to *King* for the abbreviated change-of-command ceremony, conducted in the wardroom, and then had Mose pack up his uniforms and other personal gear for transfer to *Barrett*. The CO of *Barrett*, Commander Kelly Angstrom, had already moved up to his sea cabin when the previous commodore had first embarked, so Sluff's move aboard didn't cause any further perturbations.

Before finally departing *King*, Sluff had sat down with his exec, Bob Frey, and *King*'s new skipper, Commander Reese, to explain how they'd been operating, with Bob in CIC sometimes taking over the actual operational control of the division under Sluff's orders from the bridge.

"It's all about the radar," Sluff had said. "The

people in CIC have the complete picture. The captain on the bridge does not. You'll have to decide where you want to be when the shooting starts. Nothing beats the captain being on the bridge when another ship screws up and tries to cut you in two, but for the engagement, the radars and the DRT can show you everything. Bob and his CIC team know how to do that."

"When we went to GQ in *Providence*, the ship's exec was always back aft at secondary conn in case the bridge got hit," Reese pointed out. "That arrangement saved *San Francisco*, you'll remember."

"Not quite," Sluff countered. "Their secondary conn had been wiped out when that Betty hit the after director tower the day before, remember? Anyway, you're correct; that is DESPAC doctrine, too. But think of this way, Tom: Bob is the second-most-experienced officer you have on board. In fact, in the matter of night fighting with the Japs, he has more experience than most of my squadron's COs. Isn't that the guy you want running the tactical picture in CIC? Second, destroyers are much smaller than cruisers. If the bridge does get wiped out, it's likely that the entire ship is going to be wiped out, especially if we're talking about Long Lance torpedoes. I believe the trade-off is worth it."

Reese nodded. Sluff realized that he was perhaps stepping on some toes here.

"It's your ship now, Tom," he said. "You do it your way. I'm not ordering you to organize it any other way than by DESPAC doctrine."

"Thanks, Commodore," Reese said, looking relieved.

"Oh, and by the way," Sluff said. "When it all quiets down and assuming you're still afloat, you will be expected to glare at the bosun and ask for some 'damned coffee.'"

And that had been that. Another officer now commanded *his* destroyer. He now commanded six destroyers. He'd met his staff and had sent his operations officer, Lieutenant Commander Hugh Garing, to *King*, so that Bob Frey could explain how they'd been doing business once the long, black steel fish went into the water and the shells began to fly. It was totally unconventional, but the advent of shipborne radar and the Japs' lack of it, for now anyway, had changed everything.

At the moment it was LCDR Garing down in CIC. Sluff thought he'd probably be very nervous and wondering what the new squad dog wanted him to do in a gunfight. He resolved to be careful in giving orders to his "voice" down in Combat. Then he had a thought: Why couldn't *he* be down in Combat? He was no longer double-hatted as both commodore of a division and captain of a ship. *Barrett*'s captain could take care of keeping *Barrett* from getting into collisions and other calamities, while he, the boss, could be down in

CIC, if he wanted to, and with the complete tactical picture laid out on the DRT and the radarscope. Where he could *see*.

He glanced across the pilothouse, where Commander Langstrom, *Barrett*'s CO, was sitting, a red flashlight perched on his left shoulder illuminating a message board in his lap.

"Skipper?" Sluff said.

"Commodore?"

"I've decided that I want to be in Combat when the game starts," Sluff said.

"Yes, sir," Langstrom replied. Then the bitch-box lit up.

"Bridge, Combat, radar contact, three four zero, range fifteen miles, composition four to six, course one seven zero, speed three-five."

Sluff reached for the 21MC in front of him but then stopped. Combat had called the bridge, not the commodore. Commander Langstrom was looking across the pilothouse. Sluff grinned at him, indicated that he should acknowledge, and then he went below.

TWENTY

New Georgia Island

"Commodore's in Combat," a voice called out as Sluff pushed into the crowded space. The center of attention was the dead-reckoning tracer, or DRT, the lighted plotting table where pencil-wielding plotters created spidery tracks on the tracing paper that indicated where both friendly and enemy ships were in relation to one another. Lieutenant Commander Garing sat on a stool at the head of the table. *Barrett*'s navigation officer sat at the other end, with two plotters on either side creating the tactical picture on the table. A radarman sat on a stool in front of the planned-position indicator scope, a dinner-plate-sized, round glass display that showed the actual contacts as bright green pips every time the rotating beam washed over them. The operator could position a cursor on a target, and the dials on the scope would read out that contact's distance and true bearing. He would then mutter that data into a sound-powered phone to the plotters, who would mark that position on the paper and then draw a line between the newest position and the last one, thus creating the track. The room was under red-light conditions to enhance the radarscope's presentation.

As Sluff joined the intent crowd at the DRT, Garing laid it out for him. "Five, maybe six, high-speed contacts, headed towards Cape Esperance, where the main Jap forces are. On our present course and speed, they will pass to the east of us at a range of about eight thousand yards."

"What do we need to intercept within our torpedo range?"

Another of Sluff's staff officers, Lieutenant Griggs, stepped in with a maneuvering board calculator in his hand. "We need to come right to one two zero, speed two-five, sir."

"Order it. Immediate execute by turn move-ment to starboard."

Garing blinked, as if to say, *Me?*

Sluff put his hand out. "TBS handset. Now."

The lieutenant scrambled to pull a radio handset out from under the DRT and handed it over to Sluff, who issued the immediate-execute order to the squadron. Once it was done and Sluff felt *Barrett* heel to port and accelerate, he gave the handset to Garing.

"I need to pay attention to the plot," he said. "Hugh, you will be my voice. You know how to issue maneuvering orders? CORPEN, TURN, immediate execute, execute to follow?"

"Uh, yes sir, I do. I just didn't—"

"I understand. Now make sure everybody got the last signal. Check the tracks."

Both Garing and Lieutenant Griggs jumped to

examine the DRT tracks to make sure that none of their brood was continuing to sail off to the east at twelve knots while the rest of the squadron bore away to the southeast.

"Does *Providence* hold the contacts?"

"Yes, sir," *Barrett*'s CIC officer reported.

"Okay, then here's the plan. We close into launch position, each ship will then fire five torpedoes, high speed, two-degree spread, five-foot depth." He saw Griggs writing furiously in his notebook. "Then we will turn together to three five zero, speed two-five, and run until torpedoes start going off, at which point we will turn together to zero five zero and open fire. Prepare the maneuvering signals and give me that handset. What's our collective and what's my call sign?"

"Sir, the squadron's collective call sign is Smoke; your call sign is Bear."

Sluff smiled at that. Should have been wolf, but the smoke part was right. Then he keyed the radio.

"Smoke, this is Bear. Prep torpedo attack on my signal. Five fish. High speed. Spread two. Depth five feet. Turn away after launch on my signal. Open fire with guns after hits observed. Break. Acknowledge."

One after the other the squadron ships acknowledged receipt with the simple word "Wilco."

"Time to launch point?"

"Four minutes, Commodore," Griggs said. Sluff made a note to learn more about Lieutenant

Griggs. The youngster was anticipating his questions. He scanned the plot. The Jap destroyers were in a loose column, speeding southeast through the darkness, headed for the cape and apparently oblivious to the approaching danger. His own squadron was sprinting south of east, headed for the optimum point from which to launch their torpedoes. Three minutes and counting.

"New radar contact!" shouted the PPI operator. "Bearing two five zero, range sixteen *miles,* three contacts, course zero three zero, speed three-five."

Sluff turned around and looked down over the PPI operator's shoulders. Three pips, in line-abreast formation, coming around the south end of New Georgia Island and headed right for them. Big pips, too. Cruisers?

"Notify *Providence.* Time to launch point?"

"Two minutes, thirty seconds."

Sluff thought fast. Maybe these six destroyers had been bait to lure the diminished American striking force out into a cruiser ambush. Run their tin cans right down the Slot, just like the last two times. Then pincer the Americans with a three-pack of cruisers coming from *outside* Ironbottom Sound? He suppressed a shiver.

"Range to western contacts?"

"Thirteen miles and closing."

"Okay, everybody, here's the new plan: Proceed with the torpedo attack against the destroyer column, then turn due south and set up a torpedo attack against whatever's coming in from the west. We can cap their T, I do believe. Signals ready, Hugh?"

"Affirmative, Commodore."

Sluff picked up the handset again. "Smoke, this is Bear. Change One. We will launch against the destroyers, and then turn to conduct a torpedo attack against the new skunks coming in from the west. Acknowledge."

The ships replied in turn.

"One minute to launch point."

Sluff heard the *Barrett*'s forward-torpedo-mount train motors grinding away as it swung out to port. The ship's talkers were feeding ranges and bearings to the torpedo fire-control station and to *Barrett*'s gun plot.

"Smoke, this is Bear. One minute." He looked down at the plot. The Jap column was still going southeast while his destroyers were closing in on the acute-angle course that led to the best launch point. The ships approaching from the west were way off on one side of the plot.

"*Mark* launch point," Garing said.

"Smoke, this is Bear. Launch."

Sluff handed the TBS handset to Garing and nodded, signaling that now was the time to issue the turn-away order. To his horror, Garing froze. "Um, north or south, sir—I'm sorry, I'm confused."

Sluff grabbed the handset back and gave the

orders himself, turning the destroyer formation away from the southbound Japanese column while setting his gang to cross the possible cruisers approaching from the west. Lieutenant Commander Garing sat down on his stool with a totally confused expression in his face.

"Smoke, this is Bear," Sluff transmitted. "Prepare to launch all remaining torpedoes at *western* enemy force."

As the destroyers acknowledged the preparatory orders, Sluff looked down at the DRT plot. His turn to the southwest now had his destroyers in an echelon formation, which meant that the ships out on the right flank were blocking the firing bearings for the rest of the destroyers. He needed to straighten out the line and said so to Lieutenant Griggs.

"Recommend turn to starboard to three four zero," Griggs said. "That'll put us back in line column with a clear shot at the incoming enemy ships."

"What's the range and bearing to those contacts?" Sluff asked.

"Two six zero, eighteen thousand yards and closing fast, Commodore," one of the plotters reported.

Sluff didn't like it. If he turned back to the northwest, his entire squadron would be wasting valuable time completing the maneuver while the Jap cruisers closed in at thirty-five knots. And, unlike American cruisers, Jap cruisers carried torpedoes.

Think. Think. *Think!*

"Combat, bridge, our torpedoes are hitting to the east. Three distinct explosions. *Providence* appears to have opened fire."

Dammit, Sluff thought. The admiral hadn't waited. If the approaching Jap cruisers hadn't known about *Providence* before this, they did now. The flashes from her six-inch guns would reveal exactly what they were up against, and, more important, exactly where she was. He hoped to God the Japs hadn't brought down eight-inch-gunned *heavy* cruisers for this little party.

He took a deep breath and keyed the TBS handset. "Smoke, this is Bear. Immediate execute, turn two six zero, speed two-seven. I say again, turn two six zero, speed two-seven. Stand by, *execute.* We're going to run right through them. Fire torpedoes as your tubes bear. Commence firing guns as soon as you launch torpedoes or they see you."

He felt *Barrett* lean into the new course, her hull thrumming with the power of fifty thousand shaft horsepower punishing the warm waters of Ironbottom Sound. He took one last look at the plot. His entire squadron was heading straight for the approaching Jap cruiser formation with a closing speed of nearly seventy miles an hour.

This would go fast, he thought, and suddenly

realized he wanted to be topside when it happened. He glanced over at his operations officer, who now had his head in his hands and his eyes closed. Deal with that problem later, he thought, and then he left CIC and scrambled up the interior ladder to the pilothouse.

As he stepped through the door into the pilothouse, the wind stream blowing in from the bridge wing made his eyes water for a second. The bosun saw him in the dim red light and announced, "Commodore's on the bridge."

Sluff saw two dim figures out on the starboard bridge wing and hastened to join them. *Barrett* had one chipped propeller, which vibrated when the ship was at high speed. Up here on the bridge the vibration was pronounced, and objects on the chart table were dancing in time to the spinning blade three hundred feet aft. As he stepped out onto the bridge wing he heard the first of five torpedoes going over the side. He looked out into the muggy darkness and saw nothing at all. *Barrett*'s skipper was staring intently through his binoculars on a bearing thirty degrees to the right of the bow. Sluff looked down on the forecastle and saw the forward two five-inch mounts quivering in radar-controlled increments, their barrels pointed out, low and flat, right where the skipper was looking. Then a star shell burst overhead and Sluff got to see what they were tangling with.

The nearest Jap ship was a Takao-class heavy cruiser, whose forward turrets were already training in their direction, just as *Barrett*'s forward five-inch let fly with the opening salvo. The range was close, very close, and Sluff could see red-hot embers that were their shells going out, lifting in a minuscule arc and then settling down to smash into the cruiser's forward superstructure. He was dimly aware of the after five-inch getting into it as their guns bore and wondered if their shells would have time to arm before hitting the oncoming cruiser. He was mesmerized by the sight of the powerful black monster steaming at them, so close that he thought he could see the faces of the officers high up in that towering pagoda structure, and then her eight-inch guns exploded right in his face.

There was an ear-crushing crash of metal as the eight-inch shells smashed into *Barrett*'s comparatively fragile superstructure. Sluff felt the deck beneath him sag and then collapse from the impact, dimly aware that the incoming shells had not exploded but rather had passed right through the destroyer's thin hull. As he clutched the bull rail, trying desperately to stay upright, he saw a waterspout rise along the cruiser's starboard side as one of their torpedoes hit. But it was a small waterspout, not the hull-puncturing blast he'd hoped for, as yet another American torpedo failed to go off. The Long Lance torpedo fired by the cruiser did not fail. An immense blow hammered *Barrett* amidships that literally lifted her out of the water for a throat-clenching second. Sluff turned to look aft. His feet were sliding aft as the ship collapsed into two pieces, and then a second salvo of eight-inch struck all along *Barrett's* starboard side, some going right through, some exploding inside the ship, all signing the eviscerated destroyer's death warrant. The ship's back half kept driving forward at twenty-seven knots, pushing the now detached front half into a swooping ninety-degree turn just before it fell over sideways, and catapulting the commodore of one day's standing out into the grasping waters of Ironbottom Sound.

He landed in the water, popped up courtesy of his kapok life jacket, and then something large and heavy hit him squarely in the head. He saw stars, a red haze, and then, almost gratefully, he blacked out.

PART TWO

THE CASTAWAY

TWENTY-ONE

Kalai Island

Something bit his elbow, then his hand. He opened his eyes and then a wave washed over his face, the salt stinging his eyes. Something bit his ankle, something with really sharp teeth this time. He looked down the length of his body, barely visible over the mound of sodden, oily kapok that had been his life jacket. He shook the water out of his eyes and his head told him to never do that again, not *ever.* It took him a full minute to wait out the pain.

Where am I? he wondered. What's happened? And then with a startling realization that made his eyes open right back up: *Who* am I? What am I doing here?

Another wave smacked him in the face. This time he blinked just in time. He was lying on something and he thought he could hear surf thumping and rolling somewhere over *there.* He looked, and saw big swells rising up out of the water as they came in, cascading into a coil of beautiful blue-green water before being demolished. It was morning, and he could see right through those coiled waves just before they crashed down.

A reef. He was lying on a reef. He put his hands down, trying to sit upright. Something bit both hands.

Coral. He was lying on a *coral* reef, and it was like taking a nap on a bed of razors. He felt the right side of his head, where the lightning bolt had come from a moment earlier. It was matted, swollen, and tender to the touch. Suddenly he wanted to lie back down and just go back to sleep. Finish this dream, then wake up and start over. He looked again at the swells assaulting the reef, no more than fifty feet away. Then he looked in the opposite direction and saw an island with alien-looking black-sand beaches across a dark and still lagoon. Coconut trees and tropical jungle came right down to the beach. Beyond that there was more jungle, and beyond that were hills and then a green mountain that rose high enough that he had to move his head to take it all in. The lightning came back when he moved his head.

He lifted his hands and saw that he was wearing a long-sleeved khaki shirt, buttoned at the wrists. His hands had several pinpricks that were weeping blood. Nothing serious, but the salt water made them sting. Strapped across his chest was a mound of gray fabric, tied together with strings. There was more of it behind his head, like some kind of soggy parka. He somehow knew that it was a life jacket, but it was soaked and much too heavy now to be of any use. He decided that he needed to get this thing off. He began working on the strings, first the chest, and then two more straps that went around his upper legs. He got one undone and then had to lie back and rest. His head was pounding now and the first rays of real sunlight had begun to assault his eyes. The surf kept up its monotonous drumbeat on one side, but that black sand beach, maybe a hundred yards away, was deathly silent. He wondered if there was anyone there, just inside that line of jungle, watching him.

Then he felt the water on the sea side swelling up, lifting him off his bed of razors and rolling him into the lagoon like a rotten log. He went under and flailed to get his head out of the water. He couldn't swim with that damned lifejacket half on, half off, but suddenly realized he could stand. The coral under his bare feet hurt like hell, but it was better than drowning. And where were his shoes? Why was he even here? Trying to ignore the walking-on-needles sensation from his feet, he lurched into a standing position and began making his way to that menacing black sand beach. The water got deeper and deeper until he finally had to launch himself into an awkward dog paddle toward the shore. At least the coral had stopped cutting his feet to ribbons.

It took forever but he finally made it to the shallows. He could smell the jungle now, wet, muddy, rotten. The beach didn't slope out into the lagoon in some gentle incline, but rose steeply, so much so that he tripped and fell headlong onto the edges of the sand, still half in, half out of the water. That excursion hurt his head so much that he began to retch, driven by waves of nausea that were gripping his innards like iron claws. He spat up what tasted mostly like salt water and watched a tiny crab scuttling away in total disgust. He lay there on his side now, the already warm sand inviting him to go back down again, to rest, to sleep, to make this all go away. The lumpy life jacket, which was still half on, half off, pressed up against his stomach like a comforter. The sun was warm. The sand under his right forearm was warm.

Ought to get up, he thought. What for, his brain asked. Let's caulk off for a while, give everything a much-needed rest. Then he drifted off, still trying to come up with an answer.

Sometime later he felt something biting him again, only this time it was a real bite, clamping down, tugging even. He opened his eyes and saw a small, multicolored fish nibbling on his exposed ankle. He sat up and swatted at the water. As he did, he heard two loud yells from behind him. He looked around to see two sets of dark brown elbows and heels disappearing into the bushes at the top of the beach. His head still hurt and now he was really thirsty. Water, water everywhere, he remembered. Now: What's my name?

Time to get out of the water, he thought. He rolled onto his hands and knees and moved up the surprisingly steep edge to dry sand. He sat for a moment and then began to try to get the soggy life jacket off. It was much harder than it should have been, he thought, as his rubbery fingers struggled with those strings. Finally he succeeded, and pushed the waterlogged lump of fabric to one side. There was black lettering stenciled on the back: CMDRE, whatever that meant. He was still wearing a long-sleeved khaki shirt, khaki trousers, black socks, and the top portion of one seaboot. There were large, dark stains on his right sleeve and shoulder. His back hurt, as if he'd done a reverse belly flop at some time. He raised his hand to the right side of his head. It felt a bit pulpy, like the shell of a turtle he'd once broken as a juvenile delinquent.

When was that? Where had that happened?

He thought he heard rustling in the bushes and looked over to see two sets of black eyes staring at him from the undergrowth.

"Hey," he called. "You got water?"

The eyes disappeared, but then, a moment later, two almost naked Melanesians stepped out of the bushes and approached, carefully. They seemed to be fascinated with his face. Or was it his head? Was it *that* bad? Brains leaking out?

He lay back onto the sand. He remembered— what? Something. An image, but it was gone. He realized he'd closed his eyes again. He opened them to find the two men kneeling next to him now, their faces close enough for him to smell them. They gave off an odor of greenery, tobacco, and what—seaweed? Smoked fish? Interesting. He made a drinking motion with his hand.

"Water?" he croaked.

They looked at each other, stood up, and backed away. As one turned to go back into the jungle, the other, the older of the two, based on his gray hair, nodded at him.

"*By'm by*," he said in a singsong voice. "*Come along watah.*"

Then they were gone. He dozed.

When he woke up again, the sun had shifted and it was probably early afternoon. He looked out to sea and saw some distant green mountains on the horizon. They seemed to float above the sea, bright green on top, then changing to a purplish hue lower down before disappearing into a gray mist at the bottom. Beautiful, he thought. This looked like the South Seas pictures he'd seen— where? He forced himself to relax on the sand, resting his right cheek on a small mound. His arms and legs seemed to work. He could wiggle both his toes and fingers. Something was moving toward him about two feet away from his face. He tried to focus but for some reason it was really hard to do that. Then he got it: another crab, a little bigger one this time.

He wiggled his fingers again, just a little, and the crab stopped. He lifted his fingers like a tarantula leaning back on its hind legs and the crab backed up, then rose into its own very similar defensive position, claws aloft, moist little mandibles working to determine whether this was dinner or danger. He slowly cupped a small handful of sand in his right hand and then threw it at the crab, saying: Boo! The crab fled. He repositioned his head. Big mistake. A lightning bolt went down the right side of his neck and out into the sand through his right shoulder. He gasped as he passed out again. Stay away, crab, he thought, as one of those distant green mountains blossomed into a large cloud that came across the sea and covered him right up.

"He's a Yank," a woman's voice said, just as clear as a bell. He tried to open his eyes but they were stuck shut, as if his eyelashes had been glued. He tried to sit up but she made a shushing sound, pressing on his chest to make him lie back. Then he felt a metal cup pressing to his lips, fresh water slopping onto his jaw, and he drank greedily.

"Slow down, now, mate, slow down," she said. He did not slow down. She withdrew the cup long enough for him to clear his throat. "Take your time, Buck-o. You've had a nasty whack, for sure. Who are you, and where'd you come from?"

"No idea," he croaked. She had an accent—

Brit? Aussie? The effort to figure out which one was just too painful. He tried to open his eyes again, but there was a crust of salt on them. She poured a little of the water on his eyelids and then he was able to see her.

"I believe that," she said, gazing at his head wound.

He felt a wet cloth pressing up against his battered head. It felt good as long as she didn't actually move the cloth. He tried to tell her that, but then heard her saying something like, Ah, damn, there he goes again. Poor fella. Altogether, *bring'im house b'long me.*

TWENTY-TWO

Lever Brothers Plantation, Kalai Island

He awoke to the sound of rain pounding on a metal roof with a roar that sounded like a load of gravel being dumped. He was able to open his eyes and look around. He was in a bedroom, which had one large window aperture but no glass. The bed was enveloped in a mosquito net and was very comfortable. He guessed by the pallor of the light outside that it was either dawn or dusk. There were a pitcher and a glass next to the bed on a nightstand. He blinked his eyes a couple of times, took a deep breath, and tried to sit up. A familiar lance of pain shot from the right side of his head down his right shoulder and arm, severe enough to make him cry out.

He lay back and closed his eyes for a moment until the pain subsided into a dull ache. Where am I? Who am I? What am I doing here? He realized he was naked in the bed. His body felt clean, which was to say no longer covered in salt and the stink of marine life. Coral. Crabs.

Marine life: he'd been in the sea, and then wedged up on a reef covered in teeth. And then on a black-sand beach, where strange-looking natives peering out of the jungle had been frightened out of their wits when he sat up and looked at them. Didn't they know he was the commodore?

Then it came rushing back. All of it.

The sudden appearance of heavy cruisers. His flagship, *Barrett*, toe-to-toe with eight-inch guns and torpedoes slashing past each other, *Barrett*'s banging off the sides of the bigger Jap ships, theirs . . . well, theirs tearing his flagship into two pieces with such power that the back half of the ship had driven right past the capsizing front half. A melee, for damn sure. He took a deep breath. He'd laid the same ambush one too many times. The Japs had figured it out and laid one for him. Oh, God, where are my ships? Did they get away?

There was a sudden blaze of yellow candlelight as the woman who'd ministered to him down on the beach came into the room, a glass-chimney candle in her hand. She was in her fifties, long dark hair tinged with gray coiled in a tight bun, a handsome, tanned, and lined face that bespoke many years out in the tropical sun. She was wearing a white, sleeveless blouse and khaki trousers. There was a large pistol strapped to her right hip in a holster. She smiled at him.

"Back from the dead, then," she said. "How's the head?"

"Fractured and willing to let me know that anytime I move," he said. He looked over at the pitcher. "Is that water?"

"Yes it is," she said, and poured him a glass. She held it to his lips while he drank the entire thing. When he'd finished she sat down on the edge of the bed, pulling the netting aside so that she could talk to him. "Remember anything?"

"Yes, I do," he said. "I'm an American naval officer; my name is Harmon Wolf. I need to get back to . . ." He hesitated.

"Yes," she said. "That *is* the question, isn't it? Get back to what? There was a great deal of shooting the previous evening. Gunfire and other explosions. We never know who's shooting whom, but ever since you lot went into Guadalcanal, there have been many unpleasant—*things*—washed ashore here."

"I can just imagine," he said.

"My name is Jennifer Matheson," she continued. "This is a Lever Brothers rubber plantation on

Kalai Island. The Japs haven't been here yet, but the word around the district is that they soon will be. My husband, Jack, is the plantation manager, but he's gone *long bush* into the hills with one of the coast watchers. I'm staying here, trying to hold things together until the Japs actually show up. Me and my boys. They're the ones who found you on the beach."

"Those natives?"

She smiled. "Melanesian is the proper term. Many of the workers here were from Malaita Island, across from Guadalcanal, but they've gone home. Those two are local Kalai men, loyal to me and the plantation, for now, anyway. If the Japs come here, that could all change. We grow rubber, here. The Japs will want all of it. Hungry?"

"No," he said, but then changed his mind. "Yes, I mean, as long as I can eat without moving my head, that is."

She got up from the bed. "I'll get you some soup," she said. "And we need to change that dressing on your head. Then I'll want your name and rank, so we can get a message off to Sydney." She paused, examining his face. "I must say, you don't look like an American," she said.

"I'm an Indian," he said. "From the Chippewa tribe."

"Well, I'll be damned," she said. "You Yanks never fail to surprise."

She left the room, calling for someone in the

house in that strange pidgin dialect he'd heard her use. He dozed until she came back with a mug of broth and one of the natives—excuse me, he mentally corrected himself, Melanesians—who was dressed in a tropical uniform of some kind.

"Try sipping this," she said. "Then the district NMP here will look at that wound. His name is David."

David, it turned out, was one of the Kalai locals who'd been trained in first aid and basic medicine by the British colonial authorities who governed the Solomon Islands. Whenever the district officer made his rounds to hold court, collect taxes, and settle administrative disputes, David went along to bring medical care and supplies, especially to the more remote tribes and villages living back in the hinterlands, known in pidgin as the *long bush*. He gently removed the bloody dressing, taking enough hair with it to make Sluff wince. He went into the adjoining bathroom and filled a bowl with water, to which he added a tincture of Mercurochrome. He gently washed the wound site. Sluff thought he could feel his skull buckling, like the plates on the side of a ship. David produced a new bandage from his kit bag, dusted it with sulfa powder, and pressed it gently against Sluff's head, holding it in place for a minute. He removed it, smelled the bandage carefully, and then put it back, this time with some tape. He looked over at Mrs. Matheson.

"Altogether sua 'e look'm aurait," he pronounced in the singsong voice. *"Mobeta 'e stayim quait insait house bilong youme, slip tumas altogether."*

David nodded politely and then withdrew, carrying the bloody bandage out with him. "Okay, what'd he say?" Sluff asked. David had never once moved his head, God bless him.

"He said the wound didn't look infected, and that it was best if you stayed right here and slept too much."

"Wow."

She smiled. She had a pretty smile, which made her look younger. "If you live here you get used to it," she said. "There's a pretty big vocabulary, actually. Now: Give me your particulars and we'll get a report off via the coast watchers' net, *quiktaim.*"

Sluff recited his full name, rank, and serial number, and then added his title of ComDesRon 21. He asked if the radio station was here on the plantation. She said no, that it was inland, but did not provide any further details. He wondered if she didn't quite believe that he was who he said he was. She told him to finish the broth and then pointed out the bedpan resting beneath the bed-side table. He frowned. There was no way he could reach down to get it. He started to say something, but she was gone.

After he finished the broth, which tasted mostly of salt and possibly a fowl of some kind, he lay back on the pillows. His head hurt. He realized that his whole body hurt from being thrown through the air and into the sea, but the head wound dominated his pain while keeping good pulsing time with his heartbeat. He wondered how the naval headquarters at Nouméa would react to the news that he was alive. He could almost visualize Halsey's choleric chief of staff, Captain Browning, rubbing his hands together and saying, Oh, good, now we can hold a proper court of inquiry about the disaster he led his squadron into. His right ear began to buzz. Why not, he thought. Masks the sound of my heartbeat. The broth was warm in his stomach. Pretty soon he'd have to deal with getting to the bedpan. Then he fell asleep again.

He dreamed. The north woods. His family. The summers logging. His father's disappearance. The academy. Coming up the line in the Navy, always aware that he was, with his Indian features, *different*. The prewar naval officers corps was pretty much a white proposition. The only dark skin one saw on a warship inevitably belonged to stewards, and Sluff's mahogany features always provoked a double take in the wardroom when another officer saw him for the first time. The gold academy ring added to the confusion: Is that guy one of *us?* Or did he steal it? When it became clear that he was at least as good as most of them, professionally, the knowing looks became more discreet. The Navy, God bless it. Advancing some of the fringes of American society for the better good of the country. You know. Roosevelt, for God's sake.

The December 7 slaughter of the spit-and-polish, bugle-blowing, brass-polishing, teak-deck-holystoning battleship navy had changed a lot of things. For one thing, far too many potential execs and skippers drowned in the burning oil fires of Pearl Harbor. The interwar years' stately parade of superannuated captains and commanders was suddenly decapitated, and then the Bureau of Navigation, which administered naval officers' careers, had to scramble. Instead of lineal numbers and dates of rank, professional ability had necessarily risen to the forefront in the calculus of promotion.

He tried to roll his memory through those years leading to command of a destroyer, but they were a blur when compared to the night with the battleships, the contemptuous looks from Halsey's staffers after that battle. And after that, another blurred passage as his mind roamed among the flashes in the night, the sound of the torpedoes launching, the terror in the sonar gangs' voices when they reported hearing the sleek monsters whining past the ship as if hunting. And then the final battle, the seeming ease of the ambush followed by that terrifying report of three big ships rounding Kalai's southern point and heading

273

straight for them. That sinister black cruiser looming out of the night, its forward eight-inch guns training over in his direction, aimed right at *him* even as his own flagship's guns were banging away, tracing hot red arcs of fire into the cruiser's superstructure. He could see the light from his own flagship's gun flashes reflected in the windows of that towering steel pagoda temple just before she opened fire and ruined everything. The noise was beyond frightful. It was overwhelming, punctuated by the cries of the wounded and the convulsive lurch of the ship as she was cut in half . . .

"Wake up, Captain," a woman's voice shouted. "Wake up. They're *here*. We must leave. *Now!*"

He tried to focus, gather his senses, and then he heard the all-too-familiar sound of naval gunfire, nine-gun salvos ripping the night apart, followed by painful explosions outside among the plantation warehouses and processing buildings. Bright fires were burning out there, and the grounds around the house shook with every salvo.

Before he could gather his wits there were natives in the room, carrying what looked like an old-fashioned World War I canvas litter. They swept the mosquito netting aside, pushed back his sheet, and then lifted him bodily onto the litter down on the floor. His skull felt like it was cracking again. He tried to protest but could only whimper, and then his bearers were hustling through the house and out to the back veranda as another salvo, closer this time, tore up trees and small outbuildings, showering them with dirt, burning palm fronds, and wooden fragments. The fires were brighter now that they were outside, and the four men carrying him broke into a jog. Sluff couldn't think, only feel the thump-thump-thump of their bare feet as they ran across the yard and headed out into the actual rubber-tree plantation along a sandy road. He grimly fought the urge to throw up as the pain in his head found something new to keep time to.

Finally the shells began to fall behind, becoming red flashes seen through the forest of rubber trees instead of the pounding blasts they'd just run through. He saw Jennifer Matheson running behind the stretcher-bearers, trotting along without even breaking a sweat, that big Webley pistol firmly in her right hand. She didn't look frightened, only determined. He became aware of other people running out alongside them as they headed back into the orderly rows of rubber trees and away from the cacophony of the attack behind them. Some of the "boys" had rifles; others were carrying canvas bags in each hand.

They've rehearsed this, he thought. This isn't panic; this was planned. He thought he heard the chatter of machine gun fire behind them and wondered if a landing party had just arrived. Then the pain in his head grew worse, much worse, and he began to cry out. The bearers never broke stride, but, suddenly, David was running alongside. Something sharp pricked the side of his neck, and then everything became much, much better.

TWENTY-THREE

Kalai Highlands

"This the chap?" a gravelly voice asked. "Looks like an oversized wog, he does."

Sluff heard Jennifer cluck her tongue. "That's rude, Jack," she scolded. "He's an American Indian. And he's a naval officer, to boot."

"Humph," Jack snorted. "I've seen pictures of wooden Indians, but from the looks of *that* wound, this one's going to be a steel-plate Indian."

Sluff could hear other people moving around them, as well as the sounds of distant gunfire. He thought it sounded like a ship's guns. He tried to open his eyes but the morphine still had him and he wasn't able to make anything work except his hearing.

"Have you reported that he's here?" Jennifer asked.

"Aye, I have," Jack replied. "Nothing back yet. From the sounds of that sea fight the other night, the Yanks are probably up to their eyeballs in Japs about now."

There was a sudden gabble of pidgin nearby. Jack muttered an uh-oh and withdrew. Sluff wondered where he was. It felt like he was on a hard bed or cot and inside a building. He could hear many footsteps of people walking on a wooden floor, and the room smelled of wet palm fronds. He tried again to open his eyes. No go. He tried to speak. To his surprise, the word "water" croaked out of his parched mouth.

"Ah, right," Jennifer, said. "Water." She snapped out something in rapid-fire pidgin and a moment later he felt a wet towel being wiped gently over his face and then there was a cup at his lips. He tried to open his mouth but he couldn't, and for some strange reason that panicked him.

"Easy, easy," she said, feeling his body tense up. Then he felt the tip of that wet towel being pressed between his lips. Slowly a wave of wetness permeated his mouth but without choking him. Better, he thought. Then he whimpered and went back under.

He awoke later to the sound of a tropical rain beating down on a metal roof. The noise was deafening but also comforting. This time his eyes did open. It was dark. The rain fell like a solid waterfall. He swallowed, or tried to. A small wave of nausea rose in his throat but then subsided. He wondered what time it was and where everyone had gone. Incredibly, the roar of the rain grew louder, and he closed his eyes again. He was still thirsty. Then he heard voices nearby, excited voices. He opened his eyes and looked around the small room. He moved his right hand and gently probed the bandage covering the side of his head. It felt like there was a broken dinner plate taped together under there that had been glued back together but only recently.

The voices grew louder and then there was a flashlight coming toward the partially opened door. Jack came in, followed by Jennifer and two Melanesians, carrying a stretcher.

"Good, you're awake," Jack said. "Look—there's a problem. We've had a message that the Japs have landed an army search party on the beach and that they'll be looking for us by sunrise."

"Oh" was all Sluff could manage through his dry mouth. Jennifer heard him croak and brought him a glass of water, which, this time, he could manage.

"We're two hours into the hills above the plantation *if* they know where to look. Based on what my boy told me I have a bad feeling that someone's blabbed and they *do* know where to look. As soon as this rain stops, we have to do a runner."

"Okay," Sluff said, and made as if to get out of bed. He felt Jennifer's hands restraining him, and then his cracked skull weighed in, convincing him to stay very still. Another native showed up in the doorway, firing away in pidgin.

"Shit!" Jack muttered when the man finished. "They've got dogs. We've got to go now. Jenny, darling, you sort out moving the Yank. I've got to dismantle the teleradio and bury the extra codebooks. Oh, and Captain: The control station says the American navy will be sending a submarine to get you. When and where to be determined. Okay. I'm off."

Jennifer instructed the two bearers to put the stretcher on the bed. While she immobilized his broken head as best she could, they transferred him from the sheets to the stretcher and strapped him to it. He tried not to cry out. He thought he could feel the bandage getting soggy, but then they were on the move again, this time out to the veranda, where they parked the stretcher between the arms of two chairs. Jennifer had formed a pillow from one of the bedsheets and got it under his neck. Then two blankets were rolled tight and put on either side of his head. Finally they parked a pith helmet over his head and face, tied it down to the stretcher poles, and then they were away into the night, walking, thank God, and not trotting. The rain drummed on the helmet as if trying to find a way to get in and drown him while the rest of his body felt actually cold.

He couldn't speak or see anything, but it felt like they were going up, with occasional downward stints to cross streams and flooded gullies before resuming the climb. He wondered if this torrent would destroy their scent. Dogs. He shivered, both from the chill of the rain and the thought of a pack of dogs catching up with them, followed by sword-wielding samurai wannabes. Then he thought about the two bearers, grunting with the effort of carrying his nearly two hundred pounds through the jungle and across mountain slopes in darkness and pouring rain. What if they dropped him? Would he roll down the hillside like a rotten log and fetch up in a swollen stream? If the sound of baying dogs rose behind them, would they drop him and run? He realized he was thinking selfishly. These men were doing there uttermost to get him away from the Japs. He tried to think of a way to repay them, or at least thank them. Then there was a bright light followed by a blast of sound as a shell exploded somewhere up the hill from them.

The bearers stopped immediately and put him down as the acrid smell of high explosive drifted down the hillside. Another shell went off, but farther away and down the hill from where they were halted. Then there were others, some close, some distant, seemingly random, as that Jap cruiser anchored off the plantation wharves fired lone shells into the hills above the plantation, just to let the coast watchers know that they were missed and being sought after. Every thirty seconds a round would sail over or under their position in the man-high grass, whistling through the torrential rain and then blowing up in a shower of wet mud and cracking trees. They're not aiming at anything, he thought. Just shooting up the hills to let us know that they're coming. The randomness of it made it even more terrifying. He heard Jennifer shout an order and then they were on the move again. The rain never let up.

Two exhausting hours later they went to ground in a cave. He knew it was a cave because one moment the rain was hammering on his body and the next it was an echo. The bearers moved much more slowly now as they picked their way over rocks and litter on the floor of the cave, which stank of bat guano and tropical mold. Finally they set him down and removed the pith helmet. To his surprise he could see. It was very early morning outside, but light enough that he could make out the dimensions of the cave and see the shadowy forms of the men who'd carried him so far. He made eye contact with one of them and mouthed the words, Thank you. The man gave him a big grin and then Jennifer came up.

"How are you feeling?" she asked, kneeling beside the stretcher. She looked exhausted, but her eyes shone with the strength of someone who's seen and dealt with worse than a night escape across the tropical escarpments of Kalai Island.

"The braces helped," he said. "Is there any more water?"

She held up a canteen and carefully fed him about a cup's worth. "We should be pretty safe, for now, anyway. Jack took the radio and his team in the opposite direction to another hide. We're hoping the rain will drown out their scent. And ours."

"How do you two communicate?" he asked.

"Runners," she said. "These boys can move through these hills like ghosts. Jack's also sent down a rifle party."

"They'd take on a Jap army patrol?"

"Oh, no," she said with a knowing smile. "They're hunters. They have instructions to shoot the dogs. Kill the dogs, and the Japs will blunder about until they run out of food and water. *Then* the boys will take them on."

"Jack says someone blabbed."

She shrugged. "Maybe," she said. "Most of the people on Kalai hate the Japs because of something that happened three years ago. But you never know—for the price of some tobacco or a rifle and some ammunition? There're bad apples on this island just like anywhere else. Besides, the Japs seem to be winning over there on Guadalcanal, so from their perspective, maybe the right move is to get on the side of the winners, you know?"

He closed his eyes for a moment, glad to have had the water. Then he remembered something about a submarine. He opened his eyes to ask her about that but she was gone. He looked over at the clutch of natives, who were obviously exhausted. They were passing a bowl of something between them, each taking three fingers of what looked like rice and then passing it on to the next man. One of them saw him looking. He got up, came over to the stretcher, and offered two fingers' worth of rice. Sluff opened his mouth and took it. It tasted fishy, as if someone had ground fish paste into it. Salty, too. Wonderful. He realized he was very hungry and hoped that that was a good sign.

The man rejoined his crew and Sluff closed his eyes again. Outside he could still hear the occasional crump of naval gunfire as that cruiser spat shells randomly into the hills, seemingly just for the fun of it. He wanted to raise a hand, feel the side of his head. He'd been seeing strange colors and was having trouble forming words in his mind.

Stop trying, he thought. Rest. He wondered if there was any more of that fishy rice. A shell went off outside, fairly close this time.

Missed, you sonsabitches, he thought, and then went down again.

He awoke to find David, the native medical practitioner, at his side, ministering to his head wound. This time he put something on the site that stung enough to make Sluff gasp. David stopped what he was doing, washed his hands in a small bowl, and then gave Sluff some water and two white pills. David took Sluff's wrist, opened his palm, and put the pills into it. Then he helped Sluff to raise his hand to his mouth. It took a surprising effort but he managed to put the pills in his mouth and then drink some water.

"Altogether goodfella," Doctor David pronounced. *"Bye-m-bye feelin' bettah."*

"Thank you," Sluff managed. The pills had had an acrid taste. He assumed they were pain pills of some kind. "Is there any food?"

David shook his head. Then his expression changed. He got up and went down toward the cave entrance. Sluff realized it was daylight outside. Five minutes later David came back with a dark brown coconut. He pulled out a large knife, whacked the top off the coconut, and then held it up to Sluff's lips. Sluff swallowed the sweet milk greedily, almost choking before he finished it. Then David produced a banana, peeled the top half, and let Sluff gum it for a few minutes. When David left to go back outside Sluff let his head go back down onto the rolled towels and closed his eyes. A minute later he heard distant rifle fire, not the single shots of bush hunters sniping Jap dogs, but a full-on fusillade of shooting that sounded like a dozen rifles were firing. The Jap patrol?

He heard a lot of local dialect erupting out in front of the cave, and then two natives came scrambling into the cave, hastily picked up Sluff's stretcher, and began climbing over the uneven, rock-strewn cave floor, taking him farther back into the cave. The ceiling began to lower as they went and the smell became much stronger, ammonia, sulfur, and general rot. They stopped when the cave ceiling had come down to only five feet. Sluff saw small brown shapes plastered to the ceiling above him. The bats made tiny squeaks of protest at all the sudden noise. The two natives laid the stretcher down at a dogleg bend in the cave and then each of them put a finger to his lips in the universal sign to be quiet. Then they backed out, stopped about fifteen feet from where he lay and began urinating on the floor as they backed down the cave toward the entrance. Why not, Sluff thought, until he realized they were laying a trail of human scent that *stopped* fifteen feet from where he lay helpless in a stretcher behind that little bend.

He could no longer hear any sounds of gunfire or anything else for that matter, and wondered if this was where it would all end. Commodore of Destroyer Squadron 21 one moment, a prospective skeleton in a cave somewhere in Melanesia the next. He fingered his two dog tags, held around his neck by a small chain. He felt the little notch at the end of each tag and remembered what it was for. On the battlefield, the medics would find a dead soldier and remove his dog tags. They'd position one of them vertically between his teeth, using that little notch. Then they'd slam his jaw shut. The other they'd hand over to the graves registration people behind the front lines. Not all bodies got back. He wondered where the hell he'd learned that grisly fact—certainly not at the Naval Academy.

The pills began to take effect and he settled into a state of semiconsciousness. He felt his breathing slow down and his limbs relax. He tried to stay awake and alert but then asked himself—why? He wasn't armed and he doubted he could even sit up if the Japs came. If they found him they'd unlimber one of those glinting swords and take his head off, and that would be that.

Then he heard a low growl out in the front part of the cave, and all thoughts of sleep vanished.

TWENTY-FOUR

Kalai Highlands

He tried to think of what to do. Move back in the cave? Stay very still? Shit or go blind? The light in the cave was failing, but darkness wouldn't fool a dog. He checked the stretcher and discovered he was still strapped in. The drug was arguing with him: Relax. There's nothing you can do.

No, he thought frantically; there *has* to be something. But there wasn't. He was helpless. No wonder the natives had fled. They didn't want to watch.

Something was definitely approaching out in the cave. He could hear pebbles being displaced, some scratching noises, and then even some panting. That damned thing was coming on.

He lay very still now, suppressing his breathing, trying not to make any sound at all. Then the dog hit the urine trail and the panting increased, along with a snuffling noise, as it tasted the bright human scent. More scrabbling across the rock-littered floor of the cave. It was darker now, must be night outside, he thought, but he could sense that damned thing getting nearer and nearer. He strained to see, watching the edge of that dogleg turn in the cave wall, clamping his breath in his throat, breathing only through his mouth, tensing against the straps.

There: a dark shape materialized at the edge of the dogleg. He could just barely make out ears, but the dog was big, really big, its nose busy vacuuming up scent. Then it froze. Oh, God, he thought: he's sensed that I'm here. Then the dog barked.

It was a big bark, a *really* big bark that caused Sluff to jump despite his best efforts to keep still. And then came the roar of a thousand brown bats launching from the walls and ceiling and inner recesses of the cave as that big bark echoed off the ancient volcanic stone. The only thing going faster than the bats was the dog, who yipped once and then fled like a bullet, pursued by a tidal wave of fluttering, squeaking bats as they thundered down the cave and exploded out the entrance.

There was thirty seconds of silence, and then someone started laughing. He heard Japanese echoing back up into the chamber, and then more men started laughing, probably at the abject state of that supposedly vicious tracking dog trying to climb a tree out on the hillside. The general hilarity lasted for another thirty seconds, and then a voice of authority sounded off, followed by several "*Hai*"s.

After that, silence. Sluff found himself up on his hands and elbows, still trying to not make a sound. He strained his eyes to see down the tunnel of greasy rock, but everything was gray. And then, his nose started working. The smell was horrific. Every one of those startled bats had done what any self-respecting startled bat would do, and he was literally covered in fresh bat guano. *That's why the damned dog ran*, he thought. *I would have, too, if I'd known, and if I could run, which I can't.* He was covered and the cave was covered. The ammonia stink made his eyes water.

Great God, he thought. *Where's the bosun's mate—I need some goddamned coffee.*

The natives came back after about an hour. Four of them made their way into the cave, slowly, apprehensively, probably expecting to find a headless white man at that dogleg bend. One of them had a flashlight, which he switched on to behold a white man who was no longer white and who stank like a phosphate plant. There was a quick conversation, and then they came into his crooked little chamber, picked him up, and literally trotted down the entire length of the cave and right out into the humid darkness on the hillside. They scrambled down the hill until they came to a noisy mountain stream and then unceremoniously set Sluff and his stretcher down into the water. One of them stepped down into the creek to hold Sluff's head up out of the water and then they waited.

The water felt wonderful—cool, not cold, but a welcome relief from the Solomon Islands' heavy air. He consulted with his right hand, which agreed to function, and then cupped handfuls of cool water to his face and guano-plastered hair. After five minutes the stench of ammonia had abated, and they lifted him out of the stream and laid him down on the bank. Then Jennifer Matheson materialized, a flashlight cupped in her hand to produce a beam sufficient for her to walk but not attract attention. David was at her side. He wrinkled his considerable nose but then fell to work cleaning the area around Sluff's head wound. The sudden smell of antiseptic filled the air. It stung but it was better than bat guano.

"Have a close call?" she asked.

"Two of them," he said. "The dog found me, but then the bats launched when he barked. Scared him and he ran out of the cave howling. That scared the bats so they lightened their loads as they gained altitude. Every one of them, as best I can tell."

She chuckled. "The Japs've gone on across the face of this mountain. I have two boys laying spoor to keep the dogs interested."

"How many in the patrol?"

"A dozen, we think," she said. "Regulars. Traveling light. They had four dogs, but we've thinned the pack down to two. Now the boys are leading them into an area of pig traps. Grave-sized holes in the ground covered in palm frond. The bottom covered in sharpened stakes. It works on pigs, and they're smarter than dogs. In the meantime, we have to go the other way."

"Ow!" he protested when David finally stripped off the dirty bandage.

"Sorry, sah," David said. " *'e gotta go altogether.*"

"Where's Jack?" Sluff asked, as David used surgical scissors to cut away matted hair. He was pretty sure he could feel his skull crackling.

"In a new hide with his teleradio and some sentries. He set up a half-dozen hides in these mountains against the day when the Japs actually landed. They know about the coast watchers, of course, so he has to keep moving."

"They using radio direction finders?"

"Control warned us of that, but Jack doesn't believe it. As far as he's concerned, they're a bunch of vicious monkeys dressed up in soldier suits."

"He'd be wrong about that," Sluff said. "We use signal flags and flashing lights right up to the moment when we *know* they've seen us. *Then* we use radio."

"Tell Jack that, then," she said. "The point is, this island's not as big as Guadalcanal, so if they persist, we may have to take to the sea and go over there."

She'd been in the islands long enough that the word there came out "dare." David finished applying a new bandage. Sluff thought his head didn't hurt quite as much as it had before. He was weary and hungry, but he thought he might be able to move his arms and legs in a coordinated fashion pretty soon. David got up, showed Jennifer that he had only one large bandage left, and then disappeared into the darkness. Two bearers took his place. She gave him a good drink of water and told him there'd be food where they were going. Somewhere in the far distance, a dog howled, the plaintive sound of a dog in serious misery. The sound gave everyone pause.

Know the feeling, dog, Sluff thought.

TWENTY-FIVE

Kalai Highlands

The new hide was just below the tops of a three-thousand-foot-high ridge some five crow-fly miles from the bat cave. The view was spectacular, extending across the lower slopes of the ridge all the way down to the black-sand beaches and then out over the northern expanse of Ironbottom Sound. A bulge of black volcanic rock overhung the coast-watcher campsite, which was nestled in a thick copse of trees, vines, and high grass. The radio's antenna had been strung through the treetops with a jungle vine wrapped around it for camouflage. Jack's teleradio equipment was in a bamboo and palm-frond hut just inside the jungle line.

Sluff's stretcher was parked up under that bulge of overhanging rock. Just before dawn, they'd arrived at the campsite, where he got his first meal in three days, a mixture of tinned meat, rice, and boiled squash. It was wonderful. There seemed to be a lot of people coming and going, although he couldn't tell much about their faces through the mosquito netting erected over his stretcher. They'd notched out a rectangle of logs and put his stretcher down on that to keep the ants at bay.

A bamboo A-frame held the netting. The slope faced southeast, so the sun was beginning to heat things up, even under the overhang.

Jennifer's rubber plantation was two ridges behind them, perhaps six miles farther up the coast. They couldn't see the Japanese ships anymore, assuming they were still there. Jennifer had told him that the patrol had lost their dogs and immediately started making their way down the slopes toward the beaches. She told him that David would keep an eye on him, as she had to go down to the coast, herself, to line up the boats they would need if the Japs came back in strength.

"Jack's been told to stay off the air for a few days," she said. "He can keep a listening watch, but they don't want him transmitting. He still thinks that's nonsense, the radio direction business. I think they might wind the station up, actually."

"Why?" he asked.

"We're so close to Guadalcanal that our warnings of approaching ships or aircraft don't actually offer much warning time. The stations up in the Shortlands and New Georgia are the ones who give the Yanks time to get fighters into the air."

"Any word on when I might see a submarine pickup?"

"Not a word," she said, with a wan smile on her face. "You may yet get to experience a ride in a sea canoe."

"Ca*noe?*" he asked.

She laughed. "It's how we get about these days. We had a schooner but a Kawanishi flying boat shot it to pieces about a month ago. We go at night, eight rowers, two passengers, and a limited amount of 'stuff.' So far, Jap warships pay us no mind, if indeed they even see us. The canoes, as we call them, are thirty to as much as fifty feet long, hollowed-out trees. The journey to Guadalcanal won't be the problem. The landing will, because the Japs have an entire army over there. How's your head?"

"Better, I think," he said, touching the bandage carefully. "I've tried sitting up but I've got a ways to go. Is there a spare canteen around?"

She said she'd see to it. "One meal a day now that we're out in the *long bush*. I've told David to bring you fruit when he can, but we're on the run, here. I'll be gone for three, mebbe four days. You have problems, stop any boy and ask for David."

"Not Jack?"

She paused for a moment. "No, not Jack," she said softly. "To him, you're a complication he doesn't need. He'll do his duty and his best to get you back to American lines, but our boys, their families—their survival come first."

"I understand," he said.

"Do you?" she asked. "Because if he has to choose . . ."

He nodded. "Like in the cave."

"*Just* like that, Captain. Your chaps don't seem to be in any great hurry to recover you, do they? Look: I'm an Aussie. Jack's a Pom. We see things differently sometimes. We Aussies think the Americans have come to save our bacon. Jack thinks the Americans are going to throw the British Colonial Service out when this is all over. So: If we have to do a runner, *I'll* try to get you over to Guadalcanal. If we manage that, your lot will be able to retrieve you a lot faster than a submarine. Or so it seems."

He smiled. "So it seems. I was in charge of what I think turned into a disaster. That might explain the delay."

Her face turned sad. "You may be right about that," she said. "Our boys collected and buried over two hundred bodies from the beaches after that night. Some Japs, but mostly Americans. Look: I must scarper. Chin up. It can only get worse."

They smiled at each other and then she was gone. A few minutes later the largest spider Sluff had ever seen climbed up the mosquito netting and looked him over. Sluff raised a hand and cocked his finger over his thumb and tried to flick it off the netting. The problem was that he couldn't quite make his fingers obey. The spider, he was very sure, was grinning at him. Jap spider, probably. Time for another nap.

He awoke sometime in the late afternoon to

voices. One of them was Jack's. He was cussing up a storm about the radio and the idiot "Ozzies" in charge of the coast-watcher operation. He stopped when he saw that Sluff was awake. He took off his bush hat, wiped his forehead with his sleeve, and came over to Sluff's improvised hospital bed. He seemed a bit unsteady on his feet.

"Bloody mandarins," he grumbled. "The whole lot of them. Safe and sound back there in Sydney, mumbling arcane theories to each other about radio eavesdropping. They tell me to stay off the air? So then what the hell am I doing here?"

"The Japs have listening stations in the home islands and probably right over there on Guadalcanal," Sluff said. "They can take a bearing on a transmitter, from as close as Guadalcanal or as far as Tokyo. Or from Singapore, Truk, Rabaul. Cross all those bearing lines, they get a position on the transmitter. Ship-based, shore-based, doesn't matter. With enough listening stations, they can pin down your radio's location within a few miles."

"Bugger that," Jack said. "I simply don't believe it. *Those* monkeys?" He belched, and Sluff caught the scent of whiskey.

"Those 'monkeys' took an entire British army at Singapore," Sluff said. "Sank all our battle-ships at Pearl Harbor. And they've been kicking some serious ass right here in the Solomons. You may not respect them, but we sure as hell do."

"That's the problem with you Yanks," Jack said.

"No offense intended, but, Jesus! You lot are doing everything piecemeal. A few ships here, a few ships there. Where's the goddamned American fleet?"

"What fleet?" Sluff asked softly. "And where's yours?"

Jack stared at him for a moment, then made a gesture as if to wave it all away. He stood up. "You should try to get up and move around," he said. "I'll send David to help. If you can't, you can't, but it would be better if you could stand and even walk."

"I'll give it my best," Sluff said. "But, please, stay off the air."

"A-a-a-a-h," he said. "Bugger that. I'm here to coast-watch, and I'll bloody well coast-watch, monkeys, or no monkeys."

David came to check on him at sundown and to bring him some fruit and fresh water. He smelled the bandage, which apparently met with his approval. Sluff told him he needed to get up and walk.

David shook his head. *"Tumora traim altogether. Tonait malolo."* He made a sleeping gesture with both hands clasped along the side of his aboriginal face. *"Nau: rum bilong was-was."*

That apparently was an invitation to take care of any urgent bodily functions. The chamber pot he handed over was a serious clue.

In the morning David was as good as his word.

He helped Sluff to get up out of the stretcher and then sit on the bunk of logs. His head spun for a moment, but then he began taking stock of his extremities, testing his arms and legs, and then finally his balance as he stood up, leaning heavily on David's ample shoulders.

It was all right, he realized. The side of his head was still this painful lump of bandage and skull fragments, but his balance came back as soon as he was standing, and there was nothing wrong with his legs. For two minutes, anyway, after which he sagged down onto his knees, much to David's amusement. Another one of the boys came over and between them they got him upright again and gently frog-marched him in a circle around his improvised hospital bed until he suddenly grew so weary that he couldn't stand up at all. They supported him long enough to get back onto the stretcher, where he fell fast asleep.

They did it all over again that afternoon. The next day, the same routine, and this time he made progress. He was worried about his skull. Pressing his fingers on the wound site made small pieces of bone crackle. But that was his skull— not his brain. Jack came to watch and nodded approvingly. He told Sluff there'd been no word about any submarine pickups but that there was still chatter about getting the white people off of Kalai. He said he'd reported that cruiser and the army patrol, but no action had been taken. There were still some bodies washing ashore, but by now they weren't recognizable as individual human beings. A mass grave had been dug on the north side of the plantation, which the Japs had abandoned after shelling it.

"Yanks and monkeys together for eternity," he said. "No help for it."

"Jennifer said you went to join another coast watcher," Sluff said. "He still here?"

"Nah," Jack said. "He scarpered when that cruiser showed up. Took a sea canoe to Guadalcanal. Good luck to him. He was never much of a watcher. Always on the run, scared of the boys, I think."

"Have you been staying quiet on the radio?"

"Pretty much," Jack said, with some disgust. "Got some specific orders, actually. But this morning I saw a damned Jap submarine on the surface, five miles off the coast. Sent that in, by God."

Sluff nodded, but decided to say nothing. These men out here were cut from a different cloth, apparently. Had to be, to stick with this isolated life.

That night he slept well, aided by a second meal of rice and fresh fish. The next morning dawned clear and five degrees cooler than the previous few days. He got up again, this time without help, did his *was-was*, and then stepped out from under the huge black overhang into the sunlight.

Below him he could see the coast watcher's shack and a hint of silver from the antenna strung out through the trees. There were perhaps a dozen natives hanging around the shack performing various morning chores, or just squatting in clumps of two or three, smoking their horrible tobacco. That's when the Kawanishi flying boat came, popping up over the nearest downhill ridge and flying straight at him, the sun at its back and its entire front half bathed in red flashes as the pilot turned loose with twenty-millimeter cannon.

Sluff backpedaled awkwardly to the relative safety of the overhang's shadow, flattening himself against the back wall behind his makeshift log bunk. He'd never seen one of these seaplanes but he'd read all about them; the Kawanishi was called an Emily in the allied reporting system. Five twenty-millimeter cannons, plus five machine guns, four engines, and a two-thousand-pound bomb capacity made this aircraft a formidable foe. The plane roared overhead, firing now from its rear-pointing cannon, which tore up the teleradio shack, the grounds around it, and every living thing caught in their cone of fire.

It was over in ten seconds. The only sound coming from out front was the crackling of flames as the coast watcher's shack burned to the ground. Sluff crawled on hands and knees to the edge of the overhang and looked down the slope. He could see several motionless bodies down there.

A small wave of flame was advancing up the hill through the dry grass. Then he felt rather than heard the thrumming of engines. He backed up again to his tiny bit of shelter under the overhang, getting flat up against the back wall as the Kawanishi came back, not shooting this time but flying low and fast back out toward the coast. He couldn't see it but he did see its shadow flit across the smoldering grass in front of the overhang. The drone of its engines diminished, but then steadied.

Oh, Lord, Sluff thought. He's turning around.

There was nothing he could do. Even if he'd had a rifle, shooting at an aircraft that could point twenty-millimeter cannons right at you would have been suicide. But why was it coming back—pictures? They'd done what they'd come to do. The engine noise increased rapidly now, as if the pilot was pulling the aircraft up into a climb.

Pulling up? Then he understood: The plane had dropped a bomb.

It turned out there were three bombs: one that went off in the jungle short of the burning shack, blasting several palm trees into the air, a second among the litter of bodies out on the ground, and a third that apparently smacked right into the face of the overhang. That blast hurt Sluff's ears, but what happened next scared him almost to death. The overhang broke off the cliff face with a biblical crack of doom as tons of volcanic rock dropped straight down onto the ground right in front of his face, accompanied by a cloud of dust and dirt that nearly smothered him.

For one terrible moment, he thought he'd been buried alive. With his eyes closed, he put his hands out in front of him. His fingers could just touch the gritty surface of the rock. He gasped when he felt it move, but then, with an earth-shaking groan, the huge black boulder, a hundred feet long and half that thick, began to roll down the hill. As the dust cleared he saw it gather speed like a giant steamroller and flatten the shattered remains of the coast-watcher station. Then it hit the jungle, where it compressed everything in its path into a green mat before dropping out of sight over the first ridge on its way to the sea. The silence that followed was momentarily absolute.

He crawled forward before realizing he didn't have to. The morning sun was beating down on his head. He looked up. A shiny black cliff rose behind him. There was a dent in the ground in front of him nearly eight feet deep, sufficiently pronounced that he could actually sit down on its edge. Below him most of the grass fire had been snuffed out by the passage of the rock. The bodies he'd seen before were no longer visible. There was a hundred-foot-wide notch cut into jungle beyond that gave a clear view down to the next ridgeline.

He sat back and tried to absorb the situation. The grass around the edges of the trough carved out by that boulder was still smoldering, and it was thick enough to sting his eyes. Wolf Who Walks in Smoke, he remembered. Sits in Smoke was more like it. Had the Mide foreseen what he'd be doing some twelve years later? At the time of his naming, Sluff had been the original skeptic about all things mystical. The Mide routinely mocked his mother's Catholic Church's panoply of ritual, robes, smoke, incense, arcane language, and elaborate ceremonies. Sluff had wondered then if the Chippewa elders' fascination with ritual dances, smoke, robes, arcane languages, and elaborate ceremonies was any different. It was a question he'd never asked, either of his frantically devout mother or his uncle.

He stared back down the hill, where the air above the crushed meadow seemed to almost vibrate with the sound of that baby mountain's passage through the coast-watcher camp. He wondered what time it was, and where he'd be able to find some water.

TWENTY-SIX

At first he decided not to go down the hill to see if there was anyone still alive. There were plenty of good reasons, first among them that the Kawanishi might come back. If he did find someone still alive, there was nothing that he, barely able to get around, could do for them, and after that black mass of rock had gone directly over them, he didn't want to see the results. Besides, he was too weak. His balance was unreliable.

You have to go, his conscience told him. You *have* to make sure. They did that for you.

He took a deep breath and slid down into the depression formed when the rock first broke off. Then he went sideways down the hill, crabbing along in the four-foot depression in the ground created by the sheer mass of that rock. He encountered the first body, that of one of the native Melanesians, thirty yards above where the shack had been. The man had been flattened into a gingerbread-man shape. Everything that had been inside was now outside. Sluff held his breath as he went past, trying hard not to retch. They were all like that, he discovered, simply flattened into the volcanic soil, two-dimensional now instead of three. At the burned area where the shack had been he found what had to be the remains of Jack, the determined coast watcher. Finally he could take no more.

He staggered off to the right, toward the edge of that distinct notch smashed into the jungle, fetching up against a palm tree and then indulging in some deep breathing. They weren't human, those remains. Just, well, there was no word for it. Then he remembered that Jennifer would be coming back—when? Today? Tomorrow? He knew he was too weak to be able to bury them all, or even some of them, but she should not have to see this.

The jungle was slowly, tentatively, coming back to life after the obscene violence on that hillside. There were small black birds investigating the results of the Japs' attack on the station. Suddenly furious, he yelled at them. They ignored him. Life and death in the jungle. There were natural rules about that.

Then he heard what sounded like crying, somewhere inside that seemingly solid wall of jungle growth, trees, and a string ball of arm-thick vines right in front of him.

Girls, he thought. Little girls, crying. Good God, he thought.

He called out, leaning against the tree now, and the crying noises stopped in mid-whimper. He called again, hoping that they'd recognize that it was a white man calling, not a *japan*, as the natives called them. His forehead pressed against the scalloped bark of the tree, and a column of ants trickled straight up the tree, an inch from his nose. After a few minutes the bushes twenty feet away parted and two young Melanesian girls emerged, one older than the other, moving so fearfully that he almost stopped breathing so as not to frighten them. They froze when they saw him. He beckoned for them to come closer and they did, one step at a time, obviously ready for an instantaneous bolt back into the jungle.

His legs began to tremble and so he sank down with his back against the tree. Apparently that made him less of a threat, because they became bolder, advancing now, gaping at all the destruction, the crushed landscape, and the motionless forms on the hillside that brought shocked fists to their mouths. He realized he was very tired and desperately thirsty in the late-morning heat. When they looked at him again he made signs that he needed water. They looked back at him and then the older one shook her head. The younger one grabbed the older one's hand and pointed back into the jungle, gabbling away in their own language, not pidgin.

The older one finally understood and they came over and helped Sluff to his feet. Walking erratically between them, he tried not to trip and fall as they took him into the jungle on what was obviously a well-used path. They went downhill until they came to a stream like the one where David and company had rid him of his bat guano. He went down prostrate on the bank of the rushing stream and drank as much as he could hold, lost most of it, then drank again. He then washed his face and hands. He could still see the images of all those good people out on the hill, and he washed and washed as if he could make them go away. He vaguely heard a thrashing noise behind him as some people came out of the jungle on the other side. It was Jennifer Matheson and her crew. He stared up at her as she approached the bank of the stream.

"We have to talk," he said from his prone position on the ground. "Everything's changed."

Three hours later he was back in his makeshift hospital bed, but no longer under the black cliff at the top of the hill. Jennifer had set up a camp down under that lower ridge where the huge rock had disappeared from sight into a shattered jungle. They were hidden in a narrow canyon created by an ancient lava flow that went back into the ridge face for about five hundred feet. The gash in the rock wasn't straight, so they'd been able to set up a campfire that could not be seen from down below the ridge or out on the sea. A tiny brook bubbled through the canyon, no more than a foot across but enough to provide water for washing and drinking. One boy was tending the campfire, hovering over it and blowing on it to ensure that there was not the faintest whiff of smoke.

Jennifer had insisted on going back to the remains of the coast-watcher station, despite Sluff's protests. She'd taken two of her "boys" with her. When they returned, she was ashen-faced and tight-lipped. Her two helpers were positively goggle-eyed. She'd then given a set of clipped orders to her crew and they'd gone off in all directions. Jennifer had left the canyon and walked into the jungle for a while. Sluff thought about trying to comfort her but decided that maybe he should just sit down and be quiet. An hour later the boys started returning, bearing bags of rice, some tinned meat, a rifle, the stretcher he'd been sleeping in, and, miraculously, what looked like David's medical bag. The Kawanishi hadn't come for Sluff, and she undoubtedly knew that. "Bugger-that" Jack had brought that attack down on himself.

The question of the hour was pretty obvious: What do we do now? He thought he knew the answer. With the coast-watcher station destroyed, the only alternative was extraction.

That meant crossing to Guadalcanal.

TWENTY-SEVEN

That night they all sat around the campfire, some eating, some not. The two boys who'd been to the site of the attack had disappeared. Nobody was talking. Everyone seemed to be totally engrossed in watching the tiny fire, whose light barely made it up the canyon walls. Sluff was sitting on his stretcher with his back up against the wall. When he could stand the silence no longer, he decided to ask the question.

"Jennifer," he said.

"What," she replied. Her tone of voice was not exactly friendly.

"We have to get out of here, right?"

"*You* have to get out of here," she said, softly.

"I don't understand."

"This island is my home," she snapped. "The plantation is lost, my husband is dead, but this island is my home. I'm staying. I'll stay *long bush* until these goddamned *japans* either leave or we kill them all."

"You said they were going to shut the station down and pull you out," he said.

"What I said is that they were going to shut the station down. It was up to us to get over to Guadalcanal. As long as Jack came out with me, I was all right with that. Now I'm not."

He nodded his head. "Can you help *me* get out then?" he asked.

"I need to think that through," she said, after a long pause. "Because there's a problem, yes?"

"What's that?" he asked.

"The way these people see it, you have been *nogut kas* here. Bad luck. You showed up, everything went to hell, and now this disaster. Half these boys here will slip away into the bush by morning after seeing what happened at the station. Some will stay loyal and exact revenge on the *japans* when they can, but many of the others have had enough of this white man's war. I know that's unfair. *We* knew that the *japans* would eventually come for the rubber, but that's how they see it." She stopped for a moment and then sighed. "My world has gone upside down. I'll think about it."

With that she turned her face away. Sluff realized there was no more talking to be done. Either she'd help him get across Ironbottom Sound to the big island, or she wouldn't. He also understood that some of her anger was really directed at Jack for defying orders, getting back on the air, and thereby beaconing an attack. Stupid she was not.

He lay back down on his stretcher and observed the natives' faces. They were all still fascinated by that fire, except when they shot furtive looks at one another, and then at Jennifer. But not at him.

Oh, boy, he thought, and then the day's exertions overcame him and he slept.

The following morning he awoke to an empty camp. The fire was long out and the brook was making the only sound. He sat up in the stretcher, carefully, so as not to annoy his battered head bone. There was a small canvas bag on the ground. It contained a pound or so of rice stuffed into an antique army mess cup, a gourd canteen, a small knife, a small metal cylinder, which he hoped contained some matches, and that last bandage that David had shown Jennifer. He thought he saw something under the bag and pulled it aside. It was a large revolver, and it looked familiar. Then he remembered: Jack had been wearing it in a holster the last time Sluff had spoken to him. Jennifer must have retrieved it. He bent over the edge of the stretcher and picked it up. It was pretty heavy, but he could see six brass rims in the cylinder.

He lifted his upper body into the stretcher and lay still until his head stopped swimming. He had his answer: She and whatever remained of her "boys" had gone *long bush,* as she termed it—into the deep backcountry on this island. He, alien bringer of *nogut kas*, was on his own.

Fair enough, he thought. There'd be more battle survivors, seamen as well as airmen, who would turn up on the beaches. She, on the other hand, would have to survive for many months here, maybe even years, until the Japs were driven out. For that she depended on the boys. He was a Jonah in their eyes, and he remembered what happened when the crews of sailing ships of old decided someone was a Jonah: They put him into a boat with some water and food and cast him away.

Okay, Jonah, he thought: Time to get under way, RFS or not. He got out of the stretcher, steadied himself, and then filled the gourd with water. He drank it all and then refilled it. He put everything back into the bag except the gun, which he put into his waistband, which in turn made his khaki trousers slide right off his hips. One way to lose weight, he decided: get stranded on a hostile island. He used the knife to poke holes in his canvas web uniform belt, re-cinched the belt, and then tried again with the heavy gun. This time everything held up, literally. He picked up the bag and started walking down the canyon toward the open meadow beyond. As he approached the opening he thought he felt something.

He stopped and listened. There was a vibration, a thrumming that seemed familiar, something powerful pummeling the tropic air.

Kawanishi, he thought.

He backed into the shadow of the canyon entrance and put the bag down. He still couldn't hear the engines, but he could definitely feel them. Approaching, too. He looked up. Even though he was in the shadow of the canyon entrance, narrow as it was, he realized that from the air they might be able to see a white man standing there. He knelt down and then went prone, putting that canvas bag over his neck so that there was no white skin showing, and pushed himself up against the canyon wall. Then he waited.

Finally he could hear the actual engines as the seaplane came up the slopes of the valley and then over the ridge containing the canyon. He lay perfectly still and watched a patch of sunlight that was ten feet from where he lay. The engines got louder and louder and then the plane roared overhead and was going away, its line of motion confirmed by the black shadow that flitted briefly across that patch of sunlight. He waited for the shrill sound of an approaching bomb, but there was nothing. The sounds of the engines diminished until they were gone, somewhere out toward the western shores of the island.

He waited some more to make sure the plane wasn't going to reappear, and then got up, gathered his small pack, and stepped out into the sunlight. Before him lay an expanse of jungle in every direction. Looking out over the descending ridgelines, he could see Ironbottom Sound, with the green cone of Savo Island to his right. Beyond that in the far distance was the gray-green eight-thousand-foot-high central massif of Guadalcanal itself. He tried to remember the charts: ten, maybe twelve miles across the sound? All he needed was one of those sea canoes. After that? Piece of cake.

Right. He gathered up his meager belongings and started down the hill toward the sea.

Seven hours later, he realized that he was done for the day and started to look for a place to hole up. A walk through the jungle forest of Kalai Island was not like a walk through the forests of Minnesota. Between the intense heat, bugs, an occasional snake, the vines, mud, and razor-edged bushes, downhill hadn't always been obvious until he finally came to a fast-moving stream. By then he'd been more than ready to just sit down in the water and submerge up to his neck. Since his compass rule was to keep going downhill, no matter what, he'd decided to just follow the stream on the assumption that all streams would lead to the South Pacific Ocean. He'd cut two bamboo walking sticks, used a vine to tie his supply bag to his chest, and begun picking his way down the streambed. Even though his navigation problem had been solved, the footing had been interesting. The best part was that his water problem had also been solved.

The good news was that he was physically able to make his way down the slopes of the island. His skull was still damaged, but the lightning bolts he'd experienced when he'd first been wounded had mostly gone away. He'd elected not to change the bandage, as there didn't seem to be any indications of infection, not that there would have been anything he could do about that. He worried about malaria from the mosquitoes and dysentery from drinking water of unknown quality. Aboard ship everyone had been taking antimalaria pills, but right now there was nothing he could do about that, either.

Finally he came upon a small sandbar along the stream where it threaded its way around an enormous boulder and decided to make camp. The rock was at least twenty feet high and twice that around. He wondered if it had come down off one of the top cliffs, like the building-sized one that had wiped out the coast-watcher station along with all of his chances for rescue. He sat down with his back to the rock and wiggled his legs into the warm sand while his sandals began drying off on the bamboo poles he'd stuck into the sand. The sun was getting lower and starting to bend long shafts of sunlight through the tops of the trees. He'd been surprised to hear none of the jungle sounds one heard in the Tarzan movies. The jungle was as silent as a tomb, and he wondered if that was because of his presence. Or perhaps someone else? He strained to hear any animal sounds at all, and then he fell asleep.

When he woke up, he found four Japanese soldiers squatting in a semicircle right in front of him, staring at him. One of them laughed when he saw the horrified expression come over Sluff's face.

TWENTY-EIGHT

They were so young, he thought, as he stared back at the soldiers. Thin, almost emaciated, dressed in khaki shirts and shorts, each holding what looked like a small-caliber rifle that appeared to be as long as they were tall. One of them had Jack's .45 pistol, which looked enormous in the man's tiny hands. They were looking at him as if trying to decide *what* he was. He was still wearing his Navy khaki uniform, with the silver eagles on his shirt collars. His officer's cap was long gone, and those eagles and his brass belt buckle were now green with tarnish. It's my face, he realized. They'd never seen an American Indian, just like the Melanesians who'd dragged him up the beach. He made as if to stand up, which resulted in four rifles being pointed at him.

One of the soldiers gave an order, and the rifles were lowered, but not by much. He then said something in Japanese to Sluff, who could not understand a word of Japanese. He put out his hands and then shrugged to indicate that fact. The soldier gestured for him to stand up, raise his arms and hands, and then turn around. As soon as he did two of them were standing behind him, one pressing his rifle barrel into Sluff's back while the other pulled Sluff's arms behind him and then wrapped some wire around his wrists. They then pushed him down into a seated position on the banks of the stream. One of them fingered his collar devices while another one searched his pockets and took his wristwatch. They inspected his bandage and then went through his supply bag, exclaiming when they found the matches and the rice, and set about making a camp for themselves. One soldier stood behind him while the other three built a fire, gathered fuel and water, and then began boiling rice. His guard smelled in equal parts of fish and fuel oil.

Once they'd eaten, they released his right arm

and then gave him his metal canteen cup filled with a handful of uncooked rice and some water. He drank the water and tried to chew the brittle bits of rice, which the soldiers found really amusing. Finally he swallowed the whole mess down and hoped it wouldn't blow up in his stomach later. Once he did that they rewired his right arm behind his back and pushed him over onto his side. They wired his feet together, put a blindfold over his eyes, and left him alone, gabbling in Japanese to one another the whole time. One of them tapped the bandage on the side of his head with some-thing hard, hissed, and walked away.

My sentiments exactly, he thought, as he fought back tears of pain. He forced his body to relax into the warm sand. He'd read all about the Japanese attitude toward prisoners of war: bayonet them and move on with the mission. So far that hadn't happened. Maybe those silver eagles were of interest. He feared to think of what might be in store for him if their superiors recognized that he was a senior officer in the American navy. The bayonet might be preferable.

He found himself breathing fast and shallow and forced himself to slow it all down. Nothing you can do about it, so relax, sleep, see what happens tomorrow. After all, what could go wrong? He dreamed of being taken aboard a Japanese heavy cruiser in chains, locked into a compartment well belowdecks, and then hearing the sound of dive-bombers.

It all did go wrong at about two the next morning, but for the Japanese soldiers, not him. He awoke to a fusillade of gunfire and the sound of bullets whipping over his head. He tried to burrow deeper into the wet sand. There were several screams, more gunfire, and then a smoky silence. He heard someone crunching across the sand toward him. Bayonet time? Soft hands undid the blindfold, and there was Jennifer. There was a big moon so he could see some of her boys, poking the inert forms of the soldiers with their rifles. Others were already stripping the bodies of weapons and ammo. She undid the wires, sat him upright, and then sat back on her haunches.

"My conscience got the better of me," she said. "Now we're going to get you, and possibly me, to Guadalcanal."

"I'm very glad to see you," he said. "May I have some water? And can you tell me what happens when you eat uncooked rice?"

He got the answer to that after the first half hour of walking, suddenly bending double with extreme stomach cramps and nausea. They gave him a lot more water and then one of the boys supported him as he used his bamboo poles to lurch down the slope alongside the stream, making the occasional contribution to said stream.

During the trek down the hillside he heard what sounded like distant thunder, except that it was a series of punching blasts, not the rolling sound of real thunder. Another night fight out on the sound? He wondered who was the commodore now.

After a few hours he was hungry again. One of the boys gave him a fistful of sticky rice, of *course,* he thought, but cooked this time and washed down with a really squishy banana. He felt a lot better until he sensed and then confirmed that his head wound was bleeding again.

They stopped at dawn and took shelter in a grove of trees he didn't recognize, but which turned out to be rubber trees. Jennifer changed his bandage from a medic kit she'd produced, seemingly out of nowhere. She, like David, smelled the wound carefully, and then went to get some yellow powder to put on it. She fired off a blast of pidgin to one of the boys, who disappeared into the bush. He came back two hours later with a gourd of some sticky substance that turned out to be honey. She lifted the bandage, smeared the honey all over the wound site, and reapplied the bandage.

"No germs can live in honey," she said. "God's magic goo, it is."

He wanted to ask for food, but then remembered the results of the uncooked rice. She saw his look. "The boys are hunting," she said. "We'll have food soon, but we have to be careful. There are *japan* patrols all over the island now." She pointed with her chin. "The beach is just there."

She stood up, stretched, and then shivered, a strange sight in the growing heat.

"I'm sorry for what happened to your husband," he offered.

"Brought it on himself, didn't he," she said, distractedly. "Wouldn't turn off that damned teleradio. Meant well, and all that, but . . . now we're for it, and that's certain."

"Can you still find a sea canoe?"

She smiled. "One-track mind, eh, there, Captain?" she said. "I don't know is the answer, but I'm going to try. Right now we have to make sure there aren't any *japan* patrols on our trail. Then we can see what's what. You rest now. We have to wait for darkness."

He awoke at sunset, disoriented but feeling better. He longed for the stretcher rig, but that was long gone. He was sitting with his back to a coconut tree, his head cushioned by a bundle of rags. He touched the right side of his neck. He felt the sticky blood clot that ran from his head wound down to his collarbone, but it was hard now, not actually bleeding. Progress, he thought, and then wondered if he'd ever get out of here alive. He was so tired that it was beginning not to matter so much. Then he heard the muted rumble of what sounded like airplane engines, except that it was coming from the sea. He recognized that sound: Packard engines, three of them, and that meant PT boats. *American* PT boats.

He called for Jennifer. Nothing happened. He yelled again. This time two of the boys came running.

"Get me to the beach, right now. Those are American PT boats."

They stared at him, uncomprehending. He swore and got himself up and almost fell down. They grabbed him, steadied him, and then he remem-bered some pidgin.

"*Bigfella was-was*," he said. Then he made a sound, which he hoped would sound like waves crashing. One of them got it. "*Nambis*," he exclaimed. "*Nambis*!"

They then frog-marched him through the trees and down onto the black-sand beach, where they obviously expected him to take care of daily functions. Instead he scanned the waters off-shore, looking hard for the PT boats.

Nothing. He could still hear them, but he couldn't see them. It sounded like they were nearby, maybe just around that point to his left, but those huge airplane engines made such a rumble that he couldn't tell exactly where. His escorts were getting nervous, and they were saying *altogether* and *japans* a lot. He felt a moment of fear: Did the Japs have MTBs down here?

No, those were Packard engines. He'd heard them while working up in Pearl, where they'd run some night exercises with the PT boat forces. The problem was that it was getting really dark.

Finally one of the boats came creeping around the point, maybe four hundred yards offshore, its low, black silhouette looking ominous against the fading light over the water. Then a second one, and then a third hove into view, hugging the coast of Kalai Island, looking for trouble.

Sluff walked out onto the narrow beach and began waving his arms to catch someone's attention. It didn't seem to be working. Then Jennifer hurried out of the tree line to join him. The boats kept going, moving slowly but inexorably past them. Sluff swore and started shouting.

From behind him came three loud gunshots. He turned around to find Jennifer holding Jack's enormous Webley .45 straight up into the air. Staring out at the boats, which hadn't stopped, she fired three more shots, this time *at* the boats, or in front of them. She aimed high, but Sluff couldn't see any splashes out there. The boat crews, however, did, and the lead boat turned in toward the beach, training out all sorts of automatic weapons. Sluff didn't know whether to hit the deck or just stand there. If the boats opened fire, they'd all be dead. All except the boys, who'd vanished when the shooting started.

The lead boat then lit up a searchlight, pinning

Sluff and Jennifer in its steely white light. The other two boats came to a stop as the lead boat inched its way inshore, wary of reefs. It stopped about a hundred yards offshore and swung sideways to the beach, and doused the light. Sluff walked down to the water, discarded his bamboo poles, and waded right in. He looked back at Jennifer, who was still standing there, that big .45 down along her right hip. She waved once, and then turned back into the jungle. Sluff got out into chest-deep water and started swimming.

Dog-paddling was more like it, and he quickly tired. Someone on the PT boat saw that he was struggling and dove into the water. Moments later strong arms enveloped him from behind and a gruff voice said: I gotcha. Sluff relaxed and let the sailor tow him backward out to the boat, where three men hauled him in like a dead fish. They were all wearing full battle gear, and a baby-faced lieutenant junior grade, catching sight of those silver eagles, blurted out a "Holy shit."

"That's 'holy shit, sir,'" Sluff said with an exhausted grin. "Now: Please take me to your base if you can. I need to contact Nouméa."

The three boats took off in an echelon formation, headed for Tulagi. Someone opened a can of beans and franks from a C ration, set it down on one of the engine manifolds for a minute, and then handed it over to Sluff, who gobbled it down in five seconds. The boats were cruising along at a sedate twenty-five knots over a flat-calm sea, for which Sluff and his broken skull were duly grateful. The JG came back after a few minutes.

"We're headed back to base," he said. "We're under radio-silence orders, so I can't tell them you're coming. But, for the record . . . ?"

"I'm Captain Harmon Wolf. I'm the commodore, or I was, anyway, of DesRon Twenty-One, until we ran into a Jap ambush up in the Slot. That was—" He paused. "I don't remember how long ago. A week? Ten days? Anyway, my flagship was torpedoed and I ended up on Kalai Island."

"Thank you, sir," the JG said. "Was *Providence* part of your formation?"

"Yes, she was. She was southeast of us when it started. Do you know about that fight?"

The JG nodded somberly. "Yes, sir, we all heard about it. Three Jap heavy cruisers came out of nowhere. They torpedoed *Providence* and then shot her to pieces. The task group lost three destroyers that night. Over six hundred men lost. The Japs lost a couple of destroyers, and one of their cruisers was supposedly damaged, not that you could tell after what happened to *Providence*."

Sluff sighed. A true disaster. He recalled hearing a story about the four-star admiral, Husband Kimmel, who had been in command at Pearl Harbor. A wayward, end-of-trajectory bullet had plinked through his office window as he stared out at the devastation of the naval base and the battleships. It hit the admiral square in the chest and bounced off. The admiral was said to have remarked that it would have been better if it had killed him. Sluff could now relate to that sentiment.

"I'm very tired," he said. "My head hurts. I'd like to sleep now."

"Absolutely, Commodore," the JG said. They arranged some life jackets around his upper body and then let him sleep underneath one of the two torpedo tubes. The muscular thrumming of those Packards had him asleep in thirty seconds.

PART THREE

THE COMMODORE

TWENTY-NINE

Nouméa Field Hospital

"Here he comes," a woman's voice said. "Captain? Captain? Can you hear me?"

Sluff tried to respond but his mouth was too dry. He grunted instead.

"Can you open your eyes for me, Captain?"

"Unh-unh," he replied.

"Oh, c'mon," she pleaded. "You can open your eyes. Just a little squint?" Then she leaned down to whisper in his ear. "I'll take my top off, how 'bout that?"

He tried to laugh but only managed a little chuffing sound. But he did open his eyes. White lights. Steel instruments. Faces, blurry, but recognizable as American. No *japans.* He smelled antiseptic. Soft hands wiped his face with a cool cloth.

Operating room. His lungs were full of something heavy, and there was a brick up on the right side of his head. The nurse leaning over him still had her mask on, but she had pretty eyes.

"Where am I?" he whispered, finally.

"You're in the recovery room of the Nouméa field hospital," she said. "You're safe now. No big torpedoes here."

"Good," he said. For some reason his ears were humming. "Water?" he croaked.

A second nurse pressed a paper cup with shaved ice to his lips. He got about an ounce of cold water. He wanted more until he realized he couldn't even swallow that. He had to let it dribble back out of his mouth, and the nurse wiped his chin. He almost cried.

"Go slow," she said. "Can you move your hands and feet?"

It was warm in the recovery room. He realized he was wrapped in a blanket, maybe even two. "What's on my head?"

"A brand-new steel plate," she replied. "A whole bunch of bandages. Some serious sutures. Now, wiggle your fingers and toes for me."

He did, and then lifted each hand about an inch. She seemed very pleased that he could do that.

Nouméa, he thought. How the hell did I get here? He tried to remember, but the effort was too much, so he dozed instead. He felt the nurse pat his shoulder gently and say: Okay, okay.

He awoke to find himself in a hospital bed out on a ward, with rows of other patients on either side of him. This time there were a different nurse and a couple of doctors standing by his bed. The weight on his head was still there, although it didn't really hurt all that much. He was partially sitting up, and he *still* wanted water. For as long as he could remember, he couldn't get enough water.

The nurse gave him another paper cup, and this time he could actually get it down. The doctors were smiling as they introduced themselves.

"Captain," one of them said. "I'm Doctor Reed, this is Doctor Hamill. We're the surgeons who repaired your skull. How you feeling? Are you in much pain?"

"Very tired," Sluff said. "No, it doesn't hurt much."

"Great," Reed said. "Postoperative, no signs of infection, and the sutures are holding well. You have a plate in your skull, but there was no obvious brain damage. The dura was apparently never breached, but there had to have been some swelling with an injury that size. You were, in a way, very lucky, because the skull fracture allowed the brain swelling to push *out* against bone fragments instead of compressing that area of your brain. Were you okay, mentally, after the injury?"

"I think so," Sluff said. "Couldn't remember anything for the first few hours after I got ashore, but then it all came back."

"Do you remember feeling better but then slipping into a coma or unconsciousness for a long period of time after the injury?"

"No," Sluff said. "I'd go in and out of consciousness, but mostly due to pain and being very tired. I was in the sea for half the night. How'd I get here?"

"You came in on a Catalina from Tulagi last night and we did your surgery right away. Basically, you're past the dangerous part of a traumatic head injury. What swelling you do have now is post-op, not brain. We'll pull those IVs once we know you're fully rehydrated. They'll start feeding you as soon as they know all the anesthesia is out of your system, but otherwise you just rest and recover. Oh, and did someone use honey on your head wound to stave off infection?"

"Yes, they did, or the native doctor did."

Reed looked at Hamill. "Told ya," he said.

"Rest sounds good," Sluff said. "And water."

"That we can do," Reed said. "Oh, and we've had a message from someone over at Halsey's headquarters who wants to talk to you, but I told them not for forty-eight hours. By then you're gonna feel a whole lot better, as long as that swelling keeps going down. Which it should."

"Thanks for that," Sluff said. "And for the forty-eight hours."

They wished him well and then moved on down the ward.

People at Halsey's headquarters wanted to talk to him; can't wait, he thought, remembering the brief tale told by the PT boat skipper.

He tried to relax. Yet another nurse came by and set up a bed-bridge table for him, complete with a glass of water and some saltine crackers. She checked the bandages, the IV, his covers, and then made some notes in his chart, smiled, and left. He looked up and down the ward, which was full. Some of the patients had curtains set up around them; others were sitting up and playing cards or talking to their neighbors. Every time he exhaled he coughed a little and then tasted something chemical in his mouth.

What were they going to ask him, he wondered. And would it be someone Halsey himself sent, or that snake, his chief of staff? What was his name—a color? White? Green? Browning, that was it. The guy who'd called him Tonto. A third nurse stopped by, took his vitals, made him drink some more water, smiled at him, looked at her watch, and then did something to one of the IVs. Then it was night-night time.

The next morning he was wheeled to a rehab room where two Navy corpsmen put him through a series of motor-skill tests to determine if he had neurological damage as well as skull damage. He was able to do everything they asked, but tired quickly. He got his first real meal since coming to the hospital, ate about a quarter of it, and felt much better after that. In the afternoon he got to take a long hot shower from the neck down. He caught a quick glimpse of his head in the bathroom mirror. The bandage was indeed pretty big and there were faint dark circles around his eyes. His head had been shaved clean.

They gave him fresh pajamas and a bathrobe, and then wheeled him to a different ward in the sprawling hospital up on the hill above the town of Nouméa. When he asked why the move, they told him they needed his bed in the postsurgery recovery ward. Apparently the war hadn't stopped in honor of his arrival. They said they'd be back in the morning for more rehab exercises.

The new ward had semiprivate rooms for senior officers, although with two beds, and he apparently qualified. It was small but comfortable, with an overhead fan, a tiny screened porch with two wooden chairs, and a bathroom, which he shared with the adjoining room. The bathroom had a mirror above the sink, so he got his second look at the new and improved Harmon Wolf. His face, which now stretched over his prominent cheekbones like an artist's canvas, startled him. His eyes were framed in dark hollows, and from the right side of his head a white, somewhat mashed volleyball made of bandages protruded. His entire skull had been shaved clean. What hairs he could make out on his scalp looked white. The mirror also showed massive bruising along the right side of his face, and his right ear felt like it was off kilter.

He sighed. He looked ancient, like one of the Mide, the tribal elders. He wondered if he could find a feather out on the lawn to stick into that mass of bandages.

His head didn't hurt much, and surprisingly, he couldn't feel the new steel plate through all that bandage material. The backs of his wrists hurt more than his head, courtesy of those IVs, which were now, thankfully, gone. He was vaguely aware of some pressure inside his skull, but wondered if he was just imagining that. On balance, though, it wasn't his body that was hurting. It was the thought of what had happened to his ships and his people out there in the upper reaches of Ironbottom Sound. He remembered Jennifer telling him about the mass graves down near the beach. Some Japs, but mostly Americans.

His Americans? He lay down on the bed, which was a nice change from the World War I canvas stretcher. He wondered where the "boys" were now, and whether or not Jennifer had decided to come out or go back into that evocative *long bush*. He slept.

The next day there was more rehab work, after which the corpsmen decided he mostly needed rest, as all his motor skills appeared to be okay. The surgeons stopped by for a cursory visit. Both of them looked exhausted. Once they determined there were no complications, they left to continue rounds.

The next morning he was in the bathroom, trying to shave, when he heard voices in the bedroom.

"Captain Wolf?" a voice inquired. He stepped

back into the bedroom to see a tall Navy captain standing in the doorway. Behind him was an enlisted man who was carrying a machine of some kind.

"Yes?" Sluff said.

"I'm Captain Bob Hollis, from SOPAC staff. I'm the deputy chief of staff for operations. Are you well enough to entertain some questions about what happened to you?"

"I suppose so," Sluff said. He realized he was just a little bit dizzy. "But I think I need to get back in that bed."

"Please," Hollis said. "We can come back if you're not up to this. They told us you had a serious head injury. If that bandage is any indication . . ."

"I think it's bigger than the damage," Sluff said, climbing gingerly into the single bed. He'd learned not to provoke the plate with too much actual exertion. He pulled the pillows behind him so that he could sit up. The captain came in, pulled up a chair, and then indicated for the petty officer with him to set up on the other side of the bed. Sluff wasn't familiar with the petty officer's rating badge, but he looked to be too old to be just a second-class.

"This is Petty Officer Woodrow. In civilian life he was a court reporter, and he's here to save me the effort of remembering what you have to say."

"A court reporter," Sluff mused. "Are these going to be legal proceedings?"

"By no means, Captain," Hollis said. "First of all, we're glad you're alive. When that report came in from Sydney it caused quite a stir. No, this is an informal fact-finding mission, nothing more. You were reported as missing in action after the battle and presumed lost, considering what happened to your flagship."

He paused. "There were not that many survivors from that engagement," he continued. "Destroyers *Cannon*, *Stayers*, *Barrett*, and *Evans*, along with *Providence*, all lost. *Malone* made it out of the engagement area, but then sank near Cactus the next morning. The only real survivor was *J. B. King*. She managed to escape the Jap cruisers and plant two torpedoes into one of the surviving Jap destroyers on her way out."

"*J. B. King*," Sluff said. "That was my old ship."

"Yes, we know. You apparently trained them well. Look, let me reiterate: This is not a court of inquiry or even a formal investigation. Your return to life offers us a signal opportunity to find out what happened. If it makes you feel any better, Rear Admiral Tyree was in charge, legally speaking, and thus the responsibility for what happened necessarily lies with him."

"And where is Caw Tyree now?" Sluff asked quietly.

"Ah, yes," Hollis said. He frowned and then nodded. "Right. I guess that makes you the senior surviving officer. But still—"

"Is Captain Browning still the chief of staff?" Sluff asked.

Hollis gave a faint smile and nodded. "Why do you ask?"

"We're not friends," Sluff said.

"I'm not sure Captain Browning has *any* friends," Hollis said. "Something you should know: I'm on this year's flag list. Waiting to make my number and then I'll be away, hopefully with an operational command. I tell you this so you'll know you'll get a fair shake from me—I want to know what happened. Correction: Halsey wants to know what happened. Captain Browning is—" He paused. "Captain Browning is not pleased that one of the officers on *his* staff made flag and he did not. Yes, my report has to go through the chief of staff, but soon . . ."

Sluff nodded. He understood. Hollis was telling him that as soon he became part of that rarefied community of naval officers who'd "made" flag, Browning would have zero leverage on him. On average, one-tenth of one percent of each Naval Academy class was selected for admiral rank. If Browning made trouble, he, Hollis, would be able to step on that trouble from within the ranks of the Navy's flag officers. The implicit other half of that deal was that Sluff was going to have to tell

Rear Admiral (select) Hollis everything, no holds barred, if he wanted some protection.

There was a polite knock on the door and then a nurse came in. She was older than most of the nurses he had seen and tiny, maybe five three if she stood very straight. Tiny, but very pretty, wearing the tropical gray-and-white-striped seersucker uniform, and obviously not happy.

"Gentlemen," she said. "I'm Assistant Superintendent Danfield. My nurses told me that there was an interview going on in here. That needs to stop until this patient has had a little more time to recover." She faced Captain Hollis. "He's had *brain* surgery, Captain. Look at his eyes—see how dry they look? See those rings? That's both exhaustion and dehydration. Can't this wait another day?"

"Of course," Hollis said, hastily getting up. "I'll check with the doctors in the morning and then we'll be over. Or not, as the case might be."

"I look forward to it," Sluff said, barely suppressing a yawn.

"Good," Hollis said. "We'll try again in the morning, then." He turned to speak to the nurse. "If that's okay with you, that is."

"The doctors will make that call, Captain," she said primly. "I'm just a nurse."

"Right," Hollis said with a wry smile. "Just a nurse."

Once they'd left she came over to the bed and

sat down in the chair. "Sorry," she said. "I know they have to debrief you, but your chart says you're still a long way from a hundred percent. You need water, sleep, and food. Water first, yes?"

He realized he was very thirsty. "Yes," he said. His voice had become raspy. She had dark hair, cut severely short, beautiful brown eyes, and a figure that must have broken more than a few hearts along the way.

She left and then came back in a couple of minutes with a pitcher of ice water and some paper cups. "Sip water as much as you can. Sleep in between. There are no signs of infection, but you're not out of that danger zone yet, either. We can't see inside your braincase, so it will be you who will tell us if there's swelling, infection, or any neurological disturbances going on. I think it would be best if you recovered for *two* more days, then let the Grand Inquisitor back in."

"Sounds like a great idea," he said. "Except they do need to know what happened before they go out and do it again."

She studied his face. "You don't look old enough to be a captain," she said finally.

"You don't look old enough to be an assistant superintendent of anything," he replied, but with a smile.

"I wield a mean syringe, *sir,*" she said. "Is it true you are an American Indian?"

"I was," he said, softly. "But now I'm just an American naval officer with a hole in his head."

"Not anymore," she said. "Now you have a steel plate in your head. Anybody who tries to scalp you is in for a big surprise."

"We Indians don't scalp anymore," he protested. "Stinks up the tipi; squaws object to the smell and then we have to sleep with the dogs. While they eat the scalp."

She gave him a patient look. "You all done?" she asked.

He smiled again. "You started it."

She grinned.

"It's the face, of course," he said. "I've been living with Indian jokes since plebe year. But here I am, just another Navy casualty, it seems."

"That captain—he looked serious enough."

"He's going to be an admiral pretty soon," Sluff said. "I was commodore of a destroyer squadron. We got our collective asses handed to us by those wily Oriental devils known as the Imperial Japanese Navy. Admiral Halsey wants to know what the hell happened. Hollis is his Grand Inquisitor, as you called him."

"That's interesting," she said. "That they'd send a flag selectee to interview you."

"Okay," he said. "Debrief. Flag selectee. You're talking like you're Navy yourself, I mean, besides as a superintendent nurse?"

She smiled, but now it was a sad smile. "My

husband was chief engineer on the *Juneau*," she said.

"*Juneau*," he said. "I'm sorry."

"I was one of the nurses in charge of the main surgical recovery unit at the naval hospital in San Diego when it happened. I requested a transfer out here. They said no. I didn't take no for an answer, and they finally relented."

"Why did you want to come out here to the ends of the earth?"

"Can't you guess?"

He thought about it for a moment and then nodded. "Of course," he said. "Poor *Juneau*. That was terrible."

"Seven hundred souls on board," she said, her voice so low he almost couldn't hear her. "*Ten* came back, I'm told."

He remembered the story: After the melee of November 13, cruisers *Helena*, *Juneau*, and *San Francisco*, all seriously damaged, had been making their way to the American repair base at Espiritu Santo when a Jap submarine had attempted to torpedo *San Francisco*. She missed the heavy cruiser, but one of her torpedoes hit *Juneau*, which disappeared in a thunderclap of flying metal and sank in thirty seconds. Then, adding insult to injury, the stragglers elected to keep going on to the distant base, wrongly assuming that no one could have survived such an explosion. One hundred or more men did, but only ten were alive when search planes finally went back to look days later.

"Well," he said. "I think I lost about as many men. Four destroyers sunk, a light cruiser sunk, an admiral killed. That's why Hollis was here. I think they're looking for someone to hang."

"Nobody was hanged for what happened to *Juneau*," she pointed out. She stood up and smoothed her skirt over her legs. "It's war, Captain, or Commodore—the Japs are just a lot better than everyone thought."

"You have no idea," he said.

"Actually," she said, with a wan smile.

He closed his eyes. "I'm sorry. I'm—"

"Exhausted and badly hurt," she said. "Water, rest, more water. I'll check on you in the morning." She pulled up the light blue cotton cover.

"I'd like that," he mumbled as the shadows drew around him. He found himself embracing them.

THIRTY

Nouméa Field Hospital

The next morning Sluff was asked if he could wheel himself to the hospital cafeteria, as the orderlies were really busy just then. He said he thought he could just walk if someone could maybe get him a cane. They did and he did, although halfway there he wondered if this had been such a good idea. Fortunately there were benches placed strategically all along the corridors.

The hospital staff was obviously pushing him to make the transition from invalid to walking wounded, and for good reason: they had more seriously injured patients to take care of. Lots more, apparently. The meat grinder that was Guadalcanal, plus the incessant bloody sea fights over Ironbottom Sound, kept the field hospitals on Tulagi going overtime all the time. His head injury was not trivial, but with the plate in and no infection or obvious cognitive impairment, he was apparently as "fixed" as anyone could expect, and we need that bed, please, sir. The only thing remaining was what one corpsman vaguely referred to as some routine skin grafts. Sluff had heard about skin grafts and wasn't looking forward to that.

After a real breakfast of canned bacon, powdered scrambled eggs, and fresh bread and butter, he felt much better and was able to find his way back to his room, where he found the same diminutive superintendent nurse waiting for him, along with one of the junior nurses. This time she was in an all-white dress uniform, with the two stripes of a Navy Nurse Corps lieutenant showing on her white cap.

"You're walking," she said. "That's good. I think. How's your balance?"

"Cane was useful," he admitted. "But getting some mostly real food helped."

They ushered him back into bed, where the younger nurse took vitals, updated his chart, and then hustled out to the next room.

"May I know your name?" Sluff asked.

"I'm Tina Danfield," she said. "My husband was Walter Danfield, class of thirty."

"I was twenty-six," Sluff said. "Just missed each other. I guess. Will the docs be back this morning?"

"They're operating right now. Been going all night. You feel ready to talk to Captain Hollis?"

He nodded. "I think so," he said.

"You don't have to," she said. "I told them two days and my docs will back me up on that."

"It's time," Sluff said. "I need to get the story out before I start forgetting stuff."

"Do you want a JAG present? That Captain Hollis looked as serious as a heart attack, and that was a court reporter with him."

"How'd you know that?"

"I got to sit in on some of the after-action proceedings about what happened to *Juneau*, and watched them ask the skipper of the *Helena*, the officer in charge of the convoy of cripples headed back to Espiritu Santo, why he didn't look for survivors. I recognized that machine."

"What did he say?" Sluff asked.

"That no one could have survived the magazine

explosion, and that none of his ships was in any condition to fight off a Jap sub."

Sluff thought about that. In the cold calculus of naval warfare, the skipper of *Helena* had probably made the correct if somewhat heartless decision. During World War I, a German submarine had torpedoed one of three British cruisers steaming in a column formation. The other two had stopped to render aid, and the U-boat skipper proceeded to pick them off in a serial mass murder even as they were lowering lifeboats to get the survivors of the first ship hit. Instead of losing one cruiser, the Brits lost all three. Sluff saw from her expression that someone had told her this story. He changed the subject.

"Hollis told me this was a fact-finding expedition, not some kind of court of inquiry. And, besides, I wasn't in charge that night—Admiral Tyree was."

"Okay," she said. "You're a big captain now. I'll make the call."

Hollis and his reporter showed up an hour later from SOPAC headquarters.

"Shall we?" Hollis said.

"By all means," Sluff replied. He'd arranged his pillows so that he could sit upright. Hollis took one chair, the yeoman a second that he'd dragged in from the hallway after first plugging in his transcription machine.

"Let's start with your appointment as ComDesRon

Twenty-One," Hollis said. "That happened aboard the flagship, correct?"

"That's right. Came as a big surprise, actually, but the admiral laid it all out for me, and there I was."

For the next hour and a half Sluff told the story, from getting the news of his promotion and taking over a destroyer squadron to the moment when he and Jennifer Matheson first heard the MTBs prowling down the coast of Kalai Island. When he had finished, Hollis waited for his reporter to catch up and then called a time-out for coffee. The yeoman went out into the corridor to hunt up some coffee, while Hollis sat back in his chair and shook his head.

"That's some adventure, Captain," he said. "Tell me, what was your academy nickname?"

Sluff told him, and what the letters stood for. Hollis smiled and then asked if Sluff had faced racial animosity during his Navy career.

"Some," Sluff said. "I tried out for flight school. Wasn't very good at it. Got into it with an instructor after he called me a woods nigger."

Hollis frowned. "Consequences?"

"I left naval aviation. He left the second floor for the ground floor through a window."

Hollis stared at him, and then cleared his throat. "Oka-a-y," he said. "Now: Would it be fair to say that the battle plan for the night in question was the admiral's plan? Or was it yours?"

Sluff felt the first tingle of alarm. What could it matter, he thought. The admiral was in charge, so it was *his* plan, his formation, and his operation. Then he realized that, with the yeoman gone, Hollis was speaking off the record, which meant that this was something he really wanted to know. Why? he wondered.

"I had told the admiral about the other two engagements and how we'd run a radar ambush followed by the tactic of waiting for the fish to hit, shooting for a minute or so, and then going dark and maneuvering at high speed to stay out of torpedo water. Once I thought we were safe, we'd open fire again, but only for a minute. They could only see us when we were shooting. We could see them the whole time."

Hollis nodded. The legal yeoman returned with three cafeteria mugs of coffee, handed them out, and then asked if he should resume the record. Hollis said no, not yet.

"It seems to me that the Japs went home after getting *their* asses kicked for a change and compared notes," Sluff continued.

"Is it possible that their third sortie down the Slot, almost an exact copy of the first two, one or two heavies wrapped in a clutch of destroyers, was the bait in an ambush of their own?" Hollis asked.

Sluff thought about it for a moment. "The way those heavy cruisers appeared right at the critical moment, from the west, from *outside* the Slot? Yes, I think that's possible."

"Me, too," Hollis said. "Those bastards are good."

"Never doubted that," Sluff said. "The radar may have seduced us into thinking we could fool 'em forever."

Hollis nodded at the legal yeoman, who resumed his duties as court reporter.

"Captain, why did you choose to drive straight at that formation of heavy cruisers?"

"I think the cruisers had put up a scout plane because suddenly there were star shells or dropped flares. At that moment, when they could finally see us, we ran out of good choices. If we went north, their destroyers and cruisers could get at us with Long Lances. Same thing if we ran south. By running right at the incoming cruisers, the destroyers to the east couldn't fire torpedoes without putting their own cruisers in danger, so, basically, I was hoping to cut down the number of torpedoes coming at us."

"But apparently their cruisers didn't offer the same consideration to their own destroyers, right?"

"I don't know where the torpedo that broke *Barrett* in half came from, to tell the truth," Sluff said. "Our torpedoes essentially bounced off. I think we were so close they didn't have enough time to arm. I'll say this, though: *Barrett* tore *up* that first cruiser's superstructure. There were at least four levels of the pagoda on fire."

"Well, that probably explains how their admiral and most of his staff died," Hollis said.

"How in the world do we know *that?*" Sluff asked.

"PacFleet Intel sent out a report. I guess they have spies in Rabaul."

"Wow."

"And after *Barrett* was hit by one or more torpedoes, you, personally, were basically out of the game?"

"Yes. She broke in half amidships. The stern half kept going, while the bow half was pushed a hundred eighty degrees around and then flipped over. I remember trying to hold on but getting thrown off the ship instead. After that . . ."

"Who would have assumed command of the squadron once you were incapacitated?"

"I don't know," Sluff had to admit. "But by that time, I think it was everybody for himself once we got into it with those cruisers."

"So there was no formal succession plan?"

"Hell, we barely had time to learn each other's radio call signs," Sluff said. "I learned I was the commodore at lunch with the admiral; we discussed tactics for a few minutes, I went back and moved from *J. B. King* to *Barrett*, summoned the ships' captains for a quick meeting, and eight hours later we were toast. Sound familiar?"

"What do you mean?" Hollis asked.

"It was a catch team, just like the night Ching Lee picked up four destroyers and led us all into a battleship engagement. *He* may have had a plan, but he didn't share it with us. And when *South Dakota* fell out of the fight, he and *Washington* went one-on-one with *Kirishima*. Behind him three of the four destroyers were sinking. Once he'd done in the Jap battleship, he just left." He paused, yawned, and then said, "One would think our whole mission that night was to soak up Jap torpedoes."

Hollis stared at him for a second and then told the yeoman to strike that last comment. Then he said he needed to speak to the captain in private. The yeoman finished typing, gathered up his equipment, and stepped out.

"I heard a story you left that formation just before the other three destroyers got hit," Hollis said. "Is that true?"

"I did. I knew Long Lances were coming, based on the Japs' maneuvers."

"Weren't you engaging with guns at that point?"

"We were, but when you think about it, we weren't contributing very much, not compared to eighteen battleship guns. We were tethered, really. Never allowed to use our biggest weapons, our own torpedoes. When Lee opened fire, the targets were still way out of our torpedo range."

"Have you thought that maybe that's why he

kept you tethered, as you put it? If he let you guys haul out and make a torpedo attack, he would have had to wait for you to clear, and thus give away his range advantage?"

"He could have let us go make a torpedo attack as soon as we gained radar contact. Run out, let the torpedoes fly and then get out of the way so that the big dogs could eat. I did that with cruiser formations a couple of times with pretty good success."

"Until they figured it out."

"Until they figured it out, yes, but you know what? On that night with Admiral Lee, my slipping off the leash did not interfere one bit with Lee's line of fire, and I was able to recover hundreds of our people after Lee sailed away. Even Halsey thought that was a good thing."

"You met with Admiral Halsey?"

"I did. We even had a drink. Captain Browning was outraged, I think."

Hollis grunted. "So would you consider yourself a protégé of Admiral Halsey?"

"*Me?* Hell, no. I doubt he even remembers my name."

"Halsey remembers everything and everyone," Hollis said. "That's why he's the guy in charge now. But that's not why I asked."

Sluff raised his eyebrows in anticipation.

"I asked because I think, given this background, you are going to need some protection, Captain.

You have some enemies on the SOPAC staff. I think they want to take the results of your last night fight and hang you out to dry. They'll call it *your* night fight because your boss got killed, or at least that's how they'll try to frame it."

"Frame," Sluff said, realizing he was getting really tired now. "Interesting choice of words."

"Calling it like I see it," Hollis said. "Didn't say it was fair."

"Well, I'll tell you, they, whoever 'they' are, can't do anything to me that comes close to the stuff I saw happen that night or on Kalai Island," Sluff said. "I came within five feet of being eaten alive by a Jap patrol dog. No staff pukes up at SOPAC ever went through something like that."

Hollis nodded, sniffed, and stood up. "As a fairly successful 'staff puke,'" he said, "I need to remind you that they can make life truly miserable for you—but only if you let them."

Sluff suddenly realized his mistake: Hollis was a staff officer up at SOPAC. He felt his face getting red.

Hollis grinned at him. "Relax. You've come awfully far, awfully fast. That breeds resentment in the Old Guard. You have to remember, before the Japs hit Pearl, promotion was a matter of living long enough and not blotting your copybook, as the Brits like to say. Upstarts like you—"

He put up his hand as he saw Sluff's reaction to the word "upstart."

"Upstarts like you are going to win this war," he continued. "Halsey wants brawlers. Officers who, when cornered, come out like a mad dog and go right for the face of their tormentors. Here's my advice: I'll turn in my 'informal' report. Browning and his cronies will indulge in some professional grinding of teeth. They may even 'lose' it. You, on the other hand, need to get in front of Halsey and tell your side. He's in Pearl now, meeting with Nimitz, but he'll be back in a couple of days."

"How in the world can I do that?" Sluff asked.

"Halsey comes up here to the hospital once a week. He walks the wards in full regalia, talks to the wounded. Tells them he appreciates their sacrifices. That he's going to make sure they're well taken care of. All that bluff and bluster, and yet here he is, like their grandfather, giving a shit. It's magic—a little touch of Harry in the night, so to speak. Find out when he's coming, and get in front of him."

Sluff took a deep breath. "The fact is, Captain Hollis, that it really was *my* plan, *my* tactic, that got everyone killed. Maybe I should just give this up and go home."

Hollis gave him a strange look. "Your call, Commodore." Then he left.

Sluff sat back and wondered if indeed any of this political plotting and scheming was worth it. How many sailors were drowned because he'd been just a bit too sure of himself, a little cocky, maybe, telling the new admiral how to do this thing, how to beat the Japs. Then he realized something: Hollis had called him Commodore.

THIRTY-ONE

Nouméa Field Hospital

The next day his two doctors came by again on their morning rounds. They told him that the large bandage on his head would be coming off, to be replaced with something that looked less like a half turban. They confirmed that he could get around as long as he was having no serious pain from the surgery. As they were leaving, the older doctor told Sluff that yet another captain over at SOPAC headquarters had called, inquiring if he could have visitors.

"Remember his name?" Sluff asked. "Hollis, maybe?"

"No. Brown, I think. Browning. Captain Browning. Said he was the chief of staff."

"Can't wait," Sluff said. The doc caught the sarcasm.

"You want, I can turn that off with a phone call," he said.

Sluff waved him off. "No, I've been expecting this. Time to get it over with."

The bandage people showed up at 0900 to take Sluff to a room adjacent to the operating suite, where they undid the mess on his head, cleaned things up with something that felt like gasoline, and then remounted a new bandage that had to be three pounds lighter. When he looked in a mirror, he could see the glint of the steel plate on the side of his head through some of the gauze. It was much bigger than he'd anticipated—"plate" was an appropriate word. He noticed that the fuzz of hair growing back was definitely white now. If that kept up he was going to look as old as he felt.

"Can I touch it?" he asked. "The plate?"

"Yes, sir," the corpsman replied. "It's harder than your own skull. It's the sutures you gotta be careful with."

"People always said I had a hard head," Sluff said. "Knucklehead, that was the word."

The corpsmen grinned, and then one asked if he was really an Indian. Sluff said he was.

"Knew it," the corpsman said. "There were a buncha guys off the destroyers that got sunk when the battleships went at it. They were talking about one skipper who dodged all those torpedoes and came back for 'em once the heavies bailed. Said he was an Indian, with the biggest—uh."

Sluff laughed out loud. "The biggest damn nose they'd ever seen since Mount Rushmore, right?"

"Uh, yes, sir, sorry, sir, I didn't—"

"It's okay, corpsman," Sluff said, with a grin. "And thanks for lightening up the bandage."

He and his cane thumped back to his room, where he showered, now that the turban was gone, and then tried to decide what to wear for the meeting with Browning. Uniform? Or hospital gear? Then he realized his uniforms were at the bottom of Ironbottom Sound. The one he'd been wearing when *Barrett* capsized was surely long gone into the trash. He got out some clean cotton pajamas, a cotton robe, and then got into his hospital bed.

He touched that steel plate again. It didn't hurt, of course, but the perimeter where they'd sewn it into his skull was really sore. He tried to examine the area of his brain underneath the plate, but felt nothing. He closed his eyes. That felt really good.

Sometime later, he woke up to a knock on his door, and then Tina came in. Her expression said: Look out for this one. Behind her, standing in the doorway like a statue, was his nemesis, the eternally choleric Captain Browning.

"Captain, you have a visitor," Tina announced, acting as if she didn't know him. "Is that going to be all right?"

Browning's severe expression must have worried her, he thought. "Of course," he said. "Why would it not be?"

Tina nodded and then backed out as Browning came in, took off his cap, and then sat down stiffly in the room's only chair. Sluff waited for him to speak.

"Your doctors tell me that you're making good progress," Browning said, his tone of voice neutral. "You are fortunate to have survived, from the looks of that."

"That was just the beginning," Sluff said. "Have you seen Captain Hollis's report yet?"

"Rear Admiral (select) Hollis gave me a verbal debrief, with a written report to follow," Browning replied, correcting him. "I have some staff people trying to conform what you told him to what else we know about the engagement, which, admittedly, isn't much. He said you think the Japs set an ambush of their own this time."

"Entirely possible," Sluff said. "Heavy cruisers rounding that point at thirty-six knots were certainly not in my plan."

"Interesting choice of words, Captain," Browning said. "*My* plan."

Sluff thought he heard someone in the adjoining bathroom, making cleaning-up noises. "I went through that with Hollis," Sluff said. "The admiral and I had talked it over and he told me to run the tactic again. The first half seemed to work— we fired torpedoes on a radar solution and things went boom in the night at the appropriate time."

"Then the cruisers showed up."

"Yes, they did."

"Your original targets were a light cruiser and some destroyers, correct?"

"We never saw them, but that's what we guessed from the radar returns."

"But instead of executing what one of your people called your Comanche circle, you turned away from them and headed west. Put another way, you broke off the action and tried to escape."

"Not exactly," Sluff said, realizing now where Browning was going with this. "As I explained to Captain Hollis, we were between a rock and a hard place once the additional cruisers arrived and their scout plane started dropping flares. We couldn't go north or south without becoming a Long Lance sandwich, so I elected to run the squadron right at the more dangerous enemy, the heavy cruisers. They could of course fire torpedoes, but their destroyers couldn't without hitting their own ships."

"And yet, in the end, they sank four of the tin cans in this fight and *Providence*."

"*Providence* gave herself away before she was supposed to. She wasn't supposed to start shooting when she did, but because she did, the Jap heavies saw her."

"We only have your word for that, seeing that Admiral Tyree did not survive the engagement."

"What's your point, Captain?" Sluff asked with a sigh.

"My point is that there are people at headquarters who are saying you ran, just like you ran when the shooting started the night of the battleship action."

"Then how did that Jap admiral get killed?"

Browning's face reddened. "How do you know about that?"

"Captain Hollis told me."

"Rear Admiral (select) Hollis was speaking out of school, then," Browning said. "That is very sensitive intelligence information."

"We weren't running *from* the enemy, Captain Browning. We were running *at* him. And not just my flagship, but *all* of my destroyers. If we were running away, we'd have turned southwest and gone dark. As it was, we drove right at them, shooting the whole time. We were just no match for twenty-odd eight-inch guns. Our five-inch couldn't penetrate their armor, but it could wreck their topside superstructure. Our torpedoes bounced off; theirs didn't. By the way, I would like to meet some of these 'people at head-quarters.' People who weren't there."

"That is out of the question. You are the senior surviving officer. Your actions are the focus of our inquiries."

"Inquiries, Captain? Getting a court of inquiry together?"

"What do you think?" Browning snapped. "A light cruiser, four destroyers sunk in return for one Jap cruiser damaged and a destroyer sunk, a second one damaged? While you conveniently went over the side in the middle of it?"

Sluff could barely contain his anger now. "Went over the side? Like I slid out a diving board and executed a perfect swan dive? You are a piece of work, are you not, Browning. You and your 'people' over at headquarters. Well, bring on your court. I can't wait."

"You *will* wait, and right here, too. Hollis hasn't turned in his report yet and Admiral Halsey's not back from Pearl. You need to understand something, Captain: You're not in charge of anything right now, if you ever were."

"Oh, go away," Sluff said. "I'm not afraid of you. I've seen and done things which would make a guy like you piss his pants. How much combat have you seen from the O-club here in Nouméa? I see now why Hollis made flag and you didn't."

Browning's face settled into a cold mask. He stood up and put on his brass hat. "You have no idea of who you're fooling with," he hissed. "We will destroy you."

Sluff smiled. "You can destroy my career, maybe," he said. "But not me. By the way, here's something to think about: When *Barrett* got blown in half, *Providence* was still shooting. That means Admiral Tyree was still the boss. Seems to me you're going after the wrong guy. Now get the hell out of my room."

Browning stared at him for a few seconds and

then left, slamming the door after him. Sluff lay back in his bed and let out a long breath. Hollis had been right. Browning *was* out to get him. Not enough to have Japs trying to kill you; now he had an admiral's staff after him as well.

His last jab had been an interesting technicality, but with Admiral Tyree asleep in the deep, no one would be wanting to file charges of incompetence against his ghost. In fact, another admiral who'd led his cruiser force to destruction had made the same maneuvering choice Sluff had made, and he'd been awarded the Medal of Honor. The truth was that he'd convinced his boss to run the same tactic he'd used too many times before and it had backfired. Who owns that, he asked himself. Go look in the mirror.

Listen to me, he thought, as he lay back into the pillows. Is everything really all about me? Is my so-called career that important? How about the men who died because of the orders I gave, on the fly, without a whole lot of thinking time. Didn't they count?

Then something occurred to him: There might be some survivors of that fight right here in the Nouméa hospital complex. Maybe he should emulate Halsey and go see them, tell them he was sorry for what happened. Quit worrying about Browning and his minions plotting to hang some dead albatross around his neck. What did Bob Frey used to say? "Screw 'em if they can't take a joke"?

THIRTY-TWO

Nouméa Field Hospital

As it turned out, there were several survivors from *Providence* and the destroyers sunk that night. Some of them were hopelessly injured—burns patients, for the most part, who were probably not going to survive. Tina Danfield had helped Sluff find them in the hospital complex, which was a sprawling collection of small buildings spread over a ten-acre area of coconut palms. The buildings were more like tropical huts, made of wood, with no heating or air-conditioning and many of them still sporting palm-frond roofs.

None of the people who'd survived the *Providence* sinking knew who he was, of course. He'd only been aboard briefly, and none of the admiral's staff had survived the torpedoing and subsequent shelling, which had turned *Providence*'s flag bridge into a flaming mass of mangled metal as she settled into her watery grave. The destroyer survivors didn't know him, either—he'd only been the New Commodore for one night, and if they remembered anything about that night, they were trying hard to forget it.

He tried to make a brave face of it, pretending to know what their ships had done that night and telling them that they'd killed the Jap admiral and his whole staff, sunk one destroyer, and damaged a heavy cruiser and another destroyer. As he went along he started making stuff up about what they'd done to the enemy, and they seemed to appreciate it, even if they had no idea of who this ugly guy in a bathrobe with an armor-plated head was.

The first time he tried it he ran out of steam halfway between two wards and had to be helped back to the senior officers' ward in a wheelchair. The next afternoon he went a little slower, working his way down a list of names provided by Tina Danfield and her contacts in the hospital admin hut. On the third afternoon she came with him. She proved a lot more popular with the troops than Sluff did. She'd taken the time and effort to apply a little war paint and even Sluff thought she was a whole lot more interesting than the ugly Indian guy with the stainless-steel scalp. The only unpleasant experience was when they visited a sailor who'd lost a leg and a forearm to a shark. He'd been retrieved onto a life raft and, with tourniquets applied, made it back to Nouméa. He wanted to know why no one had come back for the survivors. Sluff had to tell him that there weren't any ships left to come back for the survivors until the next day.

"So it's true," the man had whispered. "We got our asses kicked."

"We did," Sluff said. "And I'm partly responsible for that."

"So whaddaya want from me," the man said. "Forgiveness?"

"No, I'm just here to tell you I'm sorry. We tried, and it didn't work."

"Well, ain't that nice," the sailor said. "For you, whoever you are. *You* can still walk." Then he'd turned his face away.

Tina touched Sluff's arm and they moved on to the next sailor, who was, thankfully, a lot more friendly. When they left that ward. Sluff said he'd had enough. Once they got back to his ward, Tina said she had to go back on watch. She asked if he'd be all right.

"You know," he said with a sad smile, "that kid was partially right. Yes, I wanted to do the right thing, but I also wanted some forgiveness for my mistakes. He saw right through me, didn't he."

"You keep talking about your mistakes," she said. "It's war, Captain. You went out and fought the enemy. This time the enemy won. Next time he'll lose. It's not like you ordered your squadron to run away—you ran right at them. What did Nelson say? No captain can do much wrong if he lays his ship alongside one of the enemy's?"

Sluff stared at her. "How did you know that?" he asked.

"About Lord Nelson?"

"No, about what happened out there."

She blushed. "I was the one pretending to clean the bathroom when that Browning guy came to torment you," she said. "Walt used to talk about officers like that. He called them silver snakes."

He smiled. "Well," he said. "I was happy enough to accept the promotion to captain and the title of commodore. Now I suspect I'll have to be ready to take the consequences of losing a fight. It's how the system works, you know. You get promoted; you get a flag, the nice boat, a steward, and the big cabin. You screw it up, you get the big court."

"You're not just going to quit, are you?" she asked.

"I'm tired, Tina. I'm also a little embarrassed about touring the wards, like I was Bull Halsey or somebody. That was about me, again. Maybe it's just time to let the wheels of naval justice grind out the right answer." He paused. "Thank you for your moral support and your help. It was very much appreciated. But you might want to keep your distance. From here on out, I may attract some lightning."

She shook her head and left quietly. He looked out the lone window, which had no glass, only screens. Sunset was coming down. How appropriate, he thought. He dozed.

He woke up and discovered it was almost nine. He was suddenly hungry. He got up, washed his face, got back into his bathrobe and slippers, and went out into the hallway. He asked a passing corpsman if the chow hall was still open. The corpsman said, yes, it was always open because the medical staff worked around the clock. Sluff got his cane and headed out the door to the building that held the hospital's cafeteria. Sure enough there were some bleary-eyed doctors and nurses in their surgical gowns eating at two of the tables. He grabbed a steel tray and went through the empty line, where he got some soggy chicken, watery string beans, and mashed potatoes. He took a table in a far corner of the cafeteria, near the coffee urns, figuring the docs and nurses had probably had enough of seeing patients for one day. He forced himself to eat the mushy food and then got a mug of coffee. He saw the medical people get up and head for the door. One of the junior nurses got the duty of humping all their empty trays to the steam-line scullery.

Once they'd left he was all alone, except for the bored-looking Negro cooks back in the galley. He leaned his chair back against the wall and sipped his vintage yesterday coffee. Outside he could hear some boxy green ambulance trucks grinding their way up the hill from the port with more broken bodies. He realized it was December, heading toward Christmas.

Christmas in the war-torn South Pacific, he thought. Now there's a cosmic joke if there ever was one.

That's when Admiral Halsey and an aide came into the cafeteria and headed for the coffee station.

THIRTY-THREE

Nouméa Field Hospital

As he approached the coffee urns Halsey saw Sluff. Those bushy eyebrows went straight up.

"Jesus Christ and General Jackson!" he exclaimed. "Commodore Wolf. You *are* alive." Halsey sat down on one of the metal mess hall chairs and studied Sluff's face. "Shot at and missed, shit at and hit, I do believe, young man," he pronounced.

Sluff exhaled a long breath. "It's a long story, Admiral," he said. "And not a pretty one, I'm afraid."

"You think I don't know that, Wolf? I've seen the butcher's bill. Tell me in five minutes—what the hell happened out there?"

It ended up being thirty minutes, not five, but Halsey let him tell it. The aide, a lieutenant commander, appeared to be truly horrified by what he was hearing. When Sluff finally ran out of steam, Halsey raised a hand.

"Okay, I get the picture. There's lot to be learned

here—some of which we know, like our own goddamned torpedoes still not working, but how did those Jap heavy cruisers know *when* to come around the corner? They must be listening to our tactical radios." He paused, took a sip of coffee, grimaced, and then put the mug down. "The biggest question I have doesn't concern the night fight. How long have you been here?"

"Got picked up by a PT boat about a week ago, and came here on a Catalina."

"Surely someone reported that to my head-quarters," Halsey said.

"Don't know, Admiral. I wasn't the only casualty on the plane. Your chief of staff knew, though. He's been to visit me. Told me a court of inquiry is coming. Told me that some people at SOPAC headquarters think I gathered up my squadron and turned tail when those cruisers showed up."

Halsey's face turned to stone. For a moment, he seemed to be about to erupt; then he quickly calmed himself.

"Okay," he said. "I'll look into that. Meantime, I've got an entire theater of war to worry about, and this incident, while important, is not as important as the Japs' determination to reinforce their army on Guadalcanal. All the intel says they've got a big push coming. Are you fit for duty? Is that"—he pointed at the metal plate shining out of Sluff's head—"disqualifying?"

Sluff smiled. "Proof of what people have been saying for years," he said. "That I have a very hard head."

Halsey sighed, apparently not in the mood for humor.

"I need some physical rehab," Sluff said, quickly. "Balance, strength training. Later, some skin grafts. But my mind is up and running, and I have many Japs to kill for what they did to us that night."

"That's what I want to hear," Halsey said, nodding. "Okay—get your rehab. And get your ass ready to fight."

"Aye, aye, sir," Sluff said. "And thank you for hearing my side."

"Don't thank me yet, Harmon Wolf," he said, as he got up. "I may yet get you killed for real."

He made a face at the offending mug of coffee and turned to leave, aide in tow. He stopped halfway across the room and turned around.

"Something you should know, Wolf," he said. "You've got a very pretty ally, who buttonholed me in a ward tonight and told me where to find you. *And* what to ask about. *Juneau* widow, my aide tells me. You married?"

"No, sir."

"Well, then," Halsey said, putting one finger against his nose. And then he left.

Well, then, indeed, Sluff thought. God bless Tina Danfield—heard Halsey was in the hospital, went and found him, and steered him to their meeting. Somebody had faith in him, he thought. Now he just had to generate some faith in himself.

He blew out a long breath and then shivered as he thought about going back out to face those black ships in the night again. Unconsciously, he touched the plate on the side of his head.

For the next three days he found out that "rehab" meant hours of exercising, from what someone called passive-resistance training to actual walking, stair-climbing, breathing, and, interestingly, hand-eye coordination tests. He couldn't go straight through any of it on the first day, but by day three he was definitely getting stronger. The only sign of brain damage was his ability to distinguish between colors. It wasn't that he couldn't see color, it was that he made occasional mistakes when reading a color chart. Otherwise, he was pretty much himself, warts and all.

On the fourth morning after Halsey's visit, Tina stopped by and told him that Captain Hollis had called. He didn't have time to come up to the hospital complex, but wanted Sluff to know that a new surface-action group was being formed to deal with something important about to happen at Guadalcanal, and that he, Hollis, was going to command it.

"Well, great," Sluff said. "I think he's one of the good guys."

"He had one more thing to tell you," she said. "Browning is coming to see you. He didn't know what about, but he said to be careful."

"Ah, the original silver snake," Sluff mused. "When?"

"He didn't know," she said. "You have more rehab work to do today, and then we have to talk about discharge. We need the space."

"I understand," he said.

"It's Guadalcanal," she said. "Combat injuries but also tropical diseases: we've opened a *fifth* malaria ward. Kids are dying right and left. You should hear the stories the Marines are telling. It's awful up there."

"I know," he said. "At least a little bit. Tell me, how long will you be here in Nouméa?"

"*Me?* I'll be here until we win this thing in the Solomons. Then we'll go on to Japan."

He stared at her. "You're that sure?" he asked. "That we're gonna beat these bastards?"

"Never doubted it," she said. "And neither should you. Look, I've got to go. Watch yourself with that Browning fella."

"I will, and thank you again. I hope . . ." He ran out of words, and then she smiled at him. "It's gonna be a long war, Captain," she said. "Anything's possible."

Captain Browning arrived at noon, accompanied by two JAG lieutenant commanders and a yeoman. Sluff had been about to go down to the cafeteria. He was no longer in hospital garb, courtesy of a classmate who'd come to see him. The classmate was executive officer in a new heavy cruiser that was staging through Nouméa, and he had managed to scrounge up some khaki trousers, uniform shoes, a shirt, complete with the requisite silver eagles, and the fore-and-aft khaki hat known fondly throughout the fleet as a piss-cutter. He'd also brought along some khaki swim trunks and other exercise gear. Given a heads-up from one of the corpsmen that brass was inbound, Sluff had taken the only chair in the room and parked his cane between his knees.

Browning appeared to be surprised that Sluff was actually in uniform. Sluff didn't get up when Browning and his crew came into the room, which meant they all had to stand. Browning, who understood the slight immediately, frowned but then cleared his throat.

"I've come here to offer you a deal, Captain," he said.

"Do I need a deal?" Sluff said. "What about my court? I think a court might be to my professional benefit. You know, the truth about what happened out there and all that?"

Browning glared. The JAGs studied the floor. The yeoman looked bored.

"You do *not* want to be subjected to a court of inquiry," Browning said. "Even if totally exonerated, your career will be forever tarnished.

The facts of the destruction of your squadron cannot be waved away by any legal mumbo jumbo. So hear me out."

"I'm all ears."

"We propose that you will be medically retired as a result of a serious head injury, as evidenced by that steel plate. You will return to the States and be invalided out. You will be retired in the rank of Captain, USN, with a pension for life at that rank. You will be provided medical care for the rest of your life as a wounded veteran."

"And?"

"And, you will accede to these, um, terms, without complaint or objection. The war will be over for you, as it is for many wounded veterans. There will be no court of inquiry and no blame laid against your professional reputation."

"That's it?"

"What more could you want, Captain?" Browning asked. "Your war would be over. You will have what amounts to an honorable discharge from the service due to war wounds. You will be a casualty of that fiasco, rather than its perpetrator. What more could you want?"

"Does Halsey know of this so-called offer?" Sluff asked.

Browning put on a disdainful face. "What Admiral Halsey knows about anything at all is a matter for me to know and for you to accept. This isn't a negotiation, Captain Wolf. This is a way for you to retire from the war with your reputation intact. After all, you were a principal player in a tragic defeat at sea for the U.S. Navy."

"Not for lack of trying," Sluff said, softly. "We fought hard, actually, against heavy odds. You ever done that?"

Browning's face went red. God, Sluff thought. It was so easy to spin this snake up. Tina would have enjoyed this; he wondered if she was hiding in the bathroom again.

"The answer is no, Captain Browning," Sluff said, finally.

"You're kidding. Tell me you're not that dumb."

"I'm neither dumb nor disabled. I'm being returned to full duty."

"With *that?*" Browning exclaimed, pointing at the steel plate.

"Stronger than the original skull, Captain Browning. So: Bring your court if you want to. For now, however, we're done here. I've got some rehab to attend to, and then they tell me I'm being discharged."

Browning stared at him in total disbelief. Sluff suddenly understood something. If Browning had been given a shot at such a deal, he would have taken it. He might have been the chief of staff at SOPAC, but Sluff wondered if beneath all that angry bluster he really was just a coward. Somebody had told him that Browning had been the brains behind the victory at Midway, but

Sluff was willing to bet he hadn't been flying an airplane that day.

"You made a bad decision out there when those cruisers showed up," Browning said. "You're making another one now. At least you're consistent. And as to being returned to full duty, I'm sure we can find some suitable billet for you while we arrange the court. Perhaps at the ammo depot. Good day, sir."

Sluff gave him a polite smile and then waited for the group to leave. He looked at his watch, which had survived all of his various ordeals, even a brief stint on a Jap soldier's wrist. It was still time for lunch, and the corpsmen were saying they had real beef hamburgers today. Now, that was important news.

THIRTY-FOUR

Nouméa

Things happened fast after that. The very next day Sluff was discharged from the field hospital and given a room at one of the old French hotels downtown that had been requisitioned when Halsey had arrived and now served as a bachelor officers' quarters, or BOQ. There he found out that a new destroyer-tender ship, USS *Dixie*, had arrived in port. A destroyer tender looked like an ocean liner from a distance, and some of them had been converted from civilian trade. Inside, however, they were filled with machine shops of every description, and they could repair almost all battle damage as long as the ship concerned could make it alongside. Sluff cadged a ride down to the waterfront and went aboard to call on the captain. He explained his situation: He'd lost everything when *Barrett* went down, including service, medical, and pay records, not to mention all his personal effects.

The skipper called down to the ship's store and told them to outfit Captain Wolf with a full seabag. He said he would stand for the costs until someone in Disbursing found Sluff's pay records. Once that was done, he invited Sluff to stay for lunch in his cabin, where they discussed waterfront gossip and especially the new task group that was forming up. Sluff learned that there were three captains in contention for the destroyer squadron command: one on Halsey's staff and two others who'd recently been promoted and who were currently serving as destroyer commanding officers.

The tender's CO was of the opinion that the guy on Halsey's staff was the favorite, but all three had one problem: none of them had as yet served in ship-versus-ship combat against the Japanese. The SOPAC staff guy had been CO of a cruiser in early '42, but had been detached before that ship entered the Guadalcanal campaign, where she was subsequently sunk. The other two were fresh-caught captains coming from destroyer command in the Atlantic Fleet, which was primarily an antisubmarine effort against the U-boats currently tearing up the East Coast. He then asked Sluff what *he* was going to do next.

"I have no idea," Sluff said. "I'm either going to face a court of inquiry for the Russell Islands as fiasco, or go back out there and try it again. The elephants up at SOPAC are dancing, so right now I'm hiding out in the BOQ and waiting to see which way it goes."

"That guy, Browning, involved in this 'dance'?"

"Met him, have you?"

"I did when I brought *Dixie* in from Pearl. Made an office call to meet Halsey. Got Browning instead. Thinks highly of himself, apparently. Gave me a lecture about working around the clock, seven days a week, to support the fight at Guadalcanal. That night I found him dead drunk at the O-club, the one down at the Ducos Cove Rec Center that the *San Juan* sailors built? Asked him if he was off the clock. Told me to go to hell."

"That's him," Sluff said. "But he may have his ass in a crack about now. He never told Halsey that I'd been recovered. Halsey wasn't pleased with that."

"You know Admiral Halsey?"

"In a manner of speaking—we've talked a

couple of times. Anyhow, it's all way above my pay grade right now, so I'm just gonna lay low and see what happens. Like I said, when the elephants dance . . ."

"Yup. That's a good rule. Well, good luck with it. They're talking about sending *Dixie* up to Tulagi, to be closer to the action."

"That might be closer than you want to be," Sluff said. "At least until they thin out the Japs' Betty force. If you do go up there, you need to practice getting under way at a moment's notice and going full bore. And your gunnery, too."

The CO laughed. "A tender? What we do is anchor and then build up an island of coffee grounds underneath us from all the machine shops. When they start to foul the main condensers, then and only then do we move."

"Not kidding," Sluff said. "Bettys carry the airborne version of the Long Lance torpedo. Two of those in your guts and even this big girl would break in half."

That night Sluff signed out for the beachside rec center. He felt the need for a drink. He promised himself he'd stick to beer, but he was tired of hot single rooms in aging tropical buildings. He took the shuttle bus to the beach and went into the O-club. Now that he had some uniforms he didn't feel quite so helpless, although the steel plate and his white hair did attract some attention. He wondered if Lieutenant Tina Danfield ever made it down to the rec center. He smiled to himself: she'd be mobbed if she did. After two beers he was feeling pleasantly mellow and wondering if he should maybe call her, when a very young-looking lieutenant junior grade threaded his way across the veranda and approached his table. He was wearing a two-ring gold aiguillette on his left shoulder, indicating he was an aide to a two-star. Everyone in the fleet, except the aides, referred to those rings as loafer's loops.

"Commodore Wolf?" the JG asked expectantly. Some of the officers sitting nearby perked up at that title of commodore.

"How can I help you, Lieutenant?" Sluff said, wondering himself about that title.

"Admiral Hollis sends his compliments, sir, and requests that you join him for dinner aboard *New Orleans*, his flagship. I have a car ready outside."

Sluff finished his beer and followed the lieutenant outside, where a gray staff car was waiting. They drove down to the harbor, where a black-hulled admiral's barge was waiting at the fleet landing, two silver stars showing prominently on its bow. Sluff hoped the newly minted rear admiral wasn't planning to take this pretty boat into battle, where it would become a dangerous fire hazard.

New Orleans was a 1933 vintage heavy cruiser, with nine eight-inch guns in the main battery. She carried two floatplanes and an additional eight five-inch guns. Admiral Hollis greeted Sluff in his flag cabin and then introduced him to the cruiser's skipper, Captain Henry Hodges. The flag cabin had a separate bedroom and bath, and the admiral's office had been converted into a dining room by throwing a white tablecloth over the conference table. After dinner, the stewards cleared the table, brought in a silver-plated coffee pitcher, and then left the cabin. Hollis produced a bottle of Scotch, poured everyone two fingers into their coffee cups, and then asked Sluff to tell Hodges about his experiences fighting the Japanese since becoming a division and then a squadron commander.

Sluff took a sip of the Scotch and then started in. When he was finished, the coffee remained untouched and the Scotch bottle was down to a bit of vapor. Hodges was looking at him with an expression that made Sluff wonder if he was up to command of a heavy cruiser in a night fight with the Tokyo Express. Hollis's expression was unfathomable. Then he leaned forward to give Sluff the news.

"Admiral Halsey has made his decision to appoint you as the destroyer squadron commander in the new task group. You'll have eight ships, mostly new-construction Fletchers fresh out of training at Pearl. *J. B. King* will be among them, and you might consider making her your flagship. Your first mission will be to take them to sea for a week, assuming we get that much time, and whip them into a fighting force. No more catch teams, to use your expression. I'll have a group SOP out by tomorrow night, the comms plan out in two days."

"What's the mission up north?"

"The Japs are planning to bring an entire army division down the Slot by a heavily protected troop transport convoy—as many as eight transports. Intel says their situation on Guadalcanal is becoming tenuous. We think this will be the last big attempt to defeat the Marines. Our mission is to stop them from getting to Cactus."

"What's coming with them?"

"There are five heavy and four light cruisers in Simpson Harbor right now, along with twelve destroyers. We have to assume that they'll all come along for this show. The coast watchers will give us warning when they leave, and I've asked for some submarine support to see if we can attrite the force on its way down. The 'when,' of course, remains the big question."

"But soon."

"Yes, soon. Halsey's moving some carrier divebombers to Henderson Field to beef up the attack forces. Their mission will be those eight transports which will be carrying the bulk of the troops. Our mission will be the warships. The bombers need daylight. Against four heavy cruisers, we'll need darkness."

"I'll need a staff," Sluff said.

"Here's what I suggest," Hollis said. "Get set

up on *J. B. King*; she'll be here by morning. Then meet with your skippers and ask them each to send one lieutenant to you for temporary duty. They'll all squawk and you'll probably get four if you're lucky. *New Orleans* here has a lieutenant commander who's being detached and his relief's already on board. I'll assign him as your chief staff officer."

"His name is Larry Price," Captain Hodges said. "Gunnery guy. Good officer. On his way back to the States to become XO in new construction."

"He know about this?" Sluff asked.

"Knows and volunteered to do it," Hollis said. "Look—we're on the knife edge here. The Japs will have heavier and more experienced forces and they are desperate to get these troops ashore, not to mention the food and medicines they'll need just to stay alive on Cactus. If we can bust that up, we'll have won even if we don't win the sea fight. The few—very few—prisoners the Marines have taken came in for food. If we can turn them back, the Japs on Cactus are doomed to starvation if nothing else."

Sluff nodded. "Piece of cake," he announced, with much more confidence than he felt. Maybe it was all the booze.

Hollis gave him a long, hard look. "You up for this, Sluff?" he asked. "That's a big piece of metal in your head bone there."

"Think of it as armor, Admiral," Sluff said.

THIRTY-FIVE

The Slot

Two weeks later, not one, Sluff was ensconced in the left-hand captain's chair on the bridge of *J. B. King* as the task group pushed its way north up into the Slot at twenty knots. They'd passed the Russell Islands to port just before midnight. One heavy cruiser, two light cruisers, and six destroyers, not eight. Hollis had striven mightily for a trained and intact team with no more of this grab-a-destroyer-when-you-can business. He had succeeded, mostly, having lost two of the Fletchers to a carrier group, which was going into the Central Pacific to raise some hell. *New Orleans* remained the flagship, but the two light cruisers, *Roanoke* and *Carson City*, had joined the force only five days before word came that the Japs were finally going to make the big reinforcement push.

He'd tried not to dwell on the disaster he'd created the last time he was in these waters, but Halsey's reappointment of him as a squadron commander took some of the sting out of that. He absolutely understood that Halsey might have done that because the other captains available and vying for the job had never fought the Japs at night. The good news was that he had had an entire two weeks to take his ships out to sea off New Caledonia and put them through their paces, starting slowly in daylight, then graduating to higher speeds and more dangerous maneuvers until finally they were doing it at night, darkened ship, radio-silent, while slicing through the calm South Pacific waters at thirty-five knots.

J. B. King was still running like a well-oiled machine. The commander who'd relieved him had suffered a ruptured appendix, which meant that his old XO, Bob Frey, was now in command. Sluff's press-gang efforts to form a staff had netted him two lieutenants and one JG. Lieutenant Commander Larry Price had turned out to be a real gem, quickly organizing the officers into an effective tactical staff. By the end of the two weeks, his staff could maneuver the six-destroyer formation like pros, unlike the two light cruisers, who'd seemed to stumble through their various tactical exercises. They had come over from the Atlantic Fleet, and it showed.

"Captain's on the bridge," the bosun's mate announced. A moment later, Bob Frey material-ized alongside Sluff's chair.

"Captain," Sluff said.

"Commodore," Bob replied solemnly.

Sluff had been glad to come back to *J. B. King.* The ship ran well and had, so far, manifested truly good luck in avoiding the destruction so many of her class had suffered in the past six months. Everyone who'd ever served in destroyers knew that there were some ships that seemed to just be better than all the rest, and *King* was one of them. Bob had been genuinely relieved and glad when he found out that Sluff had not been killed when *Barrett* had gone down. Sluff had spent hours recounting his various adventures, including those with the SOPAC chief of staff. Bob had told him that Browning had been sent to command a new aircraft carrier, which was doing shakedown training on the East Coast before coming out to the South Pacific. That meant he was about ten thousand miles away, which in Sluff's opinion was just about right.

"Is this gonna work?" Frey asked.

"I sure as hell hope so," Sluff said. "It is nice to be able to go into a night fight with a plan that wasn't generated on the fly for once. Hollis is shaping up to be a damned good task group commander."

"No plan survives first contact with the enemy," Bob quoted from von Moltke.

"Yeah, but thus far, we've gone in to too many of these battles with *no* plan, period. Like the battleship action, or Callaghan's collision with the entire Jap striking force. We have a plan, and we know that once we get into it, everything will change. But at least it's going to start with a plan, an offensive action plan. That's real progress, Bob."

"Yes, sir, I agree with that," Bob said. "But I'd sure like to see some of those battleships that run with the carrier groups, those very distant carrier groups, up in the line with us. Why the hell do we always go up against heavier odds while the bigger half of the gun fleet escorts carriers?"

"I hear you," Sluff said. "We're here because we're the only forces Halsey has to do this job right now, and besides, the Solomons is just one campaign."

"The Japs sure seem to think it's important."

"I think that when the Jap admirals sit down with some sake on the midwatch, they'll be coming to grips with some stark facts: We're going to get stronger here in the Pacific and they're only going to get weaker. Little bitty island nation. No oil. Surrounded by our subs. They lose a ship they can't replace it. We can and do. Up to now, they've been meat-grinding *us* here in the Slot. Pretty soon, though, within a year, anyway, they're gonna be the meat."

"But for tonight . . ." Bob said.

"Yup," Sluff said. "Tonight they've got the weight advantage."

Bob blew out a long breath, but had nothing more to say. He went back over to his captain's chair on the starboard side of the bridge.

Sluff saw him pick up the sound-powered handset next to his chair and then turn the barrel switch. JA—Sluff just knew it. The captain's battle circuit. He surreptitiously switched his own sound-powered phone-set to the JA circuit and listened in.

"All stations, this is the captain. I want to review the battle plan for tonight. Here's what's happening. Our task group is shaped like a trident headed north into the Slot, away from Guadalcanal. The destroyers are on either side of the formation axis in two divisions of three ships each. The three cruisers are three miles behind us. As soon as any ship of the force makes radar contact with the oncoming Japanese force, the tin cans will announce the contact by flashing light and then peel off to either side, speed up, and conduct a torpedo attack. The cruisers behind us will slow down and then turn perpendicular to the oncoming Jap column in order to bring all their guns to bear."

"The right-hand three-ship division, which is us, will come right and head up the *eastern* side of the Jap formation, while the other division will turn left and then go up the *western* side. At the preplanned range and bearing, we, the eastern division, will launch thirty torpedoes at the Jap force and then we will turn to match the Japanese course and speed, going south. When our fish begin to go off, we will open fire with guns. When the Japs start shooting back, the western division will run in from the other side and launch thirty more torpedoes and then they'll come around and match the Jap formation's course and speed. When their fish start hitting they will engage with guns while we, the eastern division, run for cover. Once all that gets started the cruiser force will open on the Jap columns from dead ahead with nine eight-inch and eighteen six-inch guns. There will be no radio comms until our division's torpedoes start going off. That's the plan. Stay loose."

Sluff nodded as he listened in. Couldn't have said it better myself, he thought, as he hung up the handset. Bob Frey ought to be a commander. That's your job, he realized—commodores were supposed to get their best ship captains promoted.

He looked at his new watch, which had a radium dial so he could see it in the dark. Based on the coast watchers' reports, the Japs ought to show up on their radars anytime in the next hour. He hoped it would be soon, because they were now in the widest portion of the Slot. If they went much farther north, the channel would narrow down and then the plan would fall victim to von Moltke's famous prophecy.

"Bridge, Combat, Sigs. Signal from the flag: Radar contact, bearing three four zero, range fifteen miles, closing, fast. Composition many. Execute plan."

Sluff punched down the switch on the bitch-box. "Acknowledge," he ordered, and then called Combat. *J. B. King* was leading the three-ship formation on the eastern side of the task group. Larry Price answered immediately, and then Sluff heard the orders going up to the signal bridge for the eastern division to turn together to 030, speed thirty-five knots. This order would be sent by red flashing light to the two ships behind *J. B. King*. Ninety seconds later he heard *King*'s forced-draft blowers spooling up as the ship turned to starboard and accelerated. Time for him to go down to Combat. He climbed out of his chair and grabbed his steel helmet and life jacket as the ship went to general quarters. He had to wait for the throng of sailors crashing up the interior ladders to man their topside battle stations. Then he went below.

"Commodore's in Combat," someone announced as Sluff came into the crowded space. It seemed incongruous that men who were assigned as plotters on the DRT still had to be in life jackets and helmets, but as Sluff knew only too well, one minute you could be plotting, the next, bleeding and swimming. He pressed two fingertips to the steel plate in his head, as if to reassure himself that it was still there. The ship's shipfitters had had to hammer out a bulge in Sluff's steel helmet to accommodate the plate.

"Everybody going where they're supposed to?" he asked Lieutenant Commander Price, who was a tall, thin, and hatchet-faced New Englander.

"Yes, sir, so far so good. We've got good skin

paint on our guys; nothing yet on the bad guys."

"The *New Orleans*'s radar is another eighty feet in the air, compared to ours," Sluff said. "We'll get 'em pretty soon."

"Radar contact, bearing three three zero, range twenty-three thousand yards. Contacts are fuzzy."

"Course and speed?"

"Need three minutes to calculate, sir."

"Okay," Sluff said. "Start passing our ranges and bearings to the targets to *Morgan* and *Whitfield* until they get contact. Order prep torpedo attack."

"TBS?" Price asked.

"Not yet—keep it visual."

Price gave him a look that said sending out a flashing-light message was going to take too long, but then called the signal bridge. Sluff knew what the problem was: If the Japs were coming at their usual speed, they'd be flashing past each other before they could get torpedoes away. Sluff had asked about Hollis' orders to maintain radio silence, especially when they got close, but the admiral had been adamant. No radio until the ambush had been sprung. Period. Memories of the Russell Islands ambush, Sluff supposed.

The Japs were now eleven, maybe ten miles northwest of them.

"*Morgan* and *Whitfield* do not hold the contacts," the radar talker announced.

Sluff realized this wasn't going to work. Even if

he turned right now and headed in for a torpedo attack, as long as his other ships still didn't hold firm contacts, they couldn't attack. They needed more time. The only way to get more time was to reverse course and slow down. That way, the Jap ships would be overtaking him at ten knots of relative speed instead of roaring at them at a closing rate of sixty knots. He was explaining this to Larry when the TBS erupted. One of the light cruisers, five miles behind them, announced she had radar contact on the approaching Japs and requested permission to open fire.

"Oh, shit!" Sluff exclaimed. So much for radio silence. So much for the plan, too.

Then the flagship came up on TBS and told the cruiser formation to open fire immediately. Sluff knew what had happened: Admiral Hollis, realizing that surprise had probably been lost, had decided to start shooting.

The destroyers were on their own. Von Moltke had been right. Now it was his ballgame.

"Commodore, the Japs are on a course of one seven zero, speed thirty-five."

Sluff didn't hesitate. He picked up the TBS handset, called the collective voice radio call sign for his three-ship division, and ordered them to perform an immediate-execute turn to starboard to course one seven zero. Both ships rogered and he felt *J. B. King* heeling to port as she leaned into the turn.

"Combat, Bridge, we see gun flashes to the south." It was Bob Frey's voice. "I think the cruisers have opened fire."

"I concur, Bob," Sluff said. "We're going to come about, slow down the relative speed of advance, and then conduct a torpedo attack while the Japs are busy with the cruisers."

"What happened to the plan?"

"What always happens to the plan?" Sluff responded angrily.

Then he called Dragon Murphy, the skipper of the lead destroyer in the western division of destroyers, who was also the de facto western division commander. He told Dragon to conduct a torpedo attack as soon as he could.

"What the hell's going on?" Dragon responded. "You attacking?"

"Affirmative," Sluff replied. "Launch your fish as soon as you have a solution, give 'em time to get there, and then open with guns."

"We're gonna be in the cruisers' line of fire if we do that," Dragon said.

"We all are, Dragon," Sluff replied. "The Japs won't know what hit 'em."

"Neither will we," the voice on the other end of the TBS circuit said. "But, roger, out."

Sluff turned to look at the plot. The Jap formation was on the plot, still headed south, although he knew that, by now, the hail of six- and eight-inch shells from the three cruisers must be falling all around them. His own destroyers were headed south, but still too far out to use their own torpedoes.

"The Japs slowing down?" he asked.

"I need the next radar mark to know that, sir," the senior plotter said. Then the surface-search radar operator sounded off. "They're turning," he shouted. "Turning left. East. *Towards* us."

"Good," Sluff said.

"Uh-oh," he heard Larry mutter.

"Yeah," Sluff said, realizing that his reputation for a frontal attack had preceded him. "Compute an approach course that will put them thirty degrees off our port bows once we turn around. We'll run right at them and then salvo the torpedoes."

Larry gulped and then worked his maneuvering board. The plotters' hands were flying over the table, making their marks as the radar lit up each Jap ship for a brief second. Sluff was dimly aware of reports coming in from the other destroyers—they held the enemy, they didn't. One deck below he could hear the forward torpedo mount training out and the torpedomen yelling settings at each other. "Zero four zero at twenty-five knots," Larry said finally.

"Immediate execute," Sluff replied, and Larry issued the orders over the TBS. Once again, *King* heeled as she came about. The plotters all grabbed the edge of the table to hang on.

"Combat, Bridge, the Japs are firing star shells at the cruisers. What are *we* doing?"

"They've turned east to do two things, Bob," Sluff said. "Fire torpedoes at our cruisers and get out of the kill zone they're in right now. I'm trying to get our division close enough to launch. Can you see them?"

"Just shell flashes," Bob said. "A lot of them, though."

"Well, hopefully they can't see us yet. As soon as you can fire your fish, let 'em go."

"Better tell the rest of our division that, then, sir," Bob said.

Sluff swore. Bob was right—he'd forgotten to do that. Larry Price was already on it as *King* steadied up on the new intercept course, belting out orders on the TBS. Then all they could do was wait. He stared at the plot. Course 040 seemed to be doing the trick, although some of the Japanese tracks were wobbling all over the place, as if they were slowing down.

"Range to nearest Jap heavy?" he asked.

"Ten thousand, five hundred," the radar operator called out.

"Time to launch position?" Sluff asked.

"Calculating."

He gritted his teeth. He knew his CIC team were doing their very best, but it still took time and several radar sweeps for them to be able to calculate what the targets were doing in relation to what they were doing. Their torpedoes couldn't be fired until the target's predicted position at end-of-run was a scant two miles away.

"Big explosion to the northwest of us," Bob called down. "And another one. Somebody's getting hits."

Sluff noticed that their western division was no longer being tracked on the table. That was the price for scaling the DRT down to a picture that concentrated on his own eastern division's torpedo problem.

"Four minutes to launch position," Larry said. "Torpedo control has a solution."

Sluff thought fast. The Japs were going to see his division coming if they closed in for the two-mile attack solution. There was an alternative. He hit the bitch-box switch.

"Bob, what if we fire our fish at the slow-speed setting—their range goes to nine thousand instead of forty-five hundred, right?"

"Yes, sir," Bob replied.

"Then we could fire now, before they see us."

There was a moment's pause. "Yes, sir, we could. We need a minute or so to reset the guidance systems."

"Do that and then launch when you have a solution."

"Aye, aye, sir."

Sluff turned to Larry. "Tell the rest of our division to launch torpedoes on *slow* speed and fire when ready. Then issue an immediate execute to slow our formation to fifteen knots on a course that matches whatever the Japs are doing."

Larry got the orders out and the other two ships rogered up. He then asked Sluff why they were slowing. Ordinarily a staff officer wouldn't ask a question like that in the middle of a fight, but Sluff realized Larry was simply trying to keep up with his commodore's reasoning.

"It's a really dark night," he said. "If we go twenty-five to thirty knots, they'll see our bow waves. At fifteen there won't be any bow waves. As soon as our fish start hitting we'll open with guns and kick the speed back up."

"Sir, the longer we creep along here, the sooner our own cruisers' firing arcs are going to include us."

"I agree, so when the gunshoot starts, we are going to head *west,* not east. That's the fastest way for us to get across the cruisers' line of fire."

A talker reported that *J. B. King*'s fish were swimming. Teatime was in four minutes.

"Combat, Bridge," Bob called. "We're hearing shells passing overhead. Based on the light show north of us, they're going both ways. Those have to be heavy cruisers up there."

Sluff acknowledged and then told Larry to tell the flag where they were in relation to the Jap ships they were shooting at. His destroyers should be safe, since the distance between the two cruiser forces was nearly thirteen miles, which meant the shells were traveling high. Still, it was nerve-racking, with dozens of eight- and six-inch shells howling overhead as the cruisers conducted a long-range gunnery duel. With any luck, his eastern division would be out of the line of fire by the time their torpedoes got in among the Japs.

"Three minutes," Larry said, as they all stared at the evolving plot on the DRT. And then Bob Frey called down from the bridge, his voice audibly excited. "Explosions north of us, lots of them. Sounds like torpedoes."

Not ours, Sluff thought. Dragon had made his own attack. Good!

"Gun flashes north and west, sounds and looks like five-inch. I think Dragon's going in."

Sluff was torn. He really wanted to be out on a bridge wing right now, seeing what Bob Frey was seeing. He stared down at the lighted DRT table, not seeing it. Then he focused. *This* was the tactical picture. Up on the bridge they could hear shells and see flashes, but that was *not* the tactical picture. The smudgy No. 2 pencil squiggles on the DRT trace paper—that was the picture.

"Get your guns ready, Bob," Sluff replied. "We're almost there."

"Commodore," Larry said. "We should turn now—that way our guns will be settled on a steady course and speed when we open fire."

"Good call, Larry, get the orders out," Sluff said.

Larry put out an immediate-execute to the division, turning them due west and accelerating to twenty-seven knots now that the fish were gone. A moment later, Bob Frey called down reporting more explosions as their own torpedoes slammed home.

Sluff turned to Larry. "All ships, commence firing."

Larry had barely finished speaking into the handset when all five of *J. B. King*'s went to work, firing in rapid-continuous mode under director control, blasting away as fast as the crews could load the guns and the magazine crews could push more shells up the hoists.

Sluff blew out a long breath. He'd done his job. Now it was up to the gun crews of his three destroyers and Dragon's three destroyers, a total of thirty five-inch guns punching out fifteen rounds per minute each. Four hundred fifty rounds a minute being fired at a cluster of Jap ships who'd already been attacked by sixty torpedoes and the concentrated fire of one heavy and two light cruisers. As the status reports flew around Combat, Sluff studied the unfolding track charts. The enemy force was still headed generally east but their speed was falling off rapidly. They can see us now, he thought, and even if they're being hit, they can launch their own torpedoes, not to mention start hurling eight-inch shells at our little line of destroyers. Then he realized something, looking at the track geometry: It's not "can launch"; it's "*have* launched."

"Larry," he said, "torpedoes are coming. We have to maneuver. Turn the formation to due north by column movement. Immediate execute. As soon as we're on course, order a cease-firing."

This time Larry didn't ask any questions. He sent the corpen signal out by TBS and then executed it. *J. B. King* heeled to port as she swung around to the north, headed for a track behind the enemy cruiser-destroyer formation, with *Morgan* and *Whitfield* in hot pursuit. Her guns continued to blast away during the maneuver, making it hard to hear reports in Combat.

Sluff held his breath. Did we turn in time? The Type 93 Long Lance came at you at nearly sixty miles an hour. Larry ordered the radar tracker to report the positions of the two ships behind them every minute so that he would know when to order the cease-fire.

"*Morgan*'s made the turn," Larry said. "C'mon *Whitfield*."

Then Sluff swore. The tracker marking *Whitfield*, the third ship in his formation, started making marks on top of one another. Something had happened back there. He called Bob on the bridge.

"Can you see *Whitfield*?" he asked.

"Wait one," Bob shouted back over the banging of the two forward gun mounts. Then he was back. "She's not visible and not firing. *Morgan* is right behind us, but *Whitfield* is *not* visible."

"Track shows *Whitfield* has stopped," Larry said. "Recommend the cease-fire order now, sir."

Sluff put up his hand in a wait-one gesture. In his concern about *Whitfield*, Sluff had forgotten to give the cease-fire order. Had the Japs caught their ninety-degree course change to the north? Had those canny bastards detected the fact that the bearing to all those five-inch gun flashes had stabilized for a minute and then begun to draw north? A moment later, three solid thumps penetrated the ship's hull from near misses going off close aboard.

Yes, they had. A frantic call from Bob on the bridge confirmed what they'd heard down in Combat.

"Combat, Bridge, heavy stuff, incoming. And star shells. And something else—we just saw a big explosion south of us. Magazine-size."

One of the cruisers had eaten a Long Lance, Sluff thought. They couldn't just keep steaming in a straight line anymore, now that the Japs could see them. He had three choices: keep going north to run behind the enemy formation and start a broad weave to defeat their optical gun directors, or turn west again and try to outrun the Jap heavy cruiser's gunfire, or, finally, turn east and run right at them.

Multiple thumps erupted around them, sounding

closer this time, but from the other side. He realized at least one of their heavies had trained her entire eight-inch gun battery on them and was now bracketing and halving. Cease firing? Or keep firing?

"Range and bearing to the Jap formation?" he asked, trying to keep his voice calm.

"Zero eight one and down to eight thousand yards, Commodore," the radar operator said in a voice that was definitely not calm. Outside, *King*'s five-inch guns continued to hammer away at the Jap formation, shaking the bulkheads and causing a fine rain of dust to settle over Combat. Gun smoke had begun to infiltrate the vents.

So at least one Jap heavy cruiser was still in business, he thought, and she was focusing her guns on their little formation. An ear-thumping blast punched down through the overhead in Combat as something big exploded directly overhead, audibly raining shrapnel all over the ship. Nothing penetrated all the way into CIC, but it was obvious the Japs had found the correct range. Then the radar operator swore and announced he'd lost the picture.

Time to decide.

"Cease firing," he ordered. Larry repeated that to their one remaining ship, *Morgan*.

"Come right by column movement to one one zero, speed three-five," he ordered. Once again, Larry sent the order out to *Morgan* by TBS. Below and behind them, they could hear *King*'s forced-draft blowers spool up into a banshee scream as the ship went to full power. All the fixtures in CIC began to shake, rattle, and roll.

"Recommence firing when the turn is complete," Sluff said. "They can see us now; no reason not to shoot at them."

Larry's expression bordered on panic. The commodore was going to run right at them. Again. "Why?" he asked softly, as *King* straightened up from the turn and then settled into a thirty-five-knot lunge at their enemies.

"We can't outrun an eight-inch gun," Sluff said. "They can shoot eighteen miles; we're only four miles away. They'll expect us to run west." He looked up at the small sea of pale faces looking at him in the red light. "We're not gonna run," he said. "We're gonna go right at them and tear those bastards up."

He looked down at the plot one last time. The pencil lines were all merging. Time to go topside.

"I'm going to the bridge," he announced. "Larry, tell the flag we're headed *into* the Jap formation. Tell Dragon, too; he may be able to help."

"Aye, aye, sir," Larry said, but his face was white.

Combat, without radar, had become superfluous. The plotters, trackers, talkers, and the radar operator all stared, openmouthed, at the commodore as he left CIC.

THIRTY-SIX

The Slot

When he got to the top of the ladder leading out to the pilothouse, Sluff had to step aside as corpsmen ushered wounded men down toward the primary battle dressing station in the wardroom. He confronted a bloody scene when he finally stepped out onto the bridge. The shell that had taken out the radar had shredded much of the bridge with shrapnel, and there were still wounded men lying on the deck. He wondered why no one was attending to them and then realized it was because they were dead. He looked for the skipper.

Bob Frey was in his chair, his forearms covered in bloody bandages. The forward gun mounts were still blasting away to port into the darkness ahead of them, and the wind from their thirty-five-knot advance across the dark sea was streaming through a hundred holes in the pilothouse's bulkheads and overhead. Sluff hurried over to Frey's chair. The captain looked up at him, blinked a few times, and then passed out. Sluff saw that there was more blood seeping out from under the bottom of his life jacket and that his helmet had holes in it. Someone had fastened his seat belt, which was the only thing holding him in his chair.

Then three star shells burst in quick succession, and Sluff finally got a visual look at their enemy. A Chikuma-class heavy cruiser was off their port bow at a distance of only a few thousand yards. The ship was down by the stern and there was no bow wave visible, but the Chikumas carried all four of their twin-barreled eight-inch guns forward. Every one of them was pointed at *J. B. King*. As he stared, openmouthed in speechless horror, all eight guns fired right at them. A tornado of shells howled overhead, ripping the night sky with a hot, slashing sound. Sluff and everyone else still alive on the bridge instinctively ducked, as if that would save them.

High, he thought. They went high. He stood up. *J. B. King*'s five-inch were still firing away at the Chikuma, and they were getting hits, too, as the dull red boattails of each round bore across the close distance in a hot, flat arc and buried themselves in her superstructure, each one followed by a blast of flame that tore out parts of that fearsome pagoda structure.

He looked past the Chikuma. Behind her were the remains of what looked like four Jap destroyers. One was upside down, her dark hull covered with figures climbing out of a burning oil slick. Her propellers were clearly visible, as was an enormous hole in her midsection.

A second was in two pieces, the bow upside down and partially submerged, the back half floating calmly as if nothing had happened, but smoking from every orifice. Beyond that he saw two, possibly three more wrecks, all burning brightly. The flares burned out as *King* surged past the crippled cruiser, her guns straining aft as she tried to stay on the wounded beast. Then behind them there was a gigantic explosion, which once again lit the seascape. Sluff ran out to the port bridge wing in time to see his sole remaining destroyer, *Morgan*, disappearing in the fiery throes of a magazine explosion. He looked back at the Chikuma, which was training those eight guns in *King*'s direction again, even though she was paralyzed.

"Left full rudder," Sluff yelled, and the helmsman, so scared that he was crying, spun the wheel. *King* heeled to starboard and began to turn across the cruiser's bow, even as she got off another salvo of eight-inch. All the rounds went astern, blowing up in noisy succession right behind them. *King*'s guns, now given a clear field of fire, continued to blast raking shells at the cruiser. She was afire now from stem to stern, and even though *King*'s five-inch could not penetrate her armored spaces, there could not be too many people still alive above her main deck. Then Sluff saw one of the Chikuma's secondary, five-inch mounts spit fire in their direction. This was followed by two hits on *King*, one along her port side, which ricocheted off into the water. The second went off in the air at about bridge-wing height, once again flailing *King*'s superstructure with shrapnel. Sluff reflexively turned his head and ducked as a piece of metal smacked him right on his steel plate and made him see stars. He shook his head, stood back up, and felt the plate. There was a palpable dent. He started to laugh but then recognized incipient hysteria.

Sluff ordered the helmsman to steady up as *King* rushed through the gap between the cruiser and the two shattered destroyers. Astern, the immolation of *Morgan* subsided into a massive cloud of eerily glowing steam, which was quenching the lives of nearly three hundred officers and men.

Then they were alone, and somewhere out there in the darkness there was another ship that had managed to put a torpedo into *Morgan*.

"Cease firing," Sluff yelled to the Gun Control talker.

"Wha-a-t?" the astonished talker replied.

"God *damn* your eyes, *cease firing!*" Sluff roared, and the astonished talker relayed the message to the gunnery officer.

"Right standard rudder," he ordered. The Jap gunners tracked their gun flashes, and if they were on the ball, torpedoes were already coming for them. "All ahead standard, turns for fifteen knots."

The replacement helmsman, who was manning both the rudder and the engine order telegraph, repeated the order, and then *King* began to slow down as she slewed to starboard.

Now, he thought. We have to find that bastard. Standing by his chair, he picked up the sound-powered phone handset, switched to the JC circuit, and called Gun Control. He didn't recognize the voice that answered. He asked for a name.

"Chief Gonzalez," the voice replied. "I've got the conn up here. Gun boss, director officer are gone."

"Okay, Chief," Sluff said. "This is the commodore. I need you to put up some star shells, on an arc between three zero zero and zero five zero true. There's another Jap out there and we need to find him. We have no radar."

"Hell, Commodore," the chief said. "I know that. I'm standing on the fucking antenna. Director one is out. The mounts are in local control. Lemme see what we can do."

"Light up the sky, Chief, and then be ready to go back to work. It could be a cruiser out there."

"Good deal, Commodore."

For the next two minutes Sluff kept maneuvering the ship through various courses and speeds. Now that *King* wasn't shooting, the Japs should not be able to see them. The wounded cruiser was dropping farther behind them, her burning superstructure the only evidence of her presence. Sluff wondered where his own cruisers were, and whether or not they'd gotten the message that he was going to attack into the Jap formation. And where was Dragon?

Suddenly the two forward gun mounts began to fire, their barrels pointed high, as they punched out a series of parachute flare shells into the night sky. After a minute of this the sky lit up with the eye-searing glare of magnesium parachute-flares in all directions. Sluff stared out into the suddenly painful bright light, looking for—

There she was: a Hamakaze-class destroyer, four thousand yards away and coming at full speed, her bow wave so large that her entire front end was obscured. Without orders, the chief up in gun control ordered *King*'s five mounts to open fire on her immediately. As Sluff watched, the Jap destroyer began turning hard to port to present her guns and torpedo tubes, but as she did so, the shells from *King*'s guns hit her all along her length and she burst into flames and began to slow. She was only three thousand yards away now, but her guns were strangely silent as *King*'s guns punched shell after shell into her, some hitting low along the hull, some hitting along her main decks. When he saw live steam erupting from her sides, he knew she was done for. He was amazed at how well *King*'s gun crews were scoring hits because each one was firing in local control: a pointer and a trainer gripping their yokes in the gun houses, staring through 7 × 50 binoculars slaved to the yokes. At this close range, however, wherever they centered their crosshairs, that's where the shells went, and within a minute, the Hamakaze was a flaming wreck, steam roaring out of her shattered stacks and her twin-barreled guns pointed off at odd angles. Finally, a five-inch shell found one of her magazines, and the ship exploded in a white-hot blast.

Once Sluff could see again, she was gone. King's guns continued to fire into the glowing cloud of smoke and steam, and then, one by one, they went silent. The flares sputtered out as they fell into the sea with their parachutes on fire. With his ears ringing, Sluff ordered the helmsman to put the rudder over to port five degrees. He didn't give a course order. He wanted King to turn slowly in the darkness until he *knew* there were no more Japs out there readying torpedoes for him. Behind them they could hear the sinking Jap destroyer's depth charges going off. He called Combat.

"Heard anything from the flag?" he asked as he looked around the pilothouse, which was a blood-spattered mess. In the dimmed red lights it looked worse than it probably was.

"Negative, sir," Larry said. "We can't raise anybody. I think all our antennas are gone."

"We just sank a Jap destroyer," Sluff said. "There's a heavy cruiser somewhere behind us, but she seemed to be out of action. We've lost both *Morgan* and *Whitfield*, I'm afraid."

"We're still in the dark down here," Larry said. "I've sent some people topside to see what's happened to the radar."

"The radar antenna is physically down on the signal bridge, so we're gonna be blind for a while. I think there's one more cruiser unaccounted for."

"Well, we've totally lost the picture down here, Commodore," Larry said. "I've got the radio gang headed topside to see if they can get us a working antenna. Gun plot says we're about out of ammo for the five-inch and that they have a lot of shrapnel casualties topside among the AA gun crews. Recommend we come west and get the hell out of here."

Sluff looked at the gyrocompass repeater. They were still turning left, passing 300 degrees true.

"Okay," he said. "I'll steady up on two seven zero. Whatever exploded overhead took out a lot of the bridge and director personnel, too. The skipper is unconscious so I'm in command up here for the moment. See if you can find the ship's exec and get him up here."

"Yes, sir, I'll get on that, although his GQ station was back aft at secondary conn," Larry said. "Um, that's topside."

"Well I know," Sluff said. The exec probably would have been in Combat except for the fact that Sluff and his staff had taken up all the room. Now he was probably one of the shrapnel casualties.

"See what you can find out," he said. "But I don't want to stay on any course for too long in case there are more torpedo shooters out there. It's darker'n a well digger's ass out here. The GQ quartermaster bled all over the chart so I don't even know where we are."

"Combat, aye. We're reconstructing a DR plot from the DRT and our own nav charts. I'll keep the course recommendations coming to keep us weaving."

"Very well," Sluff said. He told the helmsman to slow to twelve knots and then began to reconstitute the bridge team. *King*'s crewmen were well trained and were doing what had to be done to get the ship back together again. There were corpsmen attending to the wounded and men from a damage-control team moving the dead out to the bridge wings. The ship's chief corpsman and two other men had removed Bob Frey to his cabin down below to assess his injuries. Sluff called main control to get a status on the main plant, which was undamaged except for holes in both stacks, which were impeding airflow to the boilers. Main Control said they could give him twenty knots, tops. He heard a phone-talker say that Combat was recommending 240 as the next course.

"Helmsman, come left to two four zero," he said, mechanically, and then went over to the unit commander's chair and sat down. He almost called for some damned coffee until he remembered that just about everyone left on the bridge had been hurt, or worse. He rested his head o the coarse canvas fabric of his life jacket collar and closed his eyes. Had they won this one, or lost? He realized he had no idea.

The ship's executive officer, Lieutenant Commander Walker, reported to the bridge. Sluff thought he had been wounded, based on all the black splotches on his life jacket and khaki trousers, but he was uninjured.

"Commodore, you sent for me, sir?"

"I did," Sluff said. "Your skipper is unconscious with undetermined injuries. Go over to the log and make an entry that you're assuming temporary command. Then go down to Combat and get the picture, such as it is, from Larry Price. Figure out a course to get us back to the cruiser formation as soon as possible."

Walker gulped and said, "Aye, aye, sir."

And good luck to you, young man, Sluff thought. He closed his eyes again and wondered if he dared get some sleep. He touched the steel plate again. It felt a bit loose, as did his brain. He tried to gather his thoughts, think out what they needed to do next, but it was hard. He mostly wanted to close his eyes.

THIRTY-SEVEN

Ironbottom Sound

"Commodore?" a voice said in an uncertain tone.

"Yup?" Sluff said, trying to sit forward in his chair without breaking his painfully stiff neck. It was still dark but he thought he saw some gray in the distance ahead of the ship. There was a strange dazzle around the perimeter of his vision.

"We have comms with the flag," the voice said. Sluff focused on the face. It was *King*'s exec. "Lieutenant Commander Price says we'll rendezvous in about an hour."

"Very well," Sluff said, automatically. "Where are we?"

"About thirty miles north-northwest of Savo," the exec said. "We're on one five zero, speed twenty. That's the best the blowers can give us."

"How's the captain?" Sluff asked.

Walker swallowed. "He died, sir, about two hours ago. Doc said he probably had a stroke from all that metal in his head. It came right through his helmet."

"Damn," Sluff said. "That's a real loss."

"Yes, sir. The ship's not that badly damaged, but we have twenty-seven killed and I don't know how many wounded from that one shell that hit the radar, alone."

Sluff could picture it. All those AA gun crews exposed up on the 01 level, plus the torpedo gang, the signalmen, the lookouts, the gunnery officer and his talkers up near the director, and the depth-charge crews back on the fantail. "You let the flag know all this?"

"Yes, sir, they want us to rendezvous and then we're all headed for Tulagi. The radiomen say they've been talking to the cruisers, back-channel. *Carson City* took three torpedoes, blew up, and sank. *New Orleans* was hit by eight-inch shellfire but is still operational, and *Roanoke* wasn't hit at all. The admiral wants you to highline to *New Orleans* when we join up."

"I'll just bet he does," Sluff said wearily. "Okay, *Captain,* carry on."

"I'm just acting, sir. I mean—"

"Believe me, I know the feeling, Mister Walker. Acting or not, you are the captain now. Start thinking like one. Appoint one of the department heads as your acting exec. Let him handle the details of running the ship's daily routine. All your officers right now are heads down, tangled in the details of recovery. You're the one who needs to think ahead—you need fuel, ammo, medical care, repairs, replacements."

"Yes, sir," Walker said. Sluff could see from Walker's expression that it was all starting to sink in. At that moment, Lieutenant Commander Walker looked to be about sixteen.

"And ask Mister Price to come see me."

Larry Price came up to the bridge a few minutes later. By then dawn was breaking and the true extent of the damages topside was becoming painfully obvious.

"Commodore," Larry said. "Big night."

"Bad night," Sluff said. "My old ship's been hurt bad."

"Yes, sir, but the Japs have been hurt worse. That convoy of army troops has been reported holding just north of the Russells. The Cactus air forces are getting ready to go kill it."

"The admiral wants me to highline over once we rendezvous," Sluff said. "You may or may not see me again."

Larry smiled. "No, sir," he said. "I don't think it's gonna be like that at all."

His chief staff officer turned out to be right. *New Orleans* herself showed a fair amount of topside damage, but apparently her vitals inside the armor belt were all still intact. Sluff noticed that there were a lot of sailors up on her main deck and 01 level who looked a lot like water-logged survivors who'd been plucked out of the water. As he climbed out of the highline chair, a doctor climbed in for the ride back to *King*. There were three corpsmen waiting to follow the doctor over.

Admiral Hollis himself greeted Sluff as he began shucking his life jacket.

"Welcome aboard, Sluff," the admiral said. "You and your destroyers did some good work last night."

Sluff was not entirely sure of what the admiral was talking about, but he went through the motions as the two of them walked forward toward flag country. He tried desperately not to yawn as they climbed the ladders to the 01 and then the 02 level, where the admiral's cabin and offices were. The small clumps of survivors backed away when they saw the admiral, some of them coming to attention while others just stared. Their dungarees were rumpled and smelled of fuel oil, and several of the men were sporting bandages. The admiral slowed and then started talking to some of them as they made their way forward on the cruiser's AA gun decks, where, Sluff noted, the gun crews were all still in place. He also saw the mounds of body bags stacked in a nice row between the stacks.

Once in the admiral's cabin Sluff sank gratefully into a chair while the admiral, who seemed to be running on a caffeine high, paced back and forth, rubbing his hands together.

"It was a victory, Sluff," he said. "We creamed them. You guys *really* creamed them, and we put down two of their heavy ships. We lost *Carson City* but I swear to God, it was her own damned fault. I turned the formation to get out of torpedo water and she did *not* follow us around. Next thing I knew there was a volcano erupting at the back of the formation and she was just—gone. But: We got into it with at least one heavy cruiser. They got some licks in, but radar won the night. We literally shelled the heavy into a flaming wreck and then got the light cruiser with her. I remembered what you'd said about torpedoes, so we'd fire for a minute, make a major turn, then start back up again."

Sluff nodded, glad to hear that something had worked out according to plan last night.

The admiral kept going. "Your initial attack was apparently devastating. We could see when your fish started hitting and it looked like the Fourth of July out there. We also saw a bunch of radar contacts turn around and head back north, so we guessed that was the troopship convoy. Marine bombers are already on their way to see what they can do."

"I split my squadron into two divisions, like we planned," Sluff said. "Three ships each. Dragon Murphy took one west, I took the other half east. *King*'s all that's left of my half, and I don't know where Dragon went after he made his torpedo attack."

"We saw his formation go in and then back out. Then he turned north, went up and around the Japs, probably firing five-inch. Then he came back down their east side, which is when I told him to stand clear because he was headed into our firing arcs. Once you went back at the Japs, though, we had to stop firing, which was a good thing because they had already fired torpedoes at our gun flashes. Like I said, I remembered your rule about going dark and making bold course changes, so that's what we did. Or two of us did, anyway. Those were *Carson City*'s survivors I was talking to out there. I've sent one of Dragon's ships back to the sinking site to make sure we got 'em all. Japs'll be busy with the Cactus air force right about now."

"Speaking of which," Sluff said. "I need to get my people in *King* attended to and then go back to pick up any survivors from *Morgan* and *Whitfield*."

"Dragon's been in the area since daybreak, doing just that," the admiral said, finally sitting down. "They're recovering a fair number, too, thank God."

Sluff closed his eyes for a moment, suddenly weary beyond telling.

"Halsey was right," the admiral said. "Putting you back in. You did exactly what he was looking for—you went *after* the sonsabitches. Dragon Murphy was told to get clear and that's what he did—got clear. You found yourself in deep shit and turned on them instead."

"At the cost of two destroyers," Sluff reminded him. "And Bob Frey. That's a real loss."

The admiral grunted but did not reply. Sluff's steel plate was bothering him for some reason, and he went to put his right hand on it, but his arm was just too heavy.

An hour and a half later a quiet Negro voice asked him if he'd like some coffee and some breakfast. Sluff started in his chair, and then realized he'd gone to sleep while talking to the admiral. The cabin was empty now, except for him and the steward, and *New Orleans* was under way with a purpose. Based on the light coming through the portholes, she was headed east.

"I'd love some of both," he said to the steward, who showed him to a side table. As he was finishing up, the cabin door opened and the admiral and three of his staff officers came in.

"Oh, good, you're awake," the admiral said, beaming.

Sluff went to stand up but the admiral waved him back into his chair. "Sorry about that, sir," Sluff said.

The admiral dismissed his apology. "We're coming into Tulagi in about twenty minutes," he said. "I took the liberty of getting your ops officer on board so that we could complete the after-action report, but the big news is that Halsey himself is flying up from Nouméa."

The admiral sat down at his desk and invited his staffers to find chairs. "Marine air got at that convoy this morning and then again a half hour ago. Tore it up pretty good, although that's based on aviator reports." There were grins all around. Everyone knew about aviator reports.

"Was there a light cruiser with them?" Sluff asked.

"There was, but not anymore," the admiral said, proudly. "Now, Halsey wants to see you, and me, of course. But apparently, mostly you. Are your uniforms on *King*?"

"Yes, sir," Sluff said, risking a look at his own bloodstained uniform. Bob Frey's blood, he realized. Jesus.

"Okay, you take a boat back to *King* when we get in and get spruced up, then return aboard here. I know you're tired. We all are, but this fight last night may have marked a turning point, especially for the Marines on the 'Canal. Does that thing hurt?"

Sluff realized he'd been probing the steel plate with his fingertips. "Not really, Admiral. It mostly feels—strange."

"Okay then, Commodore, and once again, congratulations on a nice piece of work with your destroyers." They heard the ship's forced-draft blowers slowing down, indicating they were beginning the entrance into Tulagi's harbor. "My aide will get you back to the quarterdeck. I've told *King* to lay to nearby." He looked at his watch. "The admiral will be here in about two hours."

"Aye, aye, sir," Sluff said, getting up. He found

himself a bit unsteady on his feet and realized that the staff officers were looking at him, their expression reflecting concern. "Cruisers," he said. "Don't know how to walk on a cruiser. Doesn't move around enough."

There were polite smiles all around, and then the aide was beckoning.

THIRTY-EIGHT

Tulagi Harbor

Halsey was late. It seemed he had seen the hospital vehicles moving like a heavily burdened train from the piers to the field hospital at Tulagi as his plane came in for a landing. He had jumped into a passing jeep and gone up to visit the troops. *New Orleans* swung at the hook about a half mile offshore, side boys in fresh whites sweating while waiting on the port quarterdeck. The ship's port side was clear. Hidden from view on the starboard side were ammo barges, a fuel barge, and a stores barge. Sluff and most of the admiral's staff were lounging around in the flag cabin, discreetly looking at their watches. A hurriedly cleaned-up motor whaleboat and crew bobbed at the Tulagi fleet landing waiting for their very important guest.

With Bob Frey gone, Sluff had permanently

taken over the inport cabin in *King*. Old Mose, who seemed to be genuinely older and perhaps even a little bit sad, had promptly fixed him up with a clean uniform and shined shoes. Mose had truly admired Bob Frey, and Sluff had commiserated with him for a few minutes. Mose had apologized for the lack of fat pills. The ship's baker had been a pointer on the port forty-millimeter mount when the shell had exploded over the ship.

Then he summoned the exec and got a report on *King*'s readiness for sea. She still had no radar, although there was a chance they could swap an antenna and some new waveguide out with a destroyer that was headed back to the States for an overhaul. Fuel, boiler feed-water, fresh water, and ammo were being topped off. The wounded had been sent ashore, and the dead were laid out on the fantail in preparation for burial at sea, probably this evening. The ship's baker was among them.

Now resting in an armchair in the flag cabin aboard *New Orleans*, he wondered what he would say when he saw Halsey again. There was probably going to be a medal ceremony—Halsey liked to do that. If one of his commanders hurt the enemy, Halsey would pin a medal on his shirt as soon afterward as possible. That would then allow the commander to authorize medals for individual ship captains, officers, and crewmen who had distinguished themselves in battle.

Sluff's problem was that didn't think he had distinguished himself in battle.

He remembered von Moltke's maxim and even talking to Bob Frey about it before the shooting started. He had a sneaking suspicion that Hollis and maybe even Halsey though that he, Sluff Wolf, had run some kind of brilliant tactical exercise out there in the dark, when, in fact, it had been chaos. If it hadn't been for Larry Price reminding him to do this or do that, he'd have gotten them all killed. As it was, he had two more destroyers sunk to his everlasting credit—or shame. He wondered if he'd sunk more Japs or Americans in his brief stint as commodore. He heard eight bells sound over the ship's announcing system as Hollis's aide stepped through the cabin door.

"Gentlemen, Admiral Halsey's on his way up," the aide announced. Everyone put down coffee mugs, doused cigarettes, stood up, and made sure their uniforms were shipshape.

Halsey followed Hollis through the door. He had a huge grin on his face as he looked around the cabin before fixing his eyes on Sluff.

"I took a chance on you, Harmon Wolf," he said in a loud voice. "And by God, sir, you rang the bell. *Damned* if you didn't. Come over here and stand to attention."

An aide handed Halsey a small, opened box from which he withdrew a Navy Cross, a decoration second only to the Medal of Honor. He pinned it on Sluff's shirt and then shook his hand. Then he turned to the rest of the assembled officers.

"Commodore Wolf and his destroyers found themselves between a rock and a hard place last night. Our own cruisers were shooting over his head and the Japs were spitting out torpedoes at him. What did he do? He turned on those yellow devils. Turned around and went after the biggest ship in their formation, and did so much top-side damage that *no* one was in charge of that formation for an entire hour. This is what I want when any of you meet up with the Japs at sea— attack, attack, *attack!*"

He paused for a moment to get his breath. "And by the way, we've already heard from Pearl Intel: Two heavy cruisers, one light cruiser, four destroyers sunk. Seven of the ten transports, with over six *thousand* Jap infantry on board, bombed and sunk. One light cruiser, two destroyers limping back to Rabaul, trailing oil they can't replace. The Japs don't know what hit them, but I do: sixty torpedoes, to start with. Then the concentrated fire of one heavy and two light cruisers, about whom the Japs knew *nothing!* And every time they figured it out, their tormentors went dark, maneuvered, and then came at them again from a different direction with eight-inch, six-inch, and five-inch.

"Now, there's plenty of praise to go around. Bob

Hollis, here, was in charge of this fight and it is he who can claim the victory. It wasn't without cost, of course—it never is. But let me tell you something: I think the Jap high command is squatting around their rice bowls this morning and asking themselves some very tough questions about their chances of prevailing on Guadalcanal. This was their big push—land one more fresh division on the island, along with ammo, medicines, and food, and tip the scale in their favor. It didn't happen. Because of you, because of all of *you*. My heartfelt congratulations and gratitude for a job exceedingly well done. I need some coffee."

Sluff felt more than a little embarrassed to be the only one sporting a medal. God knew there were lots more candidates out there, some of them already asleep in the deep. As the staff officers gathered around Halsey and Hollis, two stewards came in with trays of coffee. Sluff suddenly felt very tired. His steel plate was throbbing ever so slightly, so he slipped into the nearest chair, took a mug of coffee from one of the stewards, and sipped it with trembling hands.

Trembling?

That was new. Probably just physical exhaustion, he thought. Except, the colors in the cabin suddenly looked—wrong. The light coming through the portholes was really dazzling, if just the least bit out of focus. He felt a burning on his right hand and realized he was spilling hot coffee on his hand. He put the cup down on a side table and took a deep breath. He could hear the buzz of conversation all around him, Halsey vigorously gesticulating as he banged on about attack, attack, attack, and the staffers, all trying to get in front of the Boss. But he could not make out their individual words. He could hear just fine, though, loud even, but could not make out a word.

Well, Sluff thought, that was as it should be. Want to get ahead—catch the attention of the admirals. He touched the steel plate with his right hand. It felt a little wet. He withdrew his hand and looked at his fingertips.

Red. Oh, God, he thought, what now?

He held his fingers in front of his face for almost ten seconds and then felt a disturbance in his balance. He was listing, yes, that's what he was doing. Listing to starboard, and now there was a low roaring noise in the cabin, the sum of all the talk. The last thing he heard, and he could indeed make these words out: "Oh, shit—the commodore."

THIRTY-NINE

Nouméa Field Hospital

"What is it with you, Harmon Wolf," a woman's voice said. "You *like* being in this hospital?"

Sluff mumbled something and then recognized the aftereffects of general anesthesia. Again. Cotton mouth. Cold. A heaviness in his lungs. A mushy-feeling blob of bandages on the right side of his head. He opened one eye and saw a familiar face. Tina Danfield.

"You're still very pretty," he said.

She rolled her eyes but did it with a smile. "And you're still lying here with a hole in your head. I thought we were all over that nonsense."

"Apparently not," he said. He looked for some water and she handed him the familiar metal cup filled with ice shavings and a straw. "What did they do this time?"

"New plate, some brain surgery, consisting of technical medical terms I can't even pronounce, much less understand, and then orders for stroke medication."

"That's what I had on the flagship—a stroke?"

"They think so. You need to know that the entire surgical staff is talking about the fact that there was a *dent* in your original plate?"

"Jap five-inch round went off outside the pilot-house. Lots of shrapnel. I ducked, but apparently it ricocheted off the back bulkhead and got me in the head bone. One of the talkers told me that."

"So the plate saved your life, is what you're saying?"

"Apparently," he said, sipping some more ice-melt. "But you mentioned stroke, so it didn't save my fabulous naval career, did it."

She sat down on the edge of the bed and took his hand. His was cold; hers was nice and warm. "You, sir, are all done," she said. She reached inside her uniform pocket and produced the Navy Cross. She put it on his night table. "The pre-op people were putting your bloody uniform into the trash until someone saw this. Apparently you went out with a bang."

"So to speak."

She grinned. "Yeah, so to speak. We all thought you'd be sent home after the last visit here, but we know what happened to that."

"Halsey mentioned you, when he and I talked down in the mess hall. Said it was you who told him what was going on."

"I may have said a few words about that ass, Browning," she said. She hadn't turned loose of his hand and he was glad of that.

"Thank you," he said. "He sent me back out and he's pleased with the results, although if he only knew . . ."

"The 'results,' as you call it, are the biggest news of this campaign so far," she said. "However."

"Uh-oh," he said.

"However, since you've had traumatic brain injury followed by a stroke, your days as a dashing commodore are indeed over. Now—tell the truth—how do you feel about that?"

"I feel weary," he said. "I feel sad—I lost some ships. I lost some *more* ships, and a lot of men out there. I made some mistakes, which were caught and rectified, thank God, by some of my staff people, but I am definitely *not* the hero they're making me out to be."

"And?"

"And, I guess I'm a little relieved. I think maybe I was operating above my real abilities."

She smiled at that, a lovely, almost loving smile. "Nonsense," she said. "You and your ships hurt them bad. That's all that counts right now. Besides you getting some much-needed rest. Brain surgery is not trivial medicine, so you're going back to sleep now."

"I'm actually not that sleepy," he protested.

She reached for something just out of his field of vision. "You're about to be, my dear Commodore."

Lo and behold, she was right about that.

The next two weeks were harder than his previous recovery. It was not that he suffered from major disabilities such as blindness or total loss of speech. There were some little things that caught him off guard—a sudden loss of balance, the inability to correctly pronounce a word even as his brain rather forcefully commanded it, dropping something from his hand for no apparent reason, and the scariest, which only happened once, was waking up in the middle of the night, lying on his back, and unable to sit up. For a moment he'd thought he was drowning. The hell of it was that he never knew when something might happen, so now he used a cane whenever he was out of bed and he kept track of places where he could sit down on sudden notice.

Tina Danfield came around when she could, but she'd been moved up in the nursing organization to full superintendent, and business at the Nouméa field hospital was literally booming. She maintained a professional distance, and yet he was pretty sure that, under different circumstances, they would have been able to get much closer. On the other hand, didn't every patient fall at least a little bit in love with his nurses? Still.

One night she came to his room after the evening meal, handed him his hairbrush, and told him to sit up and make himself presentable. Before he could ask why, Admiral Halsey, now sporting four stars instead of three, steamed into the room and waggled those bushy eyebrows at him. There were three staff officers accompanying him, all captains, and all looking to Sluff like they might have been lieutenants just a day or so ago. This war was definitely moving on, and even more definitely without him.

"Commodore Wolf," Halsey said, "How the hell are you?"

"Doing pretty well, thank you, Admiral, considering. Have you killed some more Japs?"

Halsey laughed at the reference to one of his first fleet-wide orders when he took over SOPAC, which was for all hands to kill Japs, kill Japs, and kill more Japs. "You bet," he said. "Not in as grand a style as you did, but we've stopped the bastards and now we're going to start pushing them back, all the way to goddamned Tokyo. I have a job for you."

That took a moment to penetrate. "Yes, sir?" Sluff asked.

"Doc say you can't go back to sea, not after a stroke. They say anyone who has had a stroke is probably going to have another one at some point. So: I can't have you working the Slot anymore and that's a damned shame."

He paused for a moment to see how Sluff was going to take that news.

None of his doctors had ever mentioned that once someone has a stroke, there's a good chance he'll have another. Leave it to Halsey to lay it out for him. "Yes, sir, I understand that."

"But," Halsey continued. "I've talked to Chester,

and told him I want a special training squadron stood up at Pearl. In the next year we're going to see over five hundred new-construction ships heading this way. Right now they get shake-down training right after they're built, a week of training time at Pearl, but then they come out here without knowing shit from Shinola. So: I need a battle-hardened commodore to command that training squadron. Incoming fleet units will chop to you for two, maybe three weeks. You, and you'll have a staff, will teach them how things are really done out here so they don't all die on their first night out. When you think they're ready, you send 'em out. We'll take it from there. You up to that?"

Sluff nodded, although with some of the things that had been happening to him, he wondered if he truly was.

"Here's the thing," Halsey said. "We'll pick your initial staff. These will be officers and chiefs like yourself, who have distinguished themselves in battle but who cannot, for whatever reason, stay in the front lines anymore. No losers, no shell-shocked men, no cowards. Men who have done what you've done and have no illusions about what it takes to beat the Japs. We just can't afford to send you all the way home, although I will if you tell me you've run out of fighting steam. We need your experience, your savvy, your regrets, your nightmares, and your record so that all these new guys will listen to you. Please say yes."

"Yes," Sluff said. "Sir."

Halsey beamed. "I knew it." He turned to his staff. "Didn't I tell you? Now: you guys get this thing organized. Get the commodore back to Pearl. Make sure the right people in Pearl are ready to set him up with facilities and whatever support he needs. He'll need a liaison with PacFleet and DESPAC. Draft me a personal-for message that makes all of this clear to the Pearl Harbor people."

He turned to Sluff. "Thank you for doing this. It will make a big difference. Anything you want to tell me?"

Sluff wanted to tell him that what had happened that "glorious" night had been pure chaos, that he'd screwed things up only to be saved by his subordinates, that maybe his initial plan was good but his own execution had been flawed and that von Moltke had been absolutely right. He glanced over Halsey's shoulder and saw Tina, standing in the doorway. She silently shook her head.

"Thank you for letting me stay in the fight," Sluff said. "I'll do my best."

"Never doubted that, young man," Halsey said. He turned to his staff. "Where next?"

And then they were all gone in a whirl of moving khaki. Tina came back into the room. "Right answer," she said.

"I wanted to tell him the truth," he said.

"No," she said. "He knows the truth. When *Juneau* was lost I talked to everyone and anyone who would listen to me, trying to make sense of that. How could that happen? So many lost, when the ship went down in front of an entire task force? Why didn't they go back? What had happened the night before that left our ship broken almost in two? Everybody I talked to said the same thing—you don't understand. When the big guns get going, it's pandemonium. Chaos. Surprise after surprise, for both sides. Good luck, bad luck, whatever—*no* one's in control! Those big ships spit their various forms of fire at each other and men die. The next morning the admirals tote up the score and then lie about what happened so that the Japs can't know how bad they hurt us, while the survivors come here, so shocked and burned and broken they can't even speak of it. Until they do, good Christ."

He realized she was weeping. "Hey," he said. "Come here. I'm sorry I brought it up. Come here."

She stood three feet from his bed and shook her head. "No," she said. "If I let you comfort me I will just—dissolve. I'm needed here. I desperately need to be needed, do you understand? You go be strong. Go do this job, keep the new people safe so that they survive their first night out. After that, it's on them. I've got to go."

"Please don't," he said. "I've upset you. I—"

She paused in the doorway. "I *have* to go," she

said. "Mostly because I cannot stay. I like you, Harmon Wolf, but I am barely holding it together. I see too much, I hear too much. I simply can't—"

Then she was gone.

He lay back in the bed with a sigh and watched the sunset paint the back wall of his room in amazing colors. Damn, he thought. I took her for granted. That calm, brave, all-the-way-to-Tokyo façade, and, yet, underneath all that, she was still grieving. Her husband, his ship, all the wardroom officers they'd both known, reduced to chum by a Jap submarine as *Juneau* crawled back toward Nouméa with a broken back.

And all I can think about is me, he realized. He tried to imagine what his uncle, the Mide, would have said if he'd watched all that. Shit-fire, man, you can do better than that.

One day later the SOPAC machinery had him discharged and on a flight back to Pearl. He kept the cane.

FORTY

Pearl Harbor

"Mornin', Commodore," Mose said. "Got us some fresh hot cin-min rolls and some a that Kona coffee this mornin', yes we do."

Sluff was up, dressed, and sitting at his small

desk reading the morning message traffic that had been delivered earlier that morning. He was one of four captains living in a spacious white house at the edge of the Makalapa crater, but he was the only one who had a steward assigned. The house, one of eight laid out in a row of senior officers' quarters, was set up as a BOQ. There were four bedrooms and two baths upstairs, a kitchen, a dining room, and a living room downstairs, with a small bedroom behind the kitchen for a steward. The other three captains all worked up the hill at Nimitz's headquarters in various staff positions. Sluff was the only one who had what was technically a seagoing command. From the front porch there was an expansive view of Pearl Harbor below. On the street behind the row of BOQ houses were the much bigger flag quarters for Nimitz and his senior aides.

"Mose, thank you very much," Sluff said. "Put it all right there. Everyone else already gone to work?"

"Yes, suh, they have," Mose said. "That Cap'n Weaver, now, he gets on outa here at five thirty, every mornin', no matter what. He must be real important."

"He seems to think so, Mose," Sluff said, dryly. "Let me know when my car shows up."

"Yessuh, will do. I'm goan get us some fresh fish for supper tonight. You will be comin' back this evenin'?"

"I will, Mose," Sluff said. "The Lord willing and the creeks don't rise."

Mose grinned. "Ain't no creeks on this island, boss," he said. "So you be here."

After Mose left he sampled the coffee and one of the fat pills. He wasn't sure where Mose was getting this stuff but he wasn't going to ask any questions, either. He looked out the window, which gave him a view of the harbor some three hundred feet below the Makalapa quarters area and about a crow-fly mile away. It was January, which was to say that the days were a few degrees cooler than, say, July, but not by much. The weather never changed here, and he missed the roll of the four seasons. It would have been a spectacular view except for the blackened battleship wrecks over on Ford Island.

Gonna be here for dinner? Well, that depends, Mose, he thought. It's kind of one day at a time with this head bone of mine. Never know when it's going to fall apart and put me on the ground. Or in it.

He'd had some episodes since coming back to Pearl, but nothing too alarming. He'd been given an enthusiastic if almost embarrassing welcome when he'd arrived at Pearl, including a five-minute office call on Nimitz himself. The admiral exuded his usual quiet charm and encouraged Sluff to get his new training squadron up and running as soon as possible, because the crews

438

coming from the East Coast were seriously green. He'd also given Sluff the name of a captain on his staff who would be available when Sluff ran into any bureaucratic problems.

"When, not if," Nimitz had said. "It's not a case of obstinacy in the face of change, but rather that the demands on every resource here are overwhelming and getting bigger every day."

"We'll make do, Admiral," Sluff had replied. "We didn't have all that much out around Savo, either."

He finished his breakfast, got his cane and specially modified brass hat, and went out to the front porch to wait for his staff car. He worked a seven-day, ten-hour schedule, much like everyone else assigned to the Pacific Fleet's main base. No more hazy, lazy Sundays with just a scant duty section up and about, not after December 7, afloat or ashore. Even though a year had passed since that disaster, the smell of death and oil was always tainting the otherwise lovely tropical breeze, and the fourteen-inch guns, dismounted from some of the sunken battlewagons and then embedded up on the cliffs above Waikiki, were kept loaded.

His car drove up and the driver, a pretty young Wave named Sally Simpson, jumped out and ran around to the curb to open the right rear door. Sluff smiled at the sight, as he did every morning.

"Morning, Commodore," she chirped as she saluted.

He returned the salute and the greeting. Then they were off to the boat landing, where he would take a launch out to Ford Island and his sumptuous headquarters in a steel Quonset hut, bristling with aerials and altogether too close to the drowned nightmare that was *Arizona*, where over one thousand men lay irretrievable in her burned, armored bowels. His staff was, in his opinion, absolutely first-rate, all battle-scarred veterans of Ironbottom Sound. Officers, chiefs, and some senior enlisted, sent to him with two objectives: to pass on the lessons learned under fire against the Japs, and to have some time to heal, if possible, before going back out to rejoin the coming offensives up the Solomons chain. The thump of canes and crutches added a certain dignity to the schoolhouse atmosphere.

Sluff knew he would not be going back, but when he sat down in the evening with the skippers and execs of the new ships coming through the squadron after they'd spent the day being put through their paces by his veterans, they paid attention. That steel plate in his head, the unruly mop of bright white hair, the Navy Cross, Purple Heart, and other decorations, and the word in the Fleet about the Indian fella who'd destroyed an entire Jap squadron all helped, but he made sure they understood that he was no water-walker, and that what they would be facing could only be characterized as chaos. The ships would stay in the special training squadron for two weeks, and occasionally, three, and then head west, to be replaced by even more new faces and freshly painted ships. He was a commodore again, but his "squadron" featured an ever-changing sea of new faces. Not too different when he was out there, when he thought about it, but for much better reasons.

After the first month, Nimitz directed that, except for submarines, *all* warships and not just destroyers chopping to PacFleet for the first time would go through the special training squadron. That created the occasional problem when a cruiser skipper, technically senior to Sluff, got stiff-necked about reporting to a junior captain, even if he was called *Commodore* Wolf. When that happened, Sluff would actually go to sea, taking his three senior lieutenant commanders along. They would then put that ship through a series of drills and self-imposed casualties to both men and machinery that would usually end with the ship dead in the water and unable to function. The lieutenant commanders would wander through the ship, unplugging vital electrical circuits, telling key officers and petty officers that they were now "dead," or tripping steam machinery off the lineto simulate battle damage. After a day of that, attitudes usually changed and things went much better.

Sluff would then invite the embarrassed CO up

to his quarters or to the officers' club for a quiet dinner, one-on-one, over which he would describe his own personal experiences in and around Ironbottom Sound, to include the news that however much the skipper might think he was in control, once the eight-inch shells began to come through the bridge windows, the ship's survival would depend much more on how well the crew had been trained than on anything he, the captain, might do from the wreckage of the pilothouse. The next day, his staff would usually report a remarkable change aboard the USS whatever, and then they could get to work in earnest.

Twice a week, Sluff would have himself driven to the sprawling Army hospital complex up on Fort Shafter, situated in a valley above Pearl. It looked a lot like the field hospital in Nouméa as it frantically expanded to meet the demands created by the intensifying conflict in the South Pacific. Taking a page out of Halsey's book, he would walk through the wards of no-longer-critical patients, carrying a briefcase of the things that might be hard to get in a military hospital and an open bottle of Coke. He quickly discovered that *the* favorite thing was a cigarette, which were not allowed on most wards. Sluff would sit down among a cluster of hospital beds, talking to the men, asking them what ship or unit they were from and where they'd been hurt, while waiting for the nearest nurse to be called away, and then light up three or four cigarettes and pass them around. If the nurse was spotted returning, the cigarettes would be passed quickly back to the strange-looking Navy captain with a plate in his head and doused in the half-empty Coke bottle.

The ward nurses were, of course, on to the game, but allowed it because they were just a little bit intimidated by the muscular four-striper with his scowling Indian visage. After a while, he became a fixture as the word got around about his briefcase full of Camels, and sometimes even a ward nurse might sneak a quick puff or five, egged on by her patients. The word also got around Pearl Harbor circles because one night Chester Nimitz himself sent his car around to pick Sluff up at his quarters, and then the two of them, followed at a discreet distance by two aides and Nimitz's four Marine bodyguards, made the rounds. When they'd been there about an hour Nimitz indicated he had to get back, but he asked Sluff where he'd come up with the idea.

"Admiral Halsey does it twice a week out in Nouméa," Sluff said. "The troops are usually glad to see him, and, from what I saw, he's pretty good for their morale."

After hearing that, Nimitz set up a schedule to do the same thing. Sluff found that out when the admiral's aide called and asked which nights Sluff would be up there, so that Nimitz wouldn't interfere.

"You tell me when the admiral might be going up there and I'll just stay home," Sluff had responded.

"No, sir, Commodore, that's not what the admiral wants. You go up there Tuesday and Thursdays? He'll go up there Wednesdays. How about that?"

"Sounds good," Sluff said, marveling not for the first time at the magnanimity of C. W. Nimitz.

He was there one night in February, doing his hush-hush cigarette-girl act, when a voice from over his shoulder said, "What is it with you, Harmon Wolf? You like being in the hospital? And do I smell cigarette smoke, gentlemen?"

It was Tina, now sporting the insignia of a nurse corps lieutenant commander. The patients looked uncertainly from her face to his and then realized they knew each other. For one thing, the notorious scowl had vanished.

"No, ma'am, you do not," Sluff asserted, the Coke bottle in his hand hissing in a definitely guilty fashion. "There's no smoking allowed in this ward."

"There better not be," she said, trying hard for a severe frown, but the twinkle in her eyes gave her away. Some of the patients were nudging each other with knowing grins. "Come with me, sir," she said in her best boss-nurse voice. "While I explain this hospital's rules and why we have them."

Sluff got up, leaving the briefcase full of cigarettes, and followed her down the line until they went through the batwing doors out into the main corridor that connected the ward buildings. Seeing no one around, she gave him a big hug and then a kiss.

"God, I'm glad to see you, Harmon Wolf," she said. "I've had this terrible feeling that . . ."

He smiled down at her. "And I'm very glad you even gave me a thought," he replied. "Now, let's try that again, with feeling this time."

Her eyes widened as if she'd taken offense, but a moment later, maybe two, they parted and then, almost sheepishly, sat down on one of the benches out in the hallway.

"I've done okay," he said. "Some moments, but nothing scary. One day at a time."

She nodded. "Oh," she said, reaching into her purse and handing him a small white envelope. "This is for you."

He looked at the envelope, which had his name and rank handwritten on it, and a return address that said only: WFH. He opened the envelope. Inside was a white card with four blue stars engraved across the top. A hand-scrawled note read: Nimitz delighted with what you're doing. Wish you were here instead. Best regards, Bill Halsey. PS, I've sent you a present.

"What's it say?" she asked.

"It's from Halsey, if you can believe that," Sluff

said. "Says Nimitz is happy with the training squadron."

"Oh," she said. "That's it?"

He gave her a big grin. "No, that's not 'it.' However, we're going to have to know each other a whole lot better before I tell you. So: I have a car and a driver. I'll bet we can get a drink down at the O-club in Pearl."

She drew herself up as best she could sitting on a hallway bench. "I'm not that kind of girl, Captain," she said. "It has to be drinks *and* dinner."

"Deal," he said, feeling for the first time since his stroke that maybe, just maybe, there was a future.

Then they just sat there, grinning at each other like two idiots.

Center Point Large Print
600 Brooks Road / PO Box 1
Thorndike, ME 04986-0001 USA

(207) 568-3717

US & Canada:
1 800 929-9108
www.centerpointlargeprint.com